**To**
the Michael Reese Hospital
and its
Psychosomatic and Psychiatric Institute
Chicago
where first in the United States
the Rorschach test was used in the
scientific study of mental health.

# The Rorschach Experiment

## *Ventures in Blind Diagnosis*

### SAMUEL J. BECK, Ph.D.
Professorial Lecturer,
Departments of Psychology and Psychiatry
University of Chicago;
Staff Associate, Michael Reese Hospital, Chicago.

GRUNE & STRATTON        NEW YORK   LONDON

Library of Congress Card Catalog No. 49-11667

Printed and bound in the U.S.A. (M)

# Contents

# Foreword

Can the Rorschach test be employed with due regard for the rules of the scientific game? Rorschach himself intended that it should be. In his *Psychodiagnostik* he proposed experiments which would test out his assumptions, and he repeatedly called for the use of statistical method in establishing criteria. Oberholzer, chief collaborator to Rorschach and leading exponent of the test following its inventor's death, was scrupulously observant of strict method, always testing his interpretation against non-Rorschach information about his patient. It was from Oberholzer that Dr. David M. Levy took over the test and this was the orientation he taught when I first began to study with him in New York in 1927.

It was some three years earlier that Levy had first tried the Rorschach test out in the then nascent psychiatry department of the Michael Reese Hospital in Chicago. This medical center was thus the first in America which saw the test used in the study of mental illnesses. It is appropriate, therefore, that I inscribe this exposition of Rorschach's experiment to this Hospital and its Psychosomatic and Psychiatric Institute, and I am pleased to have the privilege of doing so.

The objective of the present book is to demonstrate the processes entering into the interpretation of a Rorschach test protocol, the path the examiner travels from the raw data of the test—the patient's "butterfly" or his "two girls dancing an oopsie-daisy"—to the clinical report which he turns over to the therapist. In so doing, I also show the clinically meaningful material that can be obtained from an adequate set of test associations obtained, that is, while adhering strictly to the test data. To do this, I have presented findings as they were originally derived, "blind," with the modifications and insights developed since the reports were first made.

Accompanying each report are extensive and detailed notes on my interpretive reasoning. It is in the notes that I amplify on the connections between the patient's associations, the technical Rorschach test variables, and the meanings of these in terms of personality traits and dynamics. Here I enlarge freely on the original interpretations, correcting and expanding as indicated in my present understanding of the test. The notes are, then, this book's essential new contribution toward Rorschach test teaching.

The illustrative cases are variously representative of the clinical problems that are met in the outpatient department of a mental clinic, in patients requiring hospitalization, and in patients treated in private practice. Three children are presented: Lenore, an outpatient; Harry, privately referred ; and Clyde, a schizophrenic whose three Rorschachs show his course in the Orthogenic School. The adults include Lenore's mother, also an outpatient; Mrs. O., from private practice, the wife in a marital boat that is being rocked; Mrs. E., a woman with brain pathology, hospitalized; and Mrs. L., hospitalized and a suicide. One other, Mr. C., also hospitalized, exemplifies my S-3 schizophrenia, which is equivalent to pseudoneurotic schizophrenia. These eight patients and their ten Rorschach tests, with the interpretations and the notes, form the core of the book.

Preceding these will be found a discussion of a major theoretic problem, one central to Rorschach's thinking about personality structure. This is his elusive *Erlebnistypus*, Experience Balance, concept. I attempt clarification of it, using a behavioral psychology as my point of departure, and I offer an extension of the concept. Following the case material, I have examined the relation of test findings to a patient's treatability. Essential to this exposition is the appraisal of the defenses, and I therefore devote some pages to the varieties of defenses which the test traces out. A final chapter, more speculative than the others in the book, is on transference. For the principles emerging as pertinent to this sphere of the defenses, their testing out, and also for fresh sharpenings of Rorschach test meanings, I credit my experience in the schizophrenia researches which I have been carrying on in recent years, for the support of which I express thanks to both the National Institute of Mental Health and the Illinois Department of Public Welfare. An appreciation of another kind is owed to my colleague in these researches, Dr. H. B. Molish, Commander, U.S.N. His keen sensitivity to the clinical meanings of Rorschach test findings have acted as an ever-quickening stimulus to my own thinking.

Finally, acknowledgments are in order to three other men. Dr. Roy R. Grinker was one of the first American psychiatrists to apprehend the Rorschach test's potential as a depth instrument. As Director of the Psychosomatic and Psychiatric Institute in the Michael Reese Hospital, he has consistently encouraged its "blind" use in clinical investigation. He has in this way been an effective force toward strengthing its scientific foundations and has permitted the very medical center in this country where the test was first tried out to become the one which has also done so much to foster its healthy growth. Dr. Knight Aldrich, also one of the early students of the test and now Chairman of the Department of Psychiatry at the University of Chicago's School of Medicine, with cordial warmth has made available to me this University's rich clinical resources. He thus continuously keeps open my opportunity for studying problems central to the human personality, this field where variety is infinite and the horizon of understanding ever receding. Then there is Dr. Henry M. Stratton, who for more than a decade and a half has published everything I have offered him, and he has been equally cordial to the Rorschach writings of other students. The test is fortunate in having the good will and understanding of a man with Dr. Stratton's place among publishers in medical psychology. In him there is the welcome assurance that the messages in Rorschach's test will be made known and heard.


*University of Chicago*                                SAMUEL J. BECK
*April, 1960*

# I.
## Theoretical

# CHAPTER 1

## The test as experiment

On the title page of the first (1921) edition of the *Psychodiagnostik*, and in every later edition, Rorschach used in the subtitle the word *Experiment*.[57] The subtitle in full is: "*Method and Results of a Perception-Diagnostic Experiment.*" The vicissitudes met by this test, both in Europe and in America, have been such as to keep alive the issue of whether the test is, in fact, an experiment. Before taking a position on this question we must first define the term. What is experimentation? Can its method apply to the field of human personality?

If one definition of experimental method is used, the human personality is not eligible for such research. This is the method whereby the object under investigation is altered or controlled in respect to some one variable in order to test out a hypothesis. It is the strict method of the laboratory. Prototypes of this in psychology, for the purpose of studying higher mental processes, are the learning experiments on animals which induce neurotic-type behavior. Experiments of this kind cannot be conducted on men and women. I am not referring here to the relatively innocuous ones, those that touch only a small sector of the person, physiologically or psychologically, but we do not planfully subject one of our own kind experimentally to those stresses which, according to theory, will bring on a hysteria, an organ neurosis, a depression, or a schizophrenic breakdown. Our morality prohibits such manipulation of some persons by others.

Yet, we are not by this condition enjoined from experimental investigation into whole human beings. The fact is that life, in the ups and downs to which it exposes us, conducts these experiments. Some persons do suffer neuroses or depressions, or they do disintegrate into schizophrenia. The experiment is being carried on without our yea or nay. The problem becomes that which Claude Bernard[18] identifies as "experimental reasoning." To quote: "A physician observing a disease in different circumstances, reasoning about the influence of these circumstances, and deducing consequences which are controlled by other observations—this physician reasons experimentally, even though he makes no experiments."

No more than any other psychiatrist was Rorschach interested in conducting controlled laboratory experiments on humans. He did not seek to vary his patient and observe what would happen under fixed conditions. But he did have varied groups of patients, and he invented an instrument which he could hold fixed. Far from subjecting his patients to any instrument, he subjected the instrument to his patients. The ten inkblots constituted his dependent variable. The different groups of patients were his independent variables. They were those "different circumstances" of which Bernard speaks. Rorschach then observed the varying behavior of his inkblots under the different circumstances, behavior which, for purposes of convenience, he labeled W, D, Dd, M, C, thought content, and the various other data of his test. This was Rorschach's experiment.

So far, however, he had only data, observations, facts that in themselves were not meaningful as human psychology. After observation the next step is reasoning. Rorschach could not but be intrigued by certain clusterings in his data. They showed a propensity for adhering in patterns, constant for each clinical condition and varying from one condition to another. This was still observation, but it went a step beyond—to what we are in the habit of calling experimental results. It is at this point in an experiment that thinking—interpretation is the word used technically—begins. Rorschach reasoned about his results in the light of his knowledge of psychopathology. He hypothesized as to the general psychologic significance of his data, the W, D, F+, M, C, and the others. Then from the patterns into which these clustered in the different clinical states, and within the framework of a certain (psychoanalytic) theory of personality, he hypothesized concerning the interrelations between these data and the whole test structural patterns. Translating these data into psychologic terms and converting his patterns into known diagnostic pictures, he arrived at his logic concerning the organization of personality. It is a fusion of Freudian psychoanalysis as developed to 1920 and of Jungian type theory. The bulk of his exposition is given over to this thinking and to the concept of the *Erlebnistypus*, or "experience type."

In my own studies with the test, I early disregarded type theory. Basing my thinking on the major psychoanalytic hypothesis of personality as an accommodation between id and ego forces, I could interpret Rorschach test findings as expressing results of an ego–affect give-and-take. The personality we see is the balance between these two dynamics. I could also justify this thinking from what is known of the brain and nervous system on the basis of Jacksonian concepts.[39] Meanwhile, Gestalt was proffering rationale in the field of psychology proper. Lewin's experiments and reasoning (field theory) added to the comfort with which I could  reason from Rorschach data to whole personality structure and convert this reasoning into clinical reasoning within the framework of Freudian and Jacksonian rationales.

A net conclusion from these theories is that the behaviors we observe in mentally ill patients are a function of the whole individual, although the actual order of observation is the contrary, i.e., from part to whole. The weight of current personality theory, which has developed out of both

Gestalt theory and psychoanalysis, has been to see behavior as what the person does. So also with the Rorschach test. We observe and record behavior data which it educes. We organize these into the whole structure. From this we reason, interpret, concerning the whole person. It is this whole person who is acting and producing the overt behaviors represented in the separate test data.

Insofar as the test and its theories are valid, its data and its whole-person findings tell in its language what a clinical description, or any other descriptions from life generally, tell in theirs.

This whole person, whether he is revealed in life or in the Rorschach test, has formed certain ways of reacting, has acquired certain ideas, holds certain values. These are the source traits in his character out of which arise the overtly visible behaviors. Broadly, they break up into his affective trends and his intellectual grasp. It is these source traits (Feigl[31]) which fuse into the organized complexity (Weaver[69]) that is the unit personality, i.e., the man or woman that we know. Ego, in the broad sense of knowing a goal and integration of the individual's abilities in the pursuit of that goal, is a concept embracing some of these traits. These traits are apparent also in the net state of unbalance which we see in the psychopathologies: the person so in the power of his feelings that his intelligence does not function, for example, is as impaired as if his brain had suffered physical damage.

In the Rorschach, then, as in the mental hospital or in life generally, the order of observation is (1) overt data, which are the work of (2) source traits, which are (3) the channels whereby (4) the unit person seeks his satisfactions. This is to say that Rorschach theory converges with psychoanalytic, neurologic, and Gestalt theories in that a statement of the personality is made manifest by elicited behaviors. In another paper,[14] I have shown these convergences in a synoptic table, which is here reproduced in a revised version (Table 1).

My reasoning concerning constancy of personality pattern, the general psychologic significance of source traits, and the meaning of overt behaviors as the work of the source traits demands substantiation with the logic of statistics. This demand is not specific for the Rorschach test; it obtains for any whole-personality theory whatever the method of investigation. The problem has had the attention of theorists in personality, theorists who can conceive of the individual as a lawful datum, e.g., Allport,[1] Holt,[38] Stephenson,[66] Beck.[13] The numerous opinions on the questions of quantifying and standardizing test behaviors were well reviewed by Sargent in 1945.[61] She astutely summarizes the situation:

> A fact which is often overlooked both by those who scorn statistics and those who reify them is that numbers do not bestow precision but are, rather, a convenient way to express it when it exists. Quantitative method might profitably be applied more ex-

TABLE 1.—*Personality structure in human behavior and in the Rorschach test in the light of theory. Overview.*

| The raw data | In the fields of behavior | In the Rorschach test |
|---|---|---|
| The observations manifest in——— | ⟋Life generally; the clinic; the laboratory and in——⟋ | ⟋The scored variables, W, F+, M, C, and the others |
| | and all these are expressions of | |
| ↓ | ↓ | ↓ |
| The source traits (Feigl) or personality forces which are——— | ⟋Either affective or intellectual psychological processes; and also——⟋ | ⟋The projected affective and intellectual test traits |
| | and these organize into | |
| ↓ | ↓ | ↓ |
| The individual as whole system | The unit personality, an organized complexity (Weaver) | Theoretic personality as balance of forces; as higher-lower brain level activity (Jackson); field forces (Lewin); ego-id (Freud). |

tensively to the properties of the projective tests themselves. ... If we think of these numerical results as adding to the *precision of the instrument itself,* instead of reading into the figures oversimplified generalizations about people, no atomistic conception of personality is implied. The clinician would not need to alter either his theory or his interpretation of certain Rorschach syndromes if he also knew more about the frequency of the component determinants, both singly and in constellations. Such knowledge would, on the contrary, serve both as an added support and as a check on his conclusions.

The climate since the above statement was published has moderated somewhat into a more benign attitude toward the idea of the individual as lawful datum, and a search for appropriate metrics has been one of the salutary consequences. A work that delves into the relevant theoretic issues is that of Brunswik.[23] Inquiry and experiment have burgeoned in the field of perception. In some instances, the contribution of Rorschach is explicitly recognized, notably Bruner[22]; in others, the influence can be detected. There has been feedback from Rorschach concepts to perception theory, and vice versa.

The present volume reports my efforts to replicate Rorschach's experiment. It does this by (a) reporting all the behavioral data emerging from administration of the test, and (b) stating in detail the reasoning whereby I arrive at my conclusions as to the significance to the personality of the data. By the data I refer not only to the structural findings set down in those signs that make up the quantitative summary—W, F+, M, and the others

—but also to all the nonmeasurable, non-normative, and entirely qualitative observations that are derived in a Rorschach test situation. These include card turning, for example, and also the minutiae of sighs, body shifts, etc., and the points in the test at which these have been observed. At the same time, "qualitative" does not mean subjective. The requirement *behavioral* is paramount. The behavior recorded must be, like Caesar's wife, above suspicion as that of the subject. An edifice such as I have built in Table 1, in which I venture to equate life data, clinical observations, and Rorschach data, can be no sounder than the rigorous nonsubjectivity of the facts that are its building materials.

The interpretation which, with the test records, form the body of this book were done entirely "blind." I never saw any of these patients. Some of the tests were administered by my wife, some by staff members in clinics. On the question of "blind" diagnosis and the test as clinical instrument, a confusion of issues persists. The issue and the confusion are those which exist between any technique as (a) an experiment and (b) its application to a practical situation in whatever field for which it has been invented, clinical or otherwise. The experimenter, to cite Bernard,[18] puts certain questions to nature and is "confronted with a real observation that he has induced and must note, like any other observation, without any preconceived idea." The preconceived idea is the dog in the manger in much clinical psychology diagnosis, and it is an especial hazard in Rorschach test diagnosis. Information in the patient's clinical chart may provide clues to the condition and so channelize the psychologist's thinking, causing him to arrive at "astounding" diagnostic formulations. These are not diagnoses from the test data, however, but from other behaviors. In "blind" diagnosis, on the other hand, the examiner uses an instrument to ask his questions. From the answers obtained, as validated by the usual method of experiment and statistics he applies himself to the problem presented by his patient. At this point, "reasoning intervenes, and the experimenter steps forward to interpret the phenomenon" (Bernard[18]) ; that is, after he has read his instrument the psychologist asks for the clinical chart and studies his test findings, which have been obtained without preconceived idea, in the light of the clinical problem. He steps out of the role of experimenter and into that of clinician. Hallowell[36] penetratingly evaluates the place of "blind" diagnosis, not only for individual diagnosis but also in contributing to theory. He summarizes:

> Important as blind analyses of a few individuals may be for certain purposes, these experiments must be clearly distinguished from investigations that are less concerned with methodological questions as such and more concerned with discovering and exploiting the full potentialities that appear to be inherent in the test results. One of the most striking and important implications of experiments in "blind" analysis has been overlooked. Insofar as life history data, direct observations of behavior, information

from other tests, *and* cultural facts have proved to be in accord with "blind" interpretations, we have much more than a validation of Rorschach principles. We have, in fact, a most enlightening, concrete demonstration, in more than a single human society, of the integral relations that are abstractly expressed by perception, personality structure, and culture, and which have so often been investigated separately. This is a discovery of major importance. It reflects the complexities of the human behavioral situation, the need for a comprehensive conceptual framework, and the usefulness of techniques that have already provided extremely important data.

The need for rigorous self-discipline in objectivity is compelling in Rorschach test administration and interpretation. The data obtained are those of a field of force constituted not of two variables only but of three: patient, test, and examiner. Several writers have explored this topic, notably Schafer,[62] Sarason,[60] and see also Brunswik. Concerning what it takes to equip oneself for sound use of the test, I unburdened myself some twenty years ago,[8] and I make bold to restate the points here in summary since they are still cardinal. They are: broad experience in psychopathology, personal psychoanalysis, experience with the Rorschach test in many clinical groups, orientation in the Rorschach-Oberholzer tradition, and a foundation in experimental psychology.

In the present book I undertake to demonstrate the workings of the Rorschach test both as an instrument for observing the overt behavior of human beings and as a method of knowing what is going on in them deep down. That is, first, what is manifest and can be described as sense data is observed. The next phase, that of reasoning, is then undertaken. These are the steps, represented in Table 1, that become the interpretations as exemplified in Chapters 3 through 10. My reasoning necessarily embraces concepts beyond those employed by Rorschach, both with reference to variables in his test and psychodynamically. We have, after all, the benefit of the thinking about the test and the dynamics of personality that has gone on since his death. And I have the fruits of my own experience. Yet, the cases reported in Chapters 3 through 10 do replicate Rorschach's experiment: using a fixed set of stimuli devised by Rorschach in accordance with certain precedent ideas, I apply them to the varying conditions provided by persons of differing clinical pictures.

The fresh thinking that enters into the interpretations is that which has been growing out of my researches in schizophrenia conducted continuously since 1947. In reading the interpretations and the notes, it will be seen that they consistently reflect my recourse to a psychology of the ego, its role in mastering affect, its defensive operations, the person's use of fantasy as communication out of this unconscious, the personal foci of conflict, and the treatment implications in the test findings.

All these are personality dynamics, or source traits, as I have been calling them; that is, they are the deep-down character forces which interact to

fuse into the personality as we know it. We know the forces from the manifest behaviors. A person is as he does. I devised a "trait universe" of 120
behavior items, later revised to one of 170, each of which is an expression
of a source trait, and this instrument has provided the guide lines for my
research.* The lists have been published elsewhere.[15, 50]

The thinking stimulated by applying the lists to research cases has increased my interpretative understanding. It is so often true that the insights derived from a research effort are the enzymes that promote the
growth of psychologic knowledge. Bleuler[19] speaks, for instance, of the concept of schizophrenia constituting a considerable part of the whole development of theoretic psychiatry. It may be added that the problems of psychopathology inherent in psychiatric theory are the problems of human life
itself.

Should the student seek, as he properly should, for clinical data validating my experimental use of the test, he will find some, but in small and
uneven quantities. So far as the purpose of this book is concerned, the dearth
of clinical data is only an incidental shortcoming. My effort here is not to
prove the test's validity but to demonstrate its working processes.

Finally, I am venturing in the case interpretations on a fresh approach
to one of Rorschach's core concepts. This is his *Erlebnistypus*, or *Experience
Balance* (EB). To employ this complex personality variable as a quantitatively established behavioral event sets up serious logical difficulties.
To understand it as psychological datum has been the most difficult of
the problems in the legacy which Rorschach has handed down to us. I
have been developing a perspective of EB which, while not new—it is
inherent in Rorschach's concept of *Ambitendenz*—will, I believe, help to
clarify its psychologic significance. I am calling this the *Experience Actual*,
EA, and the exposition of it occupies the chapter that follows.

* In the notes for one of the cases, (Harry, Chapter 9) I use some of the items and
describe their Rorschach test correlates.

# CHAPTER 2

# The experience actual

The greatest chasms in man's world are those between one personality and another. Ingenious and inventive as men are, they have not succeeded, and it is safe to say they never will, in *directly* entering one another's personalities. However close any one person is to another, spouse, parent, child, sibling, friend, each must still remain a unit psychologically apart through all his days on this earth.

Yet, the chasm can be bridged, and men have been doing so in their everyday lives from the time, we are sure, when they first evolved out of Pithecanthropus, and probably earlier. They understand one another, penetrate to one another's thinking, feeling, intentions. Men have always had to do so—or else. And among the ablest in so doing have been, not the scientists, but persons in other walks of life. Who is more astute than the political leader in penetrating the minds of his people? Who is shrewder in this than the successful businessman? And when it comes to reaching into the deeper recesses of men's lives and knowing their most fervid thoughts and their most strongly felt values, the poets remain unmatched.

Science meanwhile plods along, holding by the hand one of its youngest offspring—psychology. The child sometimes gives signs of precocity, with the usual acrid harvest to the too bright child: its elders—principally philosophy, sometimes the natural sciences—remind it of the propriety, at certain ages, of not being heard; while the older forebears, the physical sciences, condescendingly maintain a totally distant and amused smile. So psychology toddles on in the wonderland of the sciences. Like so many bright children, too, it is handicapped by its own parents. It is sometimes too much like the one, philosophy; and at times rather quaintly resembles the other, the natural sciences. Which means of course that both parents find fault with the poor dear, each blaming the other for the apparent blemishes.

In the effort at the direct crossing over into the mind of the other, psychology is presently treading cautiously. It is availing itself of its heritage from its elders. It is exploring with the caution of its parent, experimental science, the fields of thinking and perception, bridgeheads into personality. At the same time, it is boldly following along theoretic paths first marked out by three thinkers more speculative than experimental, men whose contributions are in the tradition of philosophy although their greatest value has been to psychology. The men and their particular areas of contribution were: Dilthey, on understanding; Husserl, on a purified phenomenology; Spranger, on meaning. See Klüver[44] for an illuminating exposition of these three thinkers' psychologies. On the problem of our knowing the other, Dilthey's concept of *understanding* is of central interest. It is the corner-stone of his psychology, and he sees it as our knowing the other by means of our living his experience. The affinity of this concept to Rorschach's thinking about the movement response as acting an experience innerly and thus identifying with another will be recognized. Possibly, Dilthey's in-fluence is also present in Rorschach's concept of the overtly emotion-toned response as having its roots in the unconscious.* Another idea in Dilthey familiar to a Rorschach-trained ear is that of the whole's primacy over the part in experience. It is organized wholes which, according to Dilthey, are always experienced.

Husserl, a younger contemporary of Dilthey, was closely related to him intellectually. He developed phenomenology into its systematic structure, a highly complex one. Phenomenologist though Dilthey was, he ignored Husserl's system. In it, Husserl deals with the "essentia" (*Wesenheiten*) and is not interested in a "science of facts (*Tatsachenwissenschaft*)" (Klüver, op. cit., p. 452). We are no doubt seeing vestiges here of medieval philosophy's controversy between the "nominalists" and the "realists." It is with the "realists" that Husserl seems to be sympathetic insofar as the "reality" of the medieval philosophers was that of the mental phenomena. From the viewpoint of a psychology of personality, and of Rorschach's ex-periment, Husserl's modern version of this reality has the significance, one, that it focuses on a core sector of the personality, its innermost experience, and, secondly, that it provides theoretic rationale for what is the core of Rorschach's experiment, his *Erlebnistypus*. But this Rorschach reaches by way of his objective test (my main thesis of this chapter), and with it, he builds a bridge into the *essentia* of the human mind.

Spranger is best known to American psychologists for his six types, the more so since Gordon Allport took them as his point of departure in his in-vestigation into values. But Spranger, like Dilthey and Husserl, is inter-ested primarily in what goes on within. He sees human life in terms of mean-ing. A person is as his meanings are. But meanings are inner experiences, and so Spranger's focus is also on the inner life. And this precisely is what Rorschach's *Erlebnistypus* is. Like Rorschach, although not with the same experimental orientation, Spranger rested on empiric data. He observed the overt behaviors in which people expressed their meanings. These clustered into the theoretic, economic, political, social, religious, and aesthetic values (his six types). In behaviors accenting these interests, persons objectified

---

* See his interpretations of the color-determined responses in the record of a patient in psychoanalysis as reported in a posthumous paper.[58]

their meanings. Thus, Spranger used observable data as his bridge to the innermost experience. That both Spranger and Rorschach were oriented by type psychology is, however, happenstance. There is no relation between their type concepts. Spranger's is, in fact, incidental to his basic psychology of meaning, while Rorschach's is a derivation from Jung's types. As we shall shortly see, Rorschach's type exposition, too, is not central to his thinking. His *Erlebnistypus* is a concept much more helpful in describing what goes on within and much more fruitful as an aid toward understanding some clinical pictures.

The philosophical quality in these three systems is evident. For the Rorschach student, what is arresting in them is the reaching into inner experience which is nuclear to all three. The key to Rorschach's psychology of personality is the *Erlebnistypus*, and the word *Erlebnis* means *experience* as something lived innerly. It is clear too from Rorschach's detailed exposition of the *Erlebnistypus* that he intends just that—inner experience.

Yet, Rorschach was an empiricist, as Klüver notes (op. cit., p. 450). Rorschach reveals this in his insistence on statistical criteria for some of the variables in his test. Oberholzer's painstaking development of the test was obsessionally empiric.* In my work, I have used the test strictly empirically, and the purpose of this book is to demonstrate such use of it. How then to reconcile the empiric-behavioral approach with the more philosophical-phenomenologic thought background? In raising this question I am not pointing to any incompatibility between experimental method and phenomenology. One need only call to mind that arch-experimentalist and also phenomenalist, Titchener; and for others, the Gestalt group, and notably Lewin. In Rorschach the contact between the two orientations, the one being the viewpoint of inner experience and the other being that of objective method, is in his *Erlebnistypus*. In the components of this cardinal finding in his test, and in their psychologic significance, he devised an empiric method for penetrating inner experience. He constructed a bridge across the chasm.

We turn to the two components of the *Erlebnistypus*: M and C, movement and color. The responses scored M are percepts of *forms* seen as if in *movement*. In the responses scored C (whether C, CF or FC) the color contributes in varying degrees toward determining the subject's association. Of the assumptions that have reference to the M responses, we are here principally concerned with two. They are (a) that the subject is en-

* Oberholzer's failure to publish more than he did was due to his compelling need for substantiation of his results. I recall while working with him in Zürich that he needed "just two more" Rorschachs of a certain clinical group to be sure of the pattern. He already had nearly a hundred. This self-imposed restriction has been a source of profound regret to all Rorschach students and of frustration to his publisher.

gaging mentally in the activity which he reports as being in the test figure, and that (b) he invests certain feelings varying in intensity from one M to another in the association. With regard to the C-determined percepts, the principal assumption of interest here is that it tells of feelings that are (a) outwardly expressed as (b) reaction to something in the environment. The intensity of these feelings varies, as does the quality of the relation to the environment. The reports (Chapters 3–10) that form the bulk of the present book offer some case evidence regarding the psychologic significance of M and C. For further evidence and discussion I can only refer the reader to the body of literature, case material as well as theoretic, that has grown so voluminously in these past thirty years. However convinced or not the reader may be by all these writings, I ask him to accept the assumptions above for the purpose of the reasoning that follows.

M starts with being a cognitive activity; the subject perceives a form. It is, further, a report of an experience, something which the subject has done, is doing, or would like to do. "Would like" includes also "would not like." The idea may be a wish or a fear. In either event, it is a representation of action. Being ideas, M are presumably innervated in the cortex at the level of the highest mental processes.

C reports the pleasure-toned feeling sensations, the warm glows that are called out by a brilliant sunset, a freshly blooming flower, a charming woman. Of the same affective quality are the excitements of shared events, as when one is present at a large athletic spectacle or a public celebration. Included among these feelings are certain primitive excitements that "carry us off our feet" or, which is the equivalent, make us "lose our heads." So intense are these that they approach the unbearable and affectively exceed the pleasure level. They can become painful. These feelings are presumably innervated by the autonomic nervous system, most likely the sympathetic.

The total of M responses in a Rorschach test record together with the weighted total of the C responses are the constituents of the *Erlebnistypus*. That is, certain operationally describable test behaviors, identified by the signs M and C, structuralize the *Erlebnistypus*. The indispensable technical requisite is that the examiner sharply define the test behaviors which he labels with these signs, the boundaries that he draws around the verbal behavior in a test record which he so scores, assuring himself that he always so scores such test behavior and never so does for any other test behaviors. How sound the final *Erlebnistypus* arrived at will necessarily depend on how sound were the observations on which the M and C decisions were based. Assuming a scrupulously self-disciplined identifying of these responses, we are able by means of these behaviors so scored, to penetrate to the psychologic activities for which they stand: the wished or feared idea and the pleasure-toned emotion in relation to something external. That is, we build a bridge out of behavioral data into those layers of another's personality which are most himself.

The M and C behaviors do not inform us as to the personal dynamics, but they are a means of entry and light up the psychologic processes as processes. They tell what the person is like in terms of process, or psychologic structure. Rorschach likes the term *"apparat."* The concept appears to be at one with Freud's "psychologic economy," and Rorshach's psychoanalytic thinking was well within Freud's orientation. From the M and the C we know the degree to which feelings play a role in the person's living pattern, but we do not yet know what the ideas are which they energize. We know how much the subject contains his wishes and fears in an imagined activity, but we do not know what he wishes for nor what he fears. We need, therefore, to examine the thought content as well in the M and the C responses. It is in this sense that, in Spranger's theorizing, *meaning* is the medium whereby we know the other, since only the meanings of our inner experiences can, according to Spranger, be communicated from person to person.* (See Klüver's exposition.)

Overt behaviors in the Rorschach test are M and C, while in life they would be the observable acts whereby we usually judge people. From acts we infer certain underlying personality activities in our friends, colleagues, or patients. How do we arrive at these inferences? We know from their words and actions the feelings and intents that accompany them because we have those feelings and intents when speaking or behaving similarly. Or, at the remotest, we have known someone who so behaved and talked and have had the opportunity to know their intents, i.e., their meanings. The essence of it is: we have lived or known the experience and related behaviors now being objectified in the subject's or patient's behavior and so can reason from his present behavior to his inner experience. Rorschach's M and C—always assuming validity—elicit these behaviors through the instrumentality of a fixed and controllable tool.

Our understanding of others is always an inferential process. Phenomenologic though the data may be, they can only be known from some behavior—whether verbal or acted out behavior. The associations to the Rorschach test are verbal behavior elicited under the standard microcosm which the ten inkblots set up. It follows from the foregoing that one's understanding of the other has as its limits his own experience potential. To the extent that the clinician, the sensitive observer in life, the Rorschach

---

* Spranger apparently did not grasp the possibility of focusing on the processes *qua* processes of another. Quoting from Klüver's discussion, "We can have in common only the *meaning* (Klüver's italics) of our subjective experiences, not the processes themselves" (p. 448). Rorschach advanced beyond Spranger in devising an instrument whereby to recognize the processes themselves.

experimenter, can himself live mentally the needs, difficulties, pains, sufferings, joys and tragedies of the other, to that extent can he be an understanding clinician or insightful writer or comprehending Rorschach student. One's ability to interpret a Rorschach test record is measurable by one's own *Erlebnistypus*.

But what is *Erlebnistypus*? A clear-cut definition is now in order for this finding—nuclear to the test yet so puzzling. The importance which Rorschach attaches to it is gauged by his having devoted 49 of the 127 pages of general text in the *Psychodiagnostik* to an exposition of its significance. The attention it has received in the test literature, and in using the test, however, has been in inverse ratio to this emphasis by Rorschach himself. This is because of the lack of a definitive description of it. Rorschach's many pages demonstrated its application but left it unclear as a defined psychologic process, or cluster of processes. The fact is that not even the students most sympathetic to his orientation have been sensitized to its possibilities. I entered a blind alley as far back as 1938[7] by translating the word *Erlebnistypus* as Experience Balance (EB). The thinking behind this was dictated by the term *typus*. However, the Rorschach test patterns I was obtaining from the variety of patients in my early work with the test, at the Boston Psychopathic Hospital, led me into theorizing about the human personality as a multidimensional system of psychologic stresses. Yet, was this *Erlebnistypus* an experience *balance*, i.e., a balance in the direction of either M or C, of introversion or extraversion? This is a steering of the *Erlebnis* into the channels of Jung's type theory. It is understandable that Rorschach should have been so influenced, living as he did when Jung's types were attracting so much interest and when he was working so close to Jung geographically. But type psychology does not do justice to the *Erlebnis* concept. It does not stimulate exploration of the research ideas with which this concept is pregnant. As a result Rorschach's brilliantly achieved insight has lain fallow.

Bash's[3] effort to define the *Erlebnistypus* mathematically, a method which would at the same time revise it to the point of discarding important forms of it, here deserves notice. Bash criticizes the concept as neither unidimensional, unitary in its significance, nor linear as measure. He comments further, "In addition, the concept carries within it a factor which, while diagnostically important, very much complicates the situation: the spread of the *Erlebnistypus*, as dilated or constricted." Bash then devises a linear measure enabling the examiner to rank the subject along an introversion-extraversion scale. He calls it *Einstellungswert* (EW), i.e., the subject's attitude measure. But, as he himself says, it is but "a partial function of the *Erlebnistypus*," since he achieves this measure by eliminating the constriction-dilation factor. In so doing, he is removing from the *Erleb-*

*nistypus* a critical differentiating datum. It is important not only in itself, i.e., for what it tells about the subject at the time of the Rorschach test, but also by reason of its varying with significant clinical change in a patient. Much as I would like to go along with Bash in his ingenious mathematical effort to provide a metric for this complex psychologic indicator which would enable us to treat it statistically, I find myself unable to do so. This proposal denatures the *Erlebnistypus*. It throws out the baby with the bath water.

Comparative findings in different personality groups point up the *Erlebnistypus* as something with potent psychologic significance. It throws critical light concerning the inner state to which his life's course has brought the patient, and its findings are pregnant with indications for the therapeutic possibilities. The findings can be compared with those now available for the several clinical conditions, for repeated tests in individual patients at different treatment points, for different intelligence levels, and for various age levels.

The findings for the same persons at different treatment points are especially enlightening. As one example, there is the Orthogenic School boy whose three Rorschachs I have previously reported.[11] Tested at the age of 7 years, 9 months, when he had been resident in the school for 26 months, his EB was recorded as 4:13 (4 M and weighted C score of 13); in his second test, at age 10 years, 11 months, after 64 months in the school, the EB was 0:1.5; in his third test, at age 13 years, 5 months, shortly before his discharge, after 94 months in the school, the EB was 2:5. Viewing each in relation to the treatment course, it can be seen that at the time of the first test the treatment had not yet achieved any appreciable progress. Eddie (as I called him in that report) was in a severely uncontrolled phase. His EB was at its most expansive. The *sum* of the two component scores rather than their balance, or ratio, best tells this side of the story. As Eddie showed up in this EB, his inner experience was very forceful, both as imagination and as expression of mobilized feelings. This was his actual experiencing state. Anything could be expected to happen with this *Erlebnis*. In fact, as his counselors would only too wryly testify, anything did (see the report of the psychiatric and social work notes from the school's files (ibid., pp. 273ff). When tested after 38 more months in the school's climate, his EB had contracted to a bare minimum (0:1.5). Eddie now showed almost no spirit. He was in that overcompensated phase which carries over into decompensation. A sluggish inner state was revealed by this second EB, which suggested that he could go through episodes in which very little would happen. The school's files included notes such as "sad, aloof, depressed" (ibid., p. 277). The EB total of 1.5 tells of the constrained inner experience state into which his malformed character was canalized under the effect of the school's treatment atmosphere. He continued in the school for another 30 months and was tested shortly before leaving. The clinical notes said about him: "Seems more mature, with more tonus in movement, speech, approach to others." The EB in his third test was 2:5. The sum of the two, 7, was that of a person with emotional freedom. Eddie had shaken off the lethargy and constraints of the interim period, and he manifested none of the undirected energy of his initial stage. His last total *Erlebnis* was at a level between the two extremes which were his portions when his mental states were at their most pathologic.

The *Erlebnis* total thus tells us what the experience processes of the subject actually are. But are they diagnostic or prognostic? Do they describe how the subject is now, or how he is shortly to become? On these questions our information is anything but decisive. The essential fact is that the experience actual—and hence my new symbol, EA—reflects the inner state in the subject's present mental phase—the inner state as total psychologic vitality, whether exerting pressure outwardly or converted into dream living. It does not necessarily inform us as to how long the phase will last. It may be something through which the subject is going; it may be his permanent way of life.

The illness may seem to shape the experience state (EA), may seem the cause of the patient's total emotional state, but this does not necessarily follow. So far as we now have the facts, the cause–effect relationship may be the contrary. It may be just as correct to say that the expanded EA at the time of Eddie's first test unleashed Eddie's primitive infantilisms; his very reduced inner experiencing at the second test point made him the torpid child he then was; and similarly for the third EA, when Eddie was ready to emerge from the school's protective walls. However, this reasoning cannot stand on present available facts either. Rorschach devotes some pages to this question of *Erlebnistypus* and illness, but all we can know is that the two sets of variations go together: the course of the illness and the Experience Actual, EA. We can add that these two sets of variations are seen together frequently enough to permit predicting from one to the other even while we remain in ignorance as to what is causing what. A third speculation would be that one common cause produces both. However this may be, we can still, using the test as our known variable, reason from it concerning the unknown variable: the style of life, as emotional experience, to expect of the subject.

Another case is that of Duncan, an adolescent who was receiving analytic therapy at Michael Reese Hospital. Two Rorschach tests were obtained, one at the beginning and one at the close of treatment (ref. 11; pp. 69–147), at ages 15 years, 11 months and 18 years, 3 months, 28 months apart. The EA were: in the first test, 11:6; in the second, 13:4. Quantitatively the EA was unchanged: 17 and 17. The changes were in the shifts within, toward introversion of his strong feelings. As reported from the test findings and as the clinical notes indicated, Duncan had made "not unmixed" progress before treatment was terminated by his induction into military service. The psychiatrist's closing notes delineate a boy bubbling with the spirits represented in the expansive EA. From these two EA findings, conclusions can be drawn as to how Duncan experiences the world. The EA does not tell us what he will do, however. That is determined by the general state of mental health, seen in the larger personality picture.

I have published other Rorschach test records and findings from repeated tests of the same persons (ref. 9; pp. 336–392). In one pair of records, a woman of 28 was at the time of the first test in one of those psychoses in which signs of schizophrenia appear in a primarily hypomanic reaction pattern. The EA of 8:8 told of a forceful emotionality that had its counterpart in the clinical picture in the hospital. She voluntarily returned 16 months later for the repeated test. Her EA in this second test was 12:11, more expansive inner living than indicated in the first.* The promise of vigorous psychologic living in the first test is more than confirmed by the EA during remission. What the second EA alone does not tell is whether this woman might break down again. She did, returning to the Boston Psychopathic Hospital in a condition essentially reproducing that in which she was at the time of her first test.

Another pair of tests was obtained from a 17 year old sentenced to life imprisonment for murder. The first was obtained within the first ten days of his entering the prison, the second 29 months later. The respective EA: 1:2.5, for a total of 3.5; and 1:0.5 for a total of 1.5. In the first we see an already dispirited state; in the second, he is even more deadened. The months of confinement were having their effect.

The other pair of records are those of a psychiatrist, one record being obtained before psychoanalysis and one during its course. He was in his early thirties at the time of his first Rorschach test; the second was given 31 months later when, he estimated, the analysis had still about one-fourth to go. The EA in the first was 3:2, an EA total of 5.0; in the second, 13:4.5, for a total of 17.5. A gain toward a much richer, freer style of day-to-day feeling can be inferred from the 17.5 in comparison to the 5.0. At the time of the first test he was nervously, cautiously inhibited; at the time of the second, as he himself stated (ibid., p. 382), he more easily expressed himself emotionally and was better able to verbalize fantasy, changes readily

---

* This is not an uncommon finding in manics. Although more talkative during an attack, they are much less organized and their total test patterns are quantitatively less productive.

traceable to the psychoanalysis. The total adjustment had not yet stabilized, of course—the subject was still "plowed up"—since the analysis was still incomplete.

The present volume includes the three test records of another child in the Orthogenic School (Clyde, pp. 155ff.). The course of the EA is, in the three tests, 0:21; 0:14; 6:9.5. The progression toward more control of his swirling inner state is the story which these EA's tell. From each, as a sum, we know about how much psychologic animation to expect. In the interpretation (pp. 172ff.) concerning Clyde, I discuss this within the framework of Clyde's other trends at each test point.

In the changes of EA in the above individuals, one constancy persists. The arresting fact is that for any one person the balance of M:C quantitatively tends to be in the same direction nearly always. In Eddie, C always exceeds M; in Duncan, M is greater than C both times; the woman with the hypomanic excitement is ambiequal both times. Only our prisoner departs from the rule: C exceeds M in his first test, and M exceeds C in the second. The psychiatrist in psychoanalysis also follows the rule, M greater than C both times. The Orthogenic School boy, Clyde, reacts with C greater than M all three times. Assuming that these trends are confirmed in large-scale statistics for repeated Rorschach tests in the same patients, these findings lend support to the type theory. Once introversive or extratensive, always introversive or extratensive.

This rule would substantiate the concept of Rorschach's *Erlebnistypus* as type, the type being indicated in the excess of M or of C over the other. Hence, too, the explanation of my own thinking of *Erlebnistypus* as balance or EB. This thinking about types or balance does not lose its descriptive value for personality by reason of the greater significance, as I now see it, of the Experience Actual (EA). As any of the examples above show, it is one thing to know that the subject possesses much experience potential. What the actual life pattern is, is another thing. Eddie in his first test, Duncan in both, the psychiatrist in his third—all are brimming with inner life. In Duncan and in the psychiatrist the introversive balance leads to an expectation of one kind of observable behavior—socially constructive behavior; in Eddie to something destructive. Similarly the quantitative course of the balance itself—will the subject stay introversive, turn extratensive, or vice versa?—is highly informative as to the personality's course (cf. in Clyde, p. 181). In any Rorschach test pattern the direction of the balance always gives decisive leads concerning the way the patient employs his psychologic resources, and the EB, Rorschach's *Erlebnistypus*, remains one of the most useful indices in understanding the total pattern.

Rorschach's attempt to correlate the experience types (EB) with the several mental illnesses has a great deal of theoretic interest. I can present much support for this from my own findings, but I can also present many cases that go contrary to the theory. Hence, it still needs much verification. Rorschach is himself cautious on the point (pp. 123f), although in his Tables IX and X (pp. 79–80) he constructs a correlational scheme of *Erlebnistypus* for all the mental diseases, and also the intelligence levels. He engages in some provocative reasoning concerning the manic-depressive groups being clinically on one continuum with the obsessive-compulsive, as well as with some well-endowed normals. In all these groups he finds an ambiequal *Erlebnistypus*. But is there a relationship between this type and the illness? Or between the EB types and the healthier personality structures? Rorschach's surmise is that if there is, we do not know whether the illness shapes the EB, or the EB predetermines the form of the illness. He hazards that both processes are probably going on.

From my own material, I can confidently say that certain *Erlebnistypus* findings regularly enough characterize certain clinical pictures to indicate a co-variance. In depressives, for example, M and C are always either absent or very low. At the other extreme, manics score with much of both M and C. Among the neurotics, however, I have found any and all *Erlebnistypus*. Rorschach reports similar findings but restricts this observation to anxiety neurotics; varieties of EB are found among "all persons, introversive as well as extratensive" (p. 125), he writes, but he adds that there are "significant differences between the anxiety neuroses of the introversives and of the extratensives" (ibid.), and he points to relationships between forms of the EB and the structures of the neuroses.

In my schizophrenic patients, the *Erlebnistypus*, or experience balance, does differentially characterize the different reaction patterns.[15] In S-1* the balance is C greater than M, which may be lacking altogether; the quantity of C varies but is likely to be higher than M. In S-2, M is very high in quantity, greater than C, although this may also be high. In S-3, C is greater than M, but the quantity of each is small. In SR-2, M is greater than C, the quantity of both being in a moderate range.†

In terms of classical diagnosis, S-1 would correspond to hebephrenic schizophrenia, for which Rorschach reports an extratensive EB. S-2 would be paranoid schizophrenia, for which Rorschach finds clear-cut introversive EB. The S-3 is the equivalent of the post-Bleuler concept of pseudoneurotic schizophrenia, a category Rorschach did not deal with, of course, as he also

* This and the following similar terms refer to categories of schizophrenia, which are explained below.

† I am omitting reference to the other two schizophrenics, SR-1 and S-G. These are both strictly children's schizophrenias, and may be a transitional phase in the children in whom they are found.

did not with SR-2, a category developed in our research on the test patterns.*

The differentiations in my own schizophrenic patterns are based on two spheres of reference. Rorschach's EB is one. But, in addition to the direction of the balance in any pattern, as well as any constant relationship between experience balance and the type of schizophrenia, the *quantities* of inner experience, as measured by the M and C totals, vary consistently for each pattern. This is the Experience Actual, EA, i.e., the present total inner force with which the patient operates. It is of import that those patterns of schizophrenia in which the Experience Actual is quantitatively highest are those in which the manifest symptoms are clinically most obvious: in order of frequency and severity, these are S-2, S-1, SR-2, and S-3. Translating from the indicated Experience Actual into clinical language, the greater the supply of inner energy, the more it is converted into pathologic symptoms, given a personality that is taking recourse to a symptomatic solution. Can one reason from either the EB, Experience Balance, or from the EA, Experience Actual, to the form of the schizophrenia? The answer must be in the negative. So far as the EB goes, I have among my test records one which I obtained from a woman in a mental hospital who had, clinically, as beautiful a set of paranoid symptoms as could be found in a textbook. But there was not a single M in her Rorschach test; pure color responses characterized it: the uninhibited feelings with which she verbally attacked all on the hospital wards—doctors and nurses indiscriminately—and her suspicions held her response total to a minimum. I can produce other examples that disturb the rules. All we can say at present is that patients with some schizophrenic reaction patterns are likely to respond with Rorschach test records of certain emotional Experience Balances but that there is a crossing over of lines by individual patients. We cannot reason from the *Erlebnis* finding to the kind of schizophrenia.

Correlation of intelligence level with the Experience Balance also cannot be counted upon. In adults, any EB may be found with any level of intelligence, i.e., the EB may be introversive, extratensive, or ambiequal, with either of the components, M or C, being high, medium or low. This generalization holds also in adolescence, and even in younger children, beginning at about age seven. Below this age, children do not produce M, apart from an occasional, very exceptional child. It may be that a constitutional factor is here in evidence, that it is an ability which does not begin to mature until this age. Or it may be of psychogenic significance: children

---

* I.e., from our Rorschach test diagnoses. The psychiatrists collaborating with us in the research recognized the clinical logic in SR-2. It is a pattern not discernible by the usual clinical observations.

may cease at about age seven to live in fantasy as if it were reality, so they develop a fantasy life, M, distinct from the real world.

In most feebleminded subjects, both M and C are lacking, although some react with much C. Very few are capable of the M response. The intelligence curve does not correlate with any distinctive EB. But it does co-vary with EA. This rule is, in fact, strikingly maintained the higher in the intelligence scale the subjects are. Rorschach constantly accented this point in relation to *dilatierte* EB.

The Experience Actual indicates what we can expect of the subject in terms of emotional force, timber, depth, range. To know what he does with this emotional equipment, or what it does with him, we need to know all the rest of his test pattern, to have before us all the other data that contribute to the interpretation of a test record: the tabulations and the qualitative structure and content. This is to say that we evaluate Experience Actual just as Rorschach evaluates Experience Balance—in the light of F+, Ap, Seq, R, V, Y, W, Z, and the others. We observe these Rorschach test signs as activity—psychologic activity—of the whole, individual subject. In their interaction they represent the facets of the entire functioning with which the subject handles his affairs. The M:C interaction participates in this functioning as the emotional constituent. The subject's total equipment is never more sound than his intellectual acuity and control and always as rich as his emotional range and sensitivity. We know both with our intellect and our emotions.*

In this knowing in which the whole person participates we recognize that *understanding* which Dilthey calls whole experience and which, in Spranger, is the innerly lived *meaning* that constitutes each of us. It is the psychologic *Ding an Sich*. But this is a phenomenalist interpretation of the psychologic events whereby we know. It appears to set the Rorschach test within the scope of phenomenology. Yet, Rorschach wanted the test to be based on statistics, of a kind which make his test a behavioral tool (pp. 23, 41, 54, 196). My own confidence in it rests on the degree to which it is amenable to behavioral method, to normative definitions as nearly operational as it is possible to make them, and to statistical controls. At the same time, there is the awareness that phenomenology cannot mix with the statistics of behavioral science, as Snygg[65] shows. How do we reconcile this discrepancy?

The inconsistency is not as serious as it may seem. Our starting point in evaluating a test record is, always, the behavior of the subject who produced it: his associations to the test and certain other activities. For

* This topic of the emotions' share in our everyday knowing, an intriguing one in itself, is considered in a separate paper.[10]

some of these behaviors statistical controls are available. Others of these behaviors can be normatively and definitively described. They are, to this extent, operational. Certain others are more qualitative but are nevertheless subject to a controlling description.

Making these behaviors our points of reference, we look for the meanings in them, meanings carried by psychologic processes which are externalized in these behaviors. We can know these meanings from two sources. One is statistical validation clinically. What do we know from extra-Rorschach sources about the persons who consistently follow certain Rorschach test patterns? And what psychologic reasoning is in order from such validating consistencies? So proceeding, we are reasoning experimentally in the way Bernard has delineated (see pp. 2f.). We have subjected the test to a variety of conditions and recorded its behaviors. This is Rorschach's experiment. Secondly, to what extent do the words, actions, and associations of the subject in reaction to this standard set of stimuli awaken in the investigator himself certain experiences? By reason of our own recall of such emotional experience and of the meaning it had to us, we understand the meaning to the subject. This is how we penetrate the personality of another by way of his manifest behavior. It is the only way. Unless we are willing to rest on such inference, there can be no communication between men, no essential understanding. From the very beginnings of the human adventure, men have always known one another by what they did. Science has been catching up and verifying this axiomatic rule; for example, Darwin's [28, 29] observation of emotion in man and lower species and the current, more systematic studies of communication, including investigations in psychopathology (cf., Ruesch[59]). There is a hazard in this inferential procedure, the hazard of mistaking a meaning which is entirely ours for one which we infer to be the subject's. Some well-known cautions, which are in the scientific equipment of the disciplined investigator, will, it is hoped, preserve him from this error.

Used operationally, the Rorschach test can be an instrument that bridges the gulf between an investigator and his patient. By means of the total *Erlebnistypus*—the Experience Actual—the test sounds the depth experience, the inner, emotionally most intense, mental life of the other. The test thus makes the bold effort of crossing the Kantian chasm to the *Ding an Sich*, doing so by means of Bridgman's operational logic. How nearly it succeeds in this is, of course, the issue always open to experimental verification.

# II.
## The persons

CHAPTER 3

# Lenore:

# A girl of eleven in a troubled withdrawal

### Response Record

*Figure I* (10″)

1. W F+ A, Ay
1.0

'Looks like a bird, on a totem pole. Looks like some kind of bird . . . the wings.' (W. D 2: bird. D 8: beak. 'Because of the bill. Shape. Looks like it is on a totem pole. One of those funny birds on a totem pole. Carved on a totem pole. This is the bottom.' Uncertain about the wings. Thought for a while of D 7 as wings.)

2. D M+ Hd

'These look like hands.' (D 1: hands. 'Look like they are grabbing something.')

*Figure II* (6″)

3. D F+ A

'Ah! Elephants!' (D 1: body. D 4: trunk, feet.)

4. D F+ Cg

'Hats. Elephants and hats.' (Returns. Encouraged.) (D 2. 'Looks like a hat. Party hats. Birthday hat. Funny shape.' No C.)

*Figure III* (15″)

5. D M+ H P
3.0

'People and a pot.' (D 9: Face. Hands. Leg. Cooking. D 4: pot. Shape. Not seen as doing something together.)

6. Dd M.FV− H

'Looks like forms of people in background.' (Dd 29. 'In the background, sitting down. Form of hat, legs, cape on.' Background? 'They are small; you can't see them very well. Not together.') 'That is all.'

*Figure IV* (20″)

7. D F− Ar

∧ ∨ ∧ ∨ ∧ 'Looks something like a fountain.' (Upper half, D 4, 'because it is coming down. Spreading up': D 3. 'Got lines going out, shooting up. Stone part. That is what it usually is. Shading gives the lines.') (Returns card. Encouraged.)

8. D F+ Adx

'Looks like dog's nose, mouth, something like it here.' (D 2. 'Shape, I guess. Tongue.')

24

*Figure V* (8″)

9. W F+ A P
   1.0

'Looks like a bat.' (W: wings; feet. 'Would be to here.' Not D 10).
'That is all.' (Returns. Encouraged.)

10. Ds F+ Ad

'Alligator, the heads of alligators.' (D 10. 'Looks like open mouth of alligator. The space here. Shape.')

*Figure VI* (37″)

11. D F+ Ad

∧ ∨ ∧ 'This looks like the back of a cat's head with the whiskers.' (D 7. 'Looks like whiskers': Dd 26. 'These could be the ears.')

12. D F+ Ad

'Bird's wings.' (D 6. 'Looks like feathers. Shape.')
'That is all.'

*Figure VII* (10″)

13. D F+ Hd P

'Head of an Indian.' (D 1. 'Got a feather': D 5. 'Nose, shape. Eye, nose, neck.')

14. D F− Ar

'A building with a round top.' (D 10. 'Half round and half square top. Looks like one. Shape. Looks like the texture of stone. The lines in it.')
'That is all.'

*Figure VIII* (6″)

15. D F+ A P

'Some kind of animal.' (D 1. 'Looks like it. Head. Little legs. Climbing up something. Mouse or something. Shape.')

16. D T.C Bt
    4.0

'Looks like vine, the animals hanging on to vine.' (D 4. 'Hanging on to the vine with their paws. Looks like vine. The texture looks like vine, the inside, lightness and darkness. And also color of vine.' Only in inquiry, C)

17. D FC.Y+ Ls

'Like rocks' (D 2. 'Shape and shading, different colors. I mean the different shades in the colors.')

*Figure IX* (Rejection)

Rejects.

'Looks like nothing. I see nothing here.' ('No.' Shaking her head.)
Shaking her head. Encouraged to keep the card. 'I see nothing.'

*Figure X* (5″)

18. D F+ A
19. D FC+ A

'Birds.' (D 2. 'Shape. No special kind.')
'Caterpillars.' (D 4. 'Shape and they are green.' FC.)
'Flowers.' (Cannot locate.)

20. D F − A          'Spiders.' (D 7. 'Spiders or frogs. Hind legs. Shape.')
21. D F + Bt         'These look like seed from a maple tree.' (D 3.' Shape.')
22. D F + Bt         'Roots.' (D 8. 'Roots or a tree'; D 14: trunk. 'Shape.')
23. Dd F Bt          'Flowers.' (Dd from D 8 up to D 14. 'Shape.')
24. D CF + A         'These are bluebirds.' (D 6. 'Color and shape.')
                     'That is all.'

Liked best card X:       'More shapes and colors.'
Liked least card IX:     'No shape on it. Just colors put together.'
                     Total Time: 11'50″

### Response Summary

R:24

| | | | | | | |
|---|---|---|---|---|---|---|
| W | 2 | M | 2 | H | 2 | F+ 81% |
| D | 20 (S:1) | M.FV− | 1 | Hd | 2 | A 50% |
| Dd | 2 | T.C | 1 | A | 8 | P 4 |
| | 24 | CF | 1 | Ad | 4 (x:1) | S 4% |
| | | FC | 1 | Ar | 2 | Af r 0.72 |
| Z f* 4 | | FC.Y | 1 | Bt | 4 | L 2.42 |
| Z sum 9.0 | | F+ | 13 | Cg | 1 | T/R 29.58 |
| Ap (W) D! Dd | | F− | 3 | Ls | 1 | T/first R 13.0 |
| Seq. methodical | | F | 1 | | 24 | Fln R 1.22 |
| | | | 24 | | | Fln T/first R 11.37 |
| | | EB 3/3.5 | | | | |
| | | EA 6.5 | | | | |

### Interpretation

A child lacking in the spontaneity, intellectual and emotional, that normally characterizes a girl of this age is the portrait drawn by this Rorschach test. A spiritless girl, at the age of eleven she lives with the psychologic tonus of a woman in her decline.

Intellectually, Lenore is sluggish [1]†, resigned, apathetic [2]. Much of her productivity maintains an invarying tempo [3], a wooden nonresilience. Her language includes perseverative trends and childish idioms such as are found in dedifferentiated and in nondifferentiated intelligences [4]. The speech pattern throughout is without the rhythm, the babbling brook tempo, so charming in every healthy child [5]. Perceptually, she frequently restricts her field of vision [6] after a pattern observed in the feeble-minded, and also in the anxious, in whom it is a functional mental deficiency. In the latter, the anxiety imposes psychological blinders, and these do to the individual what the physical blinders on his harness do

* Z f is frequency of Z, i.e., a simple count of organization responses.

† Bracketed numbers refer to Notes on Interpretation, which for this chapter will be found on pages 33–38.

to the horse. They narrow the range of the perceived world and so exclude any percepts which might be exciting—but could also make for a run-away, and the related untoward consequences.

The possibility for lively humor, although not for a run-away, is present in this girl. In her emotional life, which has been less accessible to the outer constricting forces, she can be responsive. But she puts a damper on her vivacity. Under conditions that strike a pleasurable note, her first reaction was, for example, "Ah, elephants," which is one of true childish excitement. Her thoughts go to the animal (R 3) that means the circus is coming and all the rapture which the circus holds. But she cannot follow through with the emotional tone itself [7]; she denies it (R 4, inquiry). She fails fully to express any feelings outwardly. Warm feeling pressures are nevertheless part of her. Appropriate external events [8] draw them out, and she is relatively more released under these conditions; they ring a bell in her [9]. The response is wide in its range of intensities: undelayed impulsivity, the lability of the still-growing child, but also ego restraint over the feelings [10]. She can keep her feelings under intellectual control [11], at times moderating them in consideration for others to a point where she can feel with the other [12], enough so, in fact, to uncover a maturational process that is taking place emotionally [13]. The total quantity of emotional influence which she permits herself for the entire record actually reflects release [14]. Also, the themes around which her feelings play, while not unmixed in flavor, speak of animation [15]. She is responding appropriately, i.e., to what draws out pleasurable feelings in others. The mixed flavor makes itself known as process and in content. As process it is apparent twice, minor key mood tones fusing into the cheerful ones [16]. "Mixed feelings," in the phrase of the novelists, is what we see here. Concerning the probable total quality of this fusion, see below [17]. Content carrying a lower key resonance is seen in R 16, an insecurity motif.

Of chief import in revealing her poorly organized state when it comes to dealing with her emotions is the severe shock which Lenore can suffer in an emotion-provoking situation [18]. She withdraws completely; and a question needs to be raised of hostile stirrings as she does so [19]. There is free anxiety, severe in its manifestation [20]. She reacts to a disturbing situation by rejecting it. She does not disintegrate; the ego is strong enough to prevent a break-up [21]; but the emotional impact is too much for it and cuts her off from the personality resources which this girl has.

In sum, Lenore could enjoy life, has urges thereto [22], but cannot. She is a personality damaged in that sector where we are most ourselves, our feelings.

Nor does she turn inward with her emotions in order there to indulge the satisfactions she denies herself in overt contact with the world. She is chary of imagination, reluctant even to make use of it for autistic pleasures. Again, however, she is unfree with a way of life for which she has inclination. Her total production in this sphere is, in fact, a good showing for her age [23], but she cuts it off early in the test [24] and does not return to it. Once more we see her putting a damper on satisfactions, even such as are lived without external display, i.e., in the imagination. In fact, she drags her fantasy feet even before she completely hobbles them [25]. What she liberates is slack in feeling process [26], although betraying affect in the content [27]. Only once is there a flash of vigor in her internalized world, "the hands grabbing something"—possibly projecting hostility, possibly a phobic idea (R 2).

But why is she holding the lid down so tightly on her fantasy activity? She may fear it. Both the process and the content in what she has communicated are grounds for this speculation. The process is twice regressive, neither time seriously so, but just enough to alert a circumspect ego [28] against danger of more losses. In her full clamping down on all fantasy we see the defensive feedback effect. The fact that her final such association (R 6) was regressed along more than one dimension [29] and that the content in it is critically significant in the light of the unhappy mood so dominating the child is support for my reasoning. The leads in the content—they need to be explored further for their significance to the girl—are given in her language: "people in background; small"; (the two are) "not together." Who are the people; why small? Why are they in the background, and why are the two not together? These are broodings out of this child's unconscious, the clarifying of which is likely to help explain her withdrawal, her stiffness, and her sadness. This much escaped and then she put the brakes on. Doing so, she also threw overboard a wealth of imagination that might have stood her in good stead. This one response (R 6) has just enough spark of originality to be a promise that, were this girl psychologically free and her ego directed toward healthy goals, she could transmute this resource into satisfying forms. As she is now, she throws out the baby with the bath water.

Lenore is not a happy child. A sober mood tone is her characteristic and essentially fixed affect. The somber process of passivity dims her cheerful moments [30], makes for waves of mixed feelings, usually more painful than pleasurable and carrying the quality, principally, of agitation. A giving-up, what's-the-use attitude has already sprouted out of the passivity [31]. This hallmark of the adult depressive and of many anxious adults and children stamps this girl. The anxiety which it betrays has already been made manifest in another hallmark [32]. Also, she is under pressure for self-reassurance, another indication of anxiety. This she manifests initially only [33], after which she settles into her more shut-in pattern.

The inferiority sense troubles her. She so reacts only once, to be sure, but the intensity with which our young girl suffers from this thought is very high. It stands out the more sharply in its being, in part, of an imaginative nature. Lenore thus highlights the unconscious and deep source of her worry [34]. A painful process of another variety is the one which she projects as a sense of unsatisfied longing for affectionate contact [35]. The association in which she uncovers this need is saturated with unalloyed feelings, both exciting and agitating [36], a sign of the high tension that it produces. The theme, clinging, further supports the logic as to the general significance of this determinant: an affect hunger, having its roots in the patient's needs in her infancy for direct contact with a mother person [37].

The father also contributes to the child's unhappiness. Or, rather, thoughts about him, and related ones about masculinity, do so. They generate shock [38], clear-cut even within the otherwise dispirited total life pattern [39]. In the face of a patently father-like figure [40] Lenore gives up after one response, and her hitherto moderately differentiated thought content (of the first three test figures) withers into stereotypy throughout the immediately following, and depressing, figures (i.e., figures IV, V, VI, VII; and see note 39). The exceptions are the two probable symbolisms (R 7 and R 14). Concerning the thematic significance of these as well as their structure, and how theme and structure relate to the stimuli that release them, see note 41. Of moment here is the stirring up of anxiety by thoughts centering around the male parent. To what extent these stem from some conscious or preconscious fear about him; to what extent they reflect a deeper anxiety, defensive in purpose, or an anxiety bred by the child's need for this security prop—these are questions which the test findings can only ask.

To steady herself against these corroding emotions, Lenore has developed some by now well-established defenses. They achieve their purpose but like all defenses, physical or psychological, they are erected at a cost and maintained at a sacrifice. Her passivity and withdrawal are a major strategy. What they do to her mental freedom, intellectual as well as emotional, we have seen [42]. Exercising an extracautious, rigid hold on reality, she becomes stereotyped and narrow in her thought content, in her range of vision and of attention. To insulate her conscious thought from grasping meanings too painful to her, she deadens her ability to grasp meanings in contiguous sense data [43], and in so doing she jettisons a high achievement resource. She denies or rejects the urge to a happier emotional experience [44]. She could stabilize herself, defend against the emotional pressures, by day-dreaming solutions, but Lenore early sets her face against that way out, defends against this defense. She strikes a phobic note, binding a deeper fear, in R 10; and an even more pathologic trend may be the source of the "eye" in R 13 [45]. The massive withdrawal of which she is capable in reaction to a severe enough impact of feeling has been seen [46]. She follows this complete corking up of the associative processes with what looks like a swing in the other direction, a greatly liberated productivity [47]. A reaction formation is here in evidence, one which the girl is attempting in order to make up for what she senses as an inadequate way to have met a crisis. The defenses have a binding function on the anxiety [48], and to this extent may be looked on as adjustive. Adaptive too would be her stringent hold on reality and on herself [49] did she not, in using them, sacrifice her mental freedom and her richness. Lenore also uses symbolisms [50]. Authorities differ as to whether symbolic thinking is always regressive. Its use by neurotics to screen their conflicts so as to adapt to social norms, in contrast to schizophrenics to whom a symbol is the real thing (see pp. 236f.), appears to be grounds for looking on it as serving adjustive ends. It will be noted that she forgets one "flowers" association and so she may be putting this feminine symbol out of mind. The over-all judgment of this girl's defenses is that they are less adjustive than they are pathogenic. The harm they do her outweighs their usefulness.

The damage affects Lenore's present social adjustment, both in how she uses her intellectual equipment and how she lives emotionally. Feeling herself deprived of the blessings of life, she has reacted by absorbing herself into the self. In the process she has deprived herself the more and set up a cumulative trend toward more self-absorption; a vicious circle is in the making. The intellectual damage is not in the form of breakdown but of reduction. The child is less communicative than she could be, impoverished in her interests, inefficient in using her abilities, unable to initiate any project, and aspires to no achievement [51]. Although she shows some differentiation of interest, some flashes of ability [52], and of language quality better than that of her test record, the most clear-cut stamp on her personality is that of constriction. The wine has already run out of this young jug.

Affectively the child has in her something of the ascetic. Capable of surges of pleasure, she does not obey the impulse and deprives herself of enjoyment [53]. Something within hinders her. Questions of a depressive mood trend must be raised, as young as she is [54]. She possesses enough resilience to understand others emotionally, to be in sympathetic contact with them, but again, there is the inner obstacle and she cannot now "make it." Hence, there is a limitation on her social adaptivity, which she also manifests in an inadequate intellectual rapport [55], reflecting a failure of social participation, a withdrawal from the environment. An aloofness is here uncovered that has in it the seeds of hostility. For this the test record yields only indirect evidence [56], but the child lacks overt self-assertiveness [57], a lack that has been known to screen resentment. Again, this is not a finding but an indication, a direction to be explored clinically.

Lenore, as we have seen, also refuses herself gratifying experience even in the realm of imagination [58]. She cramps her own resources along all dimensions. Ego she has. But it is a case of all too much ego. The ego has stamina since it holds the patient integrated, whatever the emotional shock, and it can call on reserve strength when the shock necessitates the reestablishment of homeostasis. The child never retreats developmentally. In freezing her own assets, however, she is seriously impairing her adaptive ability. One may even ask whether a person so realistic is not actually unrealistic: by intellectual rigidity, such a person prevents a full perception of essentials, a deficit which he aggravates by the failure at emotional understanding. He cannot see in true focus, and he cannot listen with his affective ear. His neighbors may have quite friendly intentions toward him, and yet he keeps himself stiffly aloof. The danger to our present patient is that, just at the time in her life when she is approaching the crisis of adolescence, she will settle into her present groove, unchanging and resistant to change, which is to say, to treatment. Her personality growth will be arrested at its present truncated stage. If she can grow, and the test affords evidence that she can [59], the stage—in absence of therapy—is set for one of those irreparable losses of a human resource. The climatic conditions have so far not been benign, but these conditions are themselves subject to manipulation and to change. Treatment of this child must be designed to include that of a larger human unit—the mother-child unit.

The thematic communications of this girl taken alone enable us to view her treatment outlook as favorable. There is promise in them that she seeks a more salutary total way of life than is now hers. The themes are varied in dynamic trend. Oral content recurs too often not to be meaningful. At first, it is a small voice, the "bill," "beak" of R 1; it speaks more loudly in the "dog's mouth" of R 8; and it is emphatic in the "alligator's open mouth," (R 10). More explicitly, the signal in all these images is phobic, each more convincingly so than the preceding one, and so adding support to the interpretation. The one inconsistent note is the "tongue" (R 8), which is suggestive of a gratification need. It recalls "cooking" (R 5; note 27). The "eye" (R 13), on the other hand, has more of a pathogenic flavor [60]. The "nose," in view of its recurrence (R 8, 13), may also have personal significance, although it would be a displaced one. As in much content interpretation the association may be of no dynamic import to this individual and entirely impersonal, a function of the stimulus. Only the patient herself can, in therapeutic sessions, give the answer.

The personal meaning of her two probable symbolisms is even more presumptive: the "fountain shooting up" of R 7 and the "building with round top" of R 14. What is she trying to communicate in these associations at the same time that she evades conscious awareness of what she is communicating? Again, the answer can only come out of the child. But our confidence that she is using symbolism of dynamic import is heightened by two other facts, both in the realm of process. One is the inaccuracy of her perception in these two associations, her first two inaccuracies and the only ones until the single other one in the final test figure. This girl is not given to misperceiving her world. She does so only when the personal loading is sufficient. She then sees her world less as it is and more as she is herself [61]. The same surmise is in order with reference to the "spider" or "frog" in her other misperception (R 20; and note 62). Both these animal forms have traditionally repellent connotations. In misshaping her stimulus to see these forms, the girl is telling us, in a metaphor she does not recognize as such, her feelings on some topic and that these feelings are strong enough to distort her usually accurate sight.

The second fact of dynamic significance consists of the test cards associated with the symbolisms. One of these awakens thoughts concerning a masculine (father?) figure; and the other, thoughts concerning a feminine (and very likely, a mother) figure. This girl's sensitivity at these points and their personal dynamic significance to her have already been discussed [63].

With all this, Lenore is also informing us that she can have cheerful ideas, with the inference that she can engage in pleasant pursuits. She fairly, for her, sparkles, following the "elephant" association, with ideas about hats on the elephants, party hats, birthday hats. She displays breadth and trends toward originality such as go with a relaxed state of mind in the carved totem pole (R 1) and the Indian with feathers (R 13). She strikes what may be a more dynamic note in the "climbing" mouse (R 15), a possibly hopeful theme. Whether there is a dynamic connection in the contiguity of this motif with that of insecurity (R 16; and see above, p. 28f.) is at present an unanswered question. Finally, there is an impressive concentration (in figure X) of ideas that are feminine symbolisms and may well be reflecting a prepubescent latent, healthy feminine narcissism: flowers (twice), seed, roots, bluebird. The speculation is justified that we are looking here on the psychological seedbed of the woman that this girl is ready to be, a woman both biologically and psychologically. The further logic from these conclusions is that (a) she needs treatment, and

(b) that the treatment effort, expended from the limited resources available to a community clinic, will be well invested.

The child has assets where they count most, in the inner spheres, i.e., emotional fluidity, both as outwardly expressed feelings [8, 9, 10] and as introverted emotions [23], inhibited though she becomes in this respect. Her total inner breadth [64] gives promise of change. She can be influenced by others [65], and once the need for her self-immuring defense is relieved, she may be expected to communicate more of her unconscious fears and wishes [66] and so open to the therapist's view, and to her own, the deep sources of her self-defeating life pattern.

In the intellectual sphere the assets are less obvious. But vestiges are there [50, 52, 59], and until some therapeutic effort has been made and the girl's own ego activated to use initiative in exploiting her resources, the intellectual endowment will not be known.

On the critical question of ego, the test's indications are favorable. Lenore maintains her integration in spite of apparently corroding stresses [30–32, 34–38]. She refuses to retreat to deeply regressive behaviors. Her solution is to take losses, a self-depriving total adjustment.

Situational treatment is the obvious logic of the test's findings. First should be the treatment of the mother-daughter unit [67]. But even while this is being carried on, the child herself should be placed in social situations that will activate her potential for warm relations. Lenore has the latent capacity for real self-enjoyment, can center her feelings about socially appropriate interests, and she can probably make friends. So stimulated, and tasting the rewards which such experiences are in themselves, her ego can be counted on to direct her to realistic social goals that continue to be satisfying to herself. It is in this sense that therapy will be well invested. It will redirect this girl from her present course, one in which she will at best be dour, sour, and misanthropic, to one in which she can live and enjoy the role psychologically appropriate to her as a woman.

### Notes on Interpretation

[1] The limited productivity. She is more sluggish in this respect than the 24 responses would indicate. This total is swollen by the seven responses in figure X; the fact is that figures X and VIII account for 10 out of the 24 associations. The low organization activity affords further evidence: only four instances of it, and of these four, two account for 7.0 in the total score of 9.0. In six of the test cards she does not show the drive requisite for organizing meaningful relationships. She betrays motor inadequacy in not turning the test cards except when under anxiety shock [38]; the healthy and liberated do turn them.

[2] The resignation trends, "That is all," in figures III, V, VI, VII, X.

[3] The fluctuation of productivity: exactly the same number of responses, two, in each of the first seven test figures. This inflexibility is finally broken up by the color figures, a fact which has its own separate significance.

[4] "Looks like" recurs like the fixed phraseology found in patients in senile decline; also in some with brain pathology.

[5] A total absence of embellishment of the associations; the child merely verbalizes her percept and then leaves it bare. Her language is monosyllabic.

[6] Only one x response so scored (R 8) but the child shows numerous tendencies to this kind of perceiving: the "wings" of R 1, the "face, hands, leg," of R 5; and see also R 11, 12, 15.

[7] She fails to use a color determinant, a fact the more striking in an association in which color is usually a determinant.

[8] In response to three of the all-color figures as the test's representatives of a pleasure-laden situation. Even with the rejections of figure IX she still introduces ten associations in the other two figures.

[9] The affective ratio is high, .72, well above the upper limit of the normal range, i.e., .60.

[10] She uses the three possible nuances of the color determinant: C, CF, and FC.

[11] The F in each of her CF or FC responses is F+.

[12] The F takes precedence over the C determinant, in R 17 and R 19.

[13] Of her four color-determined associations, two are FC, a high proportion, reflecting this psychological trend.

[14] In a record with 24 responses in all, four color-determined associations is high. It speaks of affective resonance.

[15] Such is the connotation in the content of all her color-determined responses. They vary, to be sure, in the degree to which they are unique for this girl and also to the extent to which the pleasurable tone in them is one that she shares with others. The "caterpillar" of R 19 and the "rocks" of R 17 are frequent. The "bluebird" of R 24, while not uncommon, has in it the flavor of the original and may therefore have a special significance to this child (see note 52). In R 16, we note an individualized theme (and see note 52).

[16] In R 17 and R 16. It is more accented in R 16, in which the girl verbalizes the texture as well as the light-dark determinants. The texture determinant, first described by Klopfer,[42] is a variation of the shading category and communicates a nuance of its mood tone. I have omitted the Y from the scoring formula in the interest of simplicity of scoring. The interpretation, however, takes account of its influence.

[17] On p. 28, concerning the child's painful affective trends.

[18] I.e., in figure IX.

[19] The clipped language in the girl's refusal and the head shaking lead to the supposition here of a resentful state of mind.

[20] The full rejection as a violent emotional response, too quick in its onset to be controlled. Full rejections of test cards are more rare in my experience than they appear to be in that of other students of the test.

[21] See below, p. 29f., concerning the defense pattern; also pp. 31, 33 concerning this girl's ego and its integrative activity.

[22] The evidence taken together with her reaction to the chromatic test figures: the number of color-dictated associations, the relative weight of form and color in them, the content in them, and the affective ratio.

[23] Her three M responses is, in fact, above the mean of that found for a group of healthy school children.[68]

[24] She scores no M after figure III.

[25] The inability to produce M in figure II, although doing so in both figures I and III, is evidence of some impediment to an ability which she has.

[26] The energy (Levy Scale*) ratings as judged from the action sensed by the patient in each M association. These are: R 2: 3, R 5: 1, R 6: 1.

[27] Probably significant to the girl in R 2; certainly so, although covertly, in R 6. In R 5, however, the child reproduces what countless other people see here. I could judge this M to be affectless except for the word "cooking," a possibly oral theme.

[28] The structures in both R 2 and R 6 are such as are found more frequently in immature persons, including children who have grown less than would be expected for their ages. This is less true for R 2, since an M with Hd is not seriously deviant for an eleven-year old. The coincidence of Dd with an M which is also an M— is of more concern. Then, too, these less mature M productions are playing too large a role among those which she produces. Also, she fails to associate with all but one of the healthy M.

[29] I.e., both in respect to Dd and F—.

[30] The Y determinant interacting with the C factor, twice, in R 16 and again in R 17. Concerning the heavy stressing of the Y element in R 16, and the reason for not scoring it, see [16].

[31] The resignation formulae in five of the test cards, and see [2]. Also, the child's wanting to give up after one association in figures IV and V.

[32] The x response; and see [6]. It is the effect of the emotions on the

---

* This scale was devised by Zubin and Young.[70] They evaluated responses obtained with the Levy Movement Blots, a series with which D. M. Levy experimented for a time. The "Movement energy scale" was one of several which they constructed for evaluating these responses. I describe this scale elsewhere.[71]

intellect, the enfeebling result, which is explicable also as a drying up
of intellectual vigor incident to the passivity represented in the Y.

[33] Really only in the very first association, in which she qualifies
more than in any other and repeats the details which justify the "bird"
and the "totem pole" percepts. Disturbance in the first test card of a kind
not later repeated will be observed in the productions of some patients,
indicating their unsettlement as they deal with the unexpected features of
this test. Descriptively I have referred to this effect as "initial shock."

[34] R 6, doubly determined by emotional processes, i.e., M and V, the
feeling in each of which I conjecture is reinforcing that in the other. Concerning the specific thoughts, the worries, with which the inferiority
feelings relate, see above, p. 28, in exposition of the content in the
fantasy living.

[35] The texture determinant in R 16.

[36] The fusion of color with a shading variable; each unmodulated by
form. See above, p. 27, concerning the feelings.

[37] This is the general psychological significance of the texture association in my opinion,[11] which differs somewhat from that of Klopfer.[42]

[38] Seen in the differential response pattern to figures IV and VI: time
for the first response is longest for these two test cards; the F— in IV.
Card turning only at these two figures tells of the unrest. Failure here of
the P associations may look like additional evidence, but this failure does
not, in this child's record, differentiate figures IV and VI from enough other
test cards. Her P count is low for the record as a whole; see above, p. 31.
In (the "mother") figure VII the first association is the usual Hd, P, and
the speed of first response is near this girl's own average, even slightly
faster. She does not here manifest anxiety shock. The F— does tell of
some disturbance, of unsteadiness, of sensitivity. But with maternal imagery she remains more comfortable than with thoughts related to masculinity.

[39] It is a provocative comment on Rorschach's test that the four
heavy black figures, IV, V, VI, VII, are differentially selective in their
effects. In a cheerful person, they do not, excepting now and then, generate
depressive mood trends. In cheerless persons, they reduce the little cheer
that may be present. These test cards and their working arouse speculation
as to how deliberately Rorschach organized them into his test, with this
mood effect as their function.

[40] Figure IV.

[41] I.e., in discussions of content, p. 31; and especially note 62.

[42] Above, concerning the intellectual sluggishness, p. 26; also concerning the passivity, p. 26.

[43] The very few organizational achievements, and see note 1. Note

especially the failure to grasp relations in R 3–4, i.e., in adjacent details with meanings which are related easily, in fact spontaneously, by healthy persons. The rejection of the meaningful relationship in R 6 is without doubt of dynamic significance to the child. See also note 1.

[44] In R 4. She explicitly denies color. The devaluing expression, "funny shape," is also a communication of denial; this denial may relate either to the thought content or to the affective value in the color.

[45] "Eye" is a frequent content in paranoid patients, but it should be confirmed by other data, which are not found in this record. Also, she is too young to make such diagnostic reasoning supportable. Yet the datum is there; she does select an "eye" where it is not commonly seen. The test is here casting the shadow of a possible coming event. It uncovers the seed of a pathologic defense which the girl will use unless treatment intervenes.

[46] See above, p. 27; and notes 18 and 19.

[47] The seven associations in figure X, more than in any other one figure; and, in fact, if we disregard figure VIII, more than in any other three figures combined. To be sure, figure X is normally a very productive one and we must ask to what extent are the seven responses a function of its potency in tapping associational processes. However, the response total here is in too great contrast with that of the other test figures to ignore, and a stepping up of the child's associational activity can be inferred.

[48] Except in figure IX, where, from the completeness of its impact, we judge it to be free.

[49] The F+ per cent is well within normal range. The hold on herself is inferred from the Approach pattern, with its too rigid adhesion to D, reflecting too unvarying a regard for the obvious and the plain.

[50] In figures IV, VII and X. For the possible significance in these for personal dynamics, see discussion of the thought content on p. 31.

[51] See note 1 concerning the constriction of the girl's communication; the impoverished interests, the lack of originality, and the high stereotypy finding (per cent of animal content); the inefficiency, in the low Z score, and the few instances of this activity. She manifests also low initiative and aspiration in the very low W score and in the poverty of interest indicated by the limited content.

[52] Sporadic original trends, i.e., the "totem pole" in figure I, the "fountain" in IV, the "building with a round top" in VII, the "vine" in VIII, the "bluebirds" in X; the unusual organization activity in R 16. The fantasy in R 6 is imaginative if not creative.

[53] See above, p. 27, concerning the child's reaction pattern to the color figures.

[54] The passivity, the resignation trends; and see p. 28 concerning her mood tone.

[55] The low P count.

[56] The withdrawal pattern, the clipped language, the morose mood tone. Here is "meta-communication" such as exponents of communication theory are highlighting in current writing. It is, however, not direct evidence such as would be shown in aggression content, in a record with higher white space count, and one decidedly extratensive in experience balance.

[57] The white space count is at minimum.

[58] The damper on the fantasy living; see exposition on p. 27f.

[59] The traces of more intellectual ability than she uses (the Z in R 16); the reaching for emotional understanding with others; the signs of latent feminine wishes. See also the discussion concerning the original thought content on p. 31f.

[60] Pathogenic because it is a percept more prevalent in patients with paranoid trends, and cf. note 45.

[61] The "personal" F−, as I call the percepts in which personal needs of the patient give rise to the inaccuracy. Thus, R 7, 14, probably 20; also the F− element in R 6.

[62] Concerning the spider as a symbol, see Fenichel.[32] It is possible that in these associations, viewed as symbolisms, the test is pinpointing the girl's frustrating affect concerning some persons, more specifically, her mother. However, the significance of any theme to the particular patient must always be established by the patient himself. Sometimes the test record provides enough other evidence to justify a conclusion with some degree of confidence, but usually it is safer to await further confirmation from the patient.

[63] In connection with the anxiety shock at figure IV, and the unsteadiness at figure VII. See also note 38.

[64] The EA, or experience actual (chapter 2), is 6.5. For a patient as constricted and self-denying as she is, this is a wide EA.

[65] The response to the color stimuli as evidence of sensitivity to influence from outside.

[66] See pp. 27–28, the description of her M responses, and the related notes.

[67] This is discussed in detail in the observations on therapeutic implications of the mother's Rorschach test (see below). The therapeutic effort, since parent-child transactions are here of the essence, should have the parent as its point of departure.

# CHAPTER 4

# Mrs. M.: Lenore's perturbed mother

## Response Record

### Figure I (10″)

'Do you want me to begin?'

1. W F+ A P
1.0
'It reminds me of an eagle.' (W. 'The general effect . . . the body and spread wing remind me, in a crude sort of way, I suppose.')
'Is that what you want? Are you supposed to turn it? 'And a butterfly.' (W. 'With tentacles in here.' D 1.)

2. D F+ Hd P
'There is a figure in the middle . . . human figure . . . bottom part of a human figure.' (D 3. 'Here you see the feet.')

3. Ws F+ An
1.0
'It looks like picture of pelvic area.' (W. 'With cavity,' i.c., Dds. 'This part would lead to the feet; spinal column in here.' Dd 27.)
'I guess that's about all.'

### Figure II (15″)

4. W M+ H P
4.5
'It looks like two dancers . . . clowns.' (W. 'Dancers facing each other. Hands are touching each other . . . one foot up and one foot out. Dressed in sacky things. Sort of clown dancers. Drips, as if throwing off emotions . . . could be fighting but does not look like that.')

5. W FV+ Ls
4.5
> 'Hm . . . It looks like reflection of an animal . . . a bear or something looking at his reflection in a pool.' (One lateral half, seen horizontally. 'The upper figure is bear and he is looking at reflection in pool.')

6. D FC.Y+ Ls
∨ 'Sun coming up or going down . . . coming up with sprayings up.' (D 3. 'Rays raying out.' Color against the black made her think of sun coming up.)

### Figure III (5″)

7. D F+ A
'Chickens without their feathers.' (D 11. 'Long neck . . . their breasts are sticking out.' Dd 27. 'Back is well defined . . . skimpy.')

8. D F+ Cg P
'Bow in middle.' (D 3. 'Bow-tie effect . . . got the center knot.') 'Whole or parts?'

9. D F+ A
'Bird effects . . . red things on side.' (D 2. 'Cock, well-feathered, more or less.')

*Figure IV* (8")

| | |
|---|---|
| 10. W FY+ A P<br>2.0 | 'I'd say . . . a bear-skin rug effect.' (W. 'Shape. . . head . . . narrowness . . . spread, without these little points, and the center shading.') |
| 11. D F+ Ad,Hh | 'This reminds me of a set of antlers . . . elk's head above fireplace.' (Upper third of whole. 'Buffalo head . . . the horns.') |
| 12. D F+ A | 'Some kind of crawling insects . . . beetles . . .' |
| 13. D F− A | 'Something with horns . . . toad or beetle.' (D 1. 'The legged effects.' Points out face as very lowermost part.) |
| 14. D YF− A | 'Reminds me of a . . . what's that black and white animal? A skunk . . . head or body.' (D 3 and section directly below. 'Two stripes down there and stripe down middle of back.') |

*Figure V* (23")

| | |
|---|---|
| 15. W F+ A P<br>1.0 | 'A bat.' (W. 'Usually have legs sticking out all over. Guess it would probably be up to here'—pointing to D 6). |
| 16. D F+ Im | 'A pair of tweezers.' (D 9. 'The shape of tweezers, pliers, or pincers.') |

*Figure VI* (7")

| | |
|---|---|
| 17. D F+ Ay | 'Indian totem pole up here.' (D 3. 'The markings . . . the spread-eagle effect . . . they show that . . . the balance.') |
| 18. D F+ A P | 'Animal skin effect down here.' (D 1. 'The shaping . . . hand, legs here, and here the rear part. All have similar bottoms where you have the openings.') (Sighs). |

*Figure VII* (38")

'I don't see anything in here.' (Encouraged.)

| | |
|---|---|
| 19. D F− A | 'There's a bug in here. The dark areas look like a little bug.' (Inner portion of D 6.) ('Has the shading out there that look like legs.') |

*Figure VIII* (13")

| | |
|---|---|
| 20. Ds F+ An P | 'This looks like a spinal column with ribs around it.' (Ds 3. 'The white part . . . these things in your spinal column . . . the separations there are like ribs . . . spinal cord.') |
| 21. D F+ A | 'Animal . . . these pink things are . . . wolf effect.' (D 1. 'The stalking wolf . . . feet out in back . . . face isn't so much of wolf.') |
| 22. D CF+ Fd | 'Decidedly looks like a nice dish of ice cream.' ('It looks like strawberry and peach ice cream'; D 2.) |

*Figure IX (27″)*

23. DW CF − An     'It looks like a diagram of human body . . . lungs in middle section.' (W: lungs, D 10: 'Pink area reminded me of lungs. Center would be digestive . . . intestines and so on. Bottom part would be sex organs with cavity in between.' On further inquiry: 'the pink . . . usually lungs are shown as pink.')

*Figure X (10″)*

24. D F+ A P     'These look like little crawling things . . . crabs.' (D 1. 'All the feelers sticking out.')

25. D F+ A     'Animals with

26. D F+ Bt     a tree.' (D 8 'are the animals and' D 14 'is the tree.
       4.0     More insect type of thing.' Tree? 'Well, it has little pieces sticking out.')

27. D CF+ A     'Snakes.' (D 4. 'Snakes or worms. The color . . . green . . . probably and the shape . . . not exactly. See, now, a rabbit in center.')

28. D CF+ Cl     'Cloud effects.' (D 9. 'The rose colors. They're spread out in that fashion when sun is going down . . . edged in red . . . pink clouds.')

29. D F+ Fd     'Wishbone.' (D 3. 'It looks like a wishbone . . . the center flat area and the two ends.')

### Response Summary

R: 29

| | | | | | | | |
|---|---|---|---|---|---|---|---|
| W | 6 (s:1) | M | 1 | H | 1 | F+ 90% | |
| DW | 1 | CF | 4 (1−) | Hd | 1 | A 52% | |
| D | 22 (s:1) | FC.Y | 1 | A | 14 | P 9 | |
| | 29 | YF− | 1 | Ad | 1 | S 7% | |
| | | FY | 1 | An | 3 | Af r 0.53 | |
| Z f | 7 | FV | 1 | Ay | 1 | L 2.22 | |
| Z sum | 18.0 | F+ | 18 | Bt | 1 | T/R (not recorded) | |
| Ap | W D (!) | F− | 2 | Cg | 1 | T/first R 15.6 | |
| Seq. | Methodical | | 29 | Cl | 1 | Fln R 1.67 | |
| | | | | Fd | 2 | Fln T/first R 15.1″ | |
| | | | | Im | 1 | | |
| | | EB | 1/4.5 | Ls | 2 | | |
| | | EA | 5.5 | | 29 | | |

## Interpretation

An apprehensive, unhappy, and, under some conditions, a perturbed woman is the impression derived from this record. Only rarely does Mrs. M. respond with a touch of cheerfulness to life's more pleasurable circumstances. She attempts a controlled exterior vis-à-vis her world, and we must infer the presence of some pride. But, stirred up by ideas related to the sources of her unhappiness, her control is breached and she presents a picture of severe upset.

Mrs. M.'s apprehensiveness is manifest both in a passivity process [1]* and in expressions of dependency with a touch of resignation [2]. Intensity of the passivity varies, and she can, usually, bring her critical perception to bear on, and soften the smart in, it [3]. Yet, in one of these reactions the feeling blends with excitement [4] to produce a mixed emotion, a disquiet sharpened by irritation. It is when the larger setting [5] sets the stage for disturbance that the usual self-mastery breaks down as the emotional process becomes more intense [6]. What makes things worse for this woman is a trace of feeling of inferiority, although she experiences this only in a small quantity [7] and to a moderate degree [8]. But the content (R 5) must arouse our curiosity. Assuming this response is a displacement and that the patient is looking at her own reflection, the questions which arise are: Why does she need to do so? Is she reliving the Narcissus myth and admiring herself? Or, as in another fairy tale, is she gazing into the mirror for what blemish she may detect? [9] Then, too, she is susceptible to the phobic, as some of her thought content shows [10], a trend which recurrently aggravates her already unhappy state of mind.

When placed in situations usually evoking pleasurable emotions and ones which impel her to reach out to others [11], she shows herself responsive to inner forces. In one of these instances, all her reactions are dominated by some affective coloring [12]. At the same time, she maintains self-mastery [13]. She does this in spite of the anxiety which the conditions stir up [14]. One inference is that this kind of situation, the impulse to an interpersonal contact, unsettles her, makes her uneasy rather than glad. What is not known is whether it is sheer loosening of feelings that produces this effect or whether it is some idea stirred up by the blot configuration or by some detail of it. Patients, both men and women, sensitive over female genitality, especially over menstruation, are among those who suffer anxiety shock here [15]. More explicit, since our patient verbalizes it, is an aggression theme (R 4), and she betrays her anxiety at the thought by denying it [16].

Mrs. M.'s upset can be even more complete (figure IX), undercutting intellectual controls. At such a time, she is not herself, seeing and thinking as a person in confusion does [17]. The anxiety which under other conditions she is able to bind courses free as the more lively emotions are being awakened. Excitement in her goes hand in hand with apprehension. The urge in this woman for emotional contact with others is at

* Bracketed numbers refer to Notes on Interpretation, which for this chapter will be found on pages 51–57.

the same time a threat to herself. On the theory that such a threat is defensive (Fenichel), it is evidence that the ego (the organizer of defenses) is in action. The ego is struggling against some trend in this individual which, by her own ego's lights, is not good for her. This is conflict, and it helps establish the whole pattern as a neurosis [18], exactly the conclusion which would be arrived at from the color shock [19].

Our patient verifies this reasoning by the key which she nearly always strikes in her feeling-determined associations: with one exception (R 6) they have the strident tone of the hypersensitive; it is an acutely felt process [20], which, however, she can usually hold under restraint [21]—usually, but not always. In one instance, either the ego was weakened or the emotional surge was too powerful [22]. In either event the balance tipped against the ego. Our patient reacts, in sum, with the feeling process most characteristic of neurotics [23] and limits her response to this range almost entirely. She does not give in to uncontrolled, impulsive discharges, but to subject her emotions to mature values is also a rarity for her [24]. She can be in affective contact with others so long as she has her way, which is an immature way of relating.

With all this, she can nevertheless give a good account of herself when stresses are brought to bear on her. Mrs. M. recovers her self-control [25] following very severe neurotic disruption, and, in so doing, tells of a reserve strength which, in crises, she can bring into play. Her mental life even while she is under strain is relatively untrammeled [26]. She remains quite effective mentally at two points at which her feelings are running high [27]. It is at these two points also that thought processes show some semblances of richness [28]. Her performance in figure II especially, in which all the associations carry an emotional tinge and all are accurate, reflects an ability to respond to a challenge. Rather than breaking her down, this exigency tapped her strength. She displays resources also in another finding: the themes in two of her color-dictated associations (R 6 and 28), i.e., the interests which stir her feelings. Both are pleasurable landscapes, themes with a note of animation of a kind that the healthy express. Three other responses tell a different story, however. They vary in significance from a possibly neutral, possibly phobic percept (the snakes of R 27), to an oral gratification topic—although it is one found occasionally among stable adults (the ice cream of R 22), to the pathologic anatomy elaboration (the lungs and intestines and sex cavity of R 23). This latter is a product specifically of her neurosis and the preoccupations which it can breed [29].

The shock absorbers with which the human personality inwardly counteracts emotional rough-going are little available to Mrs. M., that is, there is only one fantasy-determined association (R 4). Does she not

have the ability, as native endowment, to use imagination, whether healthy
or day-dreaming and regressive, or does she avoid, because she fears, the
ideas in it? Is she defensively turning off this current, or has the ability
been impaired by the neurosis? Has its source been dried up by the parch-
ing effect of the mental life generally? In her one production in this
sphere, her mental processes are intact [30]. Its content, while ordinary
run-of-the-mill material (the "clowns"), does develop an engaging whimsy
('dancing . . . the hands touching . . . the position of the feet . . . their
"sacky" dress'). She adds a very original note ("as if throwing off emotions") in which she may be further enjoying the playful scene, the clown-
ing, although of this we cannot be sure; she may here be communicating
by displacement some deeper passing trend.

     Such are the limits of Mrs. M.'s assets in the form of imagination. She
invests little energy or feeling [31] in her one fantasy; the wish fulfillment
in it is weakly enjoyed, and after this no more wish-fulfilling flights. She
provides one hint as to what is cutting it off: the theme of hostile competition. She has suppressed it (delayed until the inquiry), and after expressing it, she denies it. She is thus harboring thoughts of which she has
some fear, since she defends against them. This reasoning is supported
by what she does with figure III, where transmutation into fantasy comes
very easily to nearly everyone. Mrs. M. fails to bring it into the life
mirrored in movement. She even fails to see the human figures. And
what she does see—a female bird denuded of its covering—is all too obviously a symbol. The "breasts sticking out," a response delayed until
the inquiry, i.e., at first suppressed, is further evidence of a meaningful
communication. And who is the chicken without feathers? Does our
patient sense herself, as did Shakespeare's Wolsey, "naked to mine ene-
mies"? The test findings do not give the answer. All we can know is
that R 7 screens a thought, an attitude, from the world, and, what is
more important, screens it from the patient herself; it is something she
cannot consciously face. This is as much as our data tell us. To interpret
specifically in terms of this woman's clinical dynamics is to go beyond
the empirical facts of the test. It is at such points that the clinical investigation, the therapeutic interviews that follow, must pick up the leads which
the test provides. The two methods, test and clinical, join resources
toward understanding the patient.

     The logic is plausible that Mrs. M. has some fear of her fantasies.
When they are in conflict with her unconscious wishes, she does not permit
them expression, not even in dream form; the general neurotic adjustment by which she lives immobilizes fantasy activity. The explanation
for the small quantity of fantasy living in our patient would seem to lie
less in the factor of endowment and more in personal dynamics [32].

Whatever the cause, the actuality is that she can call upon this resource to only a very limited extent. Her inner shock absorption is very thin. It is not enough to offset the pressure outwardly indicated by the quantity and quality [33] of her feelings, not enough to stabilize her against disturbances that develop under the pressure of these feelings [34], and not enough to be a resource against the pulls and pushes which she brings on herself, the shocks generated from within [35].

Two kinds of thoughts set these shocks going: those in which the masculine figure is in high focus and those concerning women, especially women past their prime, as she is herself. She gives a better account of herself at the masculine [36]; she at first holds together when such ideas are forced upon her, breaking down only belatedly, but when the feminine imagery is flashed on the screen of her consciousness [37], she loses her control at once and even her associational flow clogs up. Here is emotional interference related to specific personal interests, and hence to particular dynamics. These two test figures, IV and VII, i.e., the ideas that they put into motion, frequently open up leads to the trouble spots in a patient. The differential behavior under these conditions, i.e., deterioration of the behavior, is the result of disturbance. This is always evidence of anxiety, i.e., of threat sensed by the individual. On the basis of the dysphoric mood moments in individuals in whom I have observed these disturbances, from fragments of clinical information about them, and from the thought content which they sometimes produce while the shock effect is on, I have been hypothesizing that the wellspring of this anxiety is the person's pained attitude about himself. It differs from disruptions the individual at times suffers at the urge to enjoy himself in an interpersonal relationship [38] in that the latter is always triggered by an outer, environmental reality and its exciting overtones. In the kind of anxiety shock which our patient is here manifesting, the stimulus is entirely within. She is ready to take a dim view of herself, to be guilty. "I myself am Heaven and Hell," Milton's Satan saw it. It is, of course, the classical psychoanalytic concept: superego.

As ideas of the masculine are activated, our patient is sensitive to the dysphoric tones [39] but maintains her poise; she is realistic, conventional, orderly [40]. But, although up to this point she has been capable of some differentiation in her thought content, she now restricts herself to the most obvious [41]. It is the price the ego pays as it closes ranks against the sensed threat. However, it must ultimately yield ground. She disregards reality [42] for the first time in the test. Then she does so a second time, and in this, her final association under these tensions, she is again sensitive to a dysphoric influence, and it is now a more intense process [43]. The high productivity here is easily understood as an undoing defense. Significant, too, is her content in the last three associations (R 12, 13, 14) as the self-mastery weakened: animals or parts of animals, with various degrees of unsavory connotations; this is again a defensive expedient, aiding the patient in mastering her anxiety [44].

Mrs. M. snaps back into full intellectual control in the two test figures immediately following [45] but she is mentally less free than under any other condition up to this point [46]. She is still under the disabling influence of the anxiety's impact, which is not an uncommon finding. One may speculate, too, whether the effort required by the undoing defense (at masculinity imagery) may not have reduced the ego's stamina, with resulting inadequate functioning at the next two stimuli. Inadequate as she is before these two, she is bankrupt at the one following them (figure VII). She at first tries to escape by rejecting. She is more retarded here intellectually than in any of the varied circumstances represented by the ten test figures [47]. Her bogged-down associational processes permit her only a single response, the only test situation that so limits her. She is inaccurate in what she does see, with the probability that she is distorting reality [48]. A free anxiety, acute in its onset, extensive in its effect, has taken possession of the woman and, for once, uprooted the ego.

Her thought content here is noteworthy, both in what she sees and where, as well as in what she does not see. She attends to the vagina form detail and calls it "a bug." Her perceptive process thus selects a most significant element, but she misshapes it [49]. What the latent meaning is in a "bug" being equated with the female genital is not answerable from the test data. One can guess, but one guess is as good as another; the only person who knows the answer, the patient, has locked it away in her unconscious. Further study of her that solves this riddle will at the same time be penetrating her therapeutically. All that we know from the test is that the reminder of the female genital holds a threat for her. She is more comfortable in seeing it as a bug than as what it is.

What Mrs. M. does *not* see at this juncture fills out the story of a woman unhappy at thoughts about women. Just about everyone [50] sees two female figures, usually in some animated conversation. She shuts out this percept. The surmise that her blindness is especially selective for imagery of women in middle life (which is also her own age point) rests on the great frequency [51] with which women in this age group are seen here. The critical question is whether she herself identifies with these characters which she so avoids. And if so, what threats do these thoughts stir up in her? However that may be, she runs away from thinking about women and from female genitality [52]. What the precise connection between this finding and that of anxiety at masculinity ideas is can only be a guess. The examiner's free associations can lead down many paths, and the patient does not point out in the record which is the true one. What her reaction pattern does describe is her generally unhappy state of mind and the distressing moments she can suffer when certain topics are forced on her attention. It is a foreboding picture as the psychologic climate for this patient's child, the girl Lenore, who was the impetus for studying this woman psychiatrically.

Against this gloomy state of mind which can throw her off balance so, Mrs. M. has been erecting some effective defenses. Unhappily, the cure is as bad as the disease. She defends by hemming in her mind's freedom and scope in a character armor pattern. She narrows the range of her thought content, stereotypes it, glaringly so at points of emotional impact [53]. She shuts down on her associational productivity [54], becomes sluggish or inhibited [55], is excessively cautious about what she says and critical of what she sees [56], adheres rigidly to reality and permits herself no feeling-toned response [57]. In the test performance generally she is stiff in the way she attends to matters that come before her [58]. Among her other expedients are denial [59], undoing [60], and displacement [61]. More pathogenic is her binding of anxiety in phobic thoughts [62]. The question may be a moot one as to where displacing ends and phobic binding begins [63]. So far as I know, there is no measure for this. Again, it is only the patient who can give the answer by clarifying the significance of the symbolisms she employs [64].

In the face of emotional experiences, this patient maintains an un-flagging alertness. She shies from events with excitement potential [65], and she wants to reject the painful import of female imagery (figure VII); there is a precipitate withdrawal, counterphobic in quality. Her vigilance against imaginative living has been noted [66]. How strongly she wards off fancies or fears that may rise into her awareness, she demonstrates in figure III. She could here release some subsurface motif, even a prosaic one [67], but she does not. At the same time, she takes the firmest possible hold on herself intellectually [68], a retreat, as it were, into a rigidly guarded position. Here is the characteristic compromise of neurosis: the patient jettisons the pleasures of the imagination in the interests of safety. She pays this price also in the coin of content, i.e., what she does not see anywhere in her test, namely, aggressive ideas and sexual topics. These will emerge in (a) patients more disorganized than she is, i.e., less de-fended, and in (b) better adjusted persons, i.e., well defended but re-laxed and more secure and hence better able to talk about intimate mat-ters. Our patient suppresses these. What all these processes, desiccating and impoverishing to the mental life, make of her as a person to live with, what kind of a mother she has to be since she is so defensively organized is the question that next attracts our interest.

The intelligence which Mrs. M. is at present bringing to bear on her life's problems is operating sluggishly [69]. She can grasp complexities but does so infrequently [70]; the flashes of intellectual energy are only enough to indicate that there is more where these came from. Everyday practicalities preoccupy her attention excessively [71]; mundane values too readily satisfy her, as reflected by the thought content [72]—hence, the viscosity of her mental activity, one effect of which is to desensitize this patient to the niceties of life [73]. Persons functioning at this tempo can for the most part ward off error; they are just heavy-footed enough not to wander frequently or far from the beaten path [74]. Yet, when the personal press is too much for the defensive guarding and for the stolidity, our patient can make mistakes. She then sees the world not as it is commonly perceived but in a misshapen fashion and as she requires it to be [75]. The instances are few, however. In fact, she too frequently sticks to the world's most accustomed paths. Her worried state of mind makes her cautious in social contacts, over-conventional [76]. It is the wariness of a woman who has been hurt or fears she may be [77], and, in consequence, she is less communicative, less open in expressing thoughts that are more characteristic of herself, halting in the use of her abilities: a withdrawing, self-contained woman.

But Mrs. M. does not withdraw into autistic living. Rather, she represses such proclivities [78], even though she obtains little direct gratification from the world [79]. Her self-containment is thus reinforced by self-denial, and restrains or interferes with pleasurable pursuits. It is a total attitude which burdens her in understanding others emotionally and impedes her participation in the daily ups and downs of their lives [80]. All this can only redound on her self-attitude and increase the unhappiness which so dominates her. In turn, this dictates more self-denial and self-containment, and again painful affect, in a never-ending, closed circuit. Clinically the formulation is a neurosis, one with enough ego stamina to indicate that she will recover from the disturbance to which she is prone and maintain herself in an integrated state for the purpose of day-to-day living in her community. The Rorschach test findings to this extent etch out a picture more benign than was feared from the preliminary clinical impression.

So much then for the processes—emotional, intellectual, imaginative—that constitute this human being. What now about the personal preoccupations, conscious or unconscious, that are motivating her as a value-holding individual? Central to these values are those rooted in what she is at the core, biologically and socially—a woman. A "pelvis" and "sex organs with cavity in between" express these thoughts as an awareness not far below consciousness [81]. The frank sex topic (R 23) gives her trouble. She tries to avoid it and the idea discomposes her [82]. Her hypersensitivity to this association highlights the emotional loading of the "pelvis" theme. Close enough to awareness to come out candidly is an anal idea: "all have similar bottoms where you have the openings" (R 18). But the tug and struggle between values reaches far deeper. Much is being screened in the "chickens without feathers," (R 7) and the "cock" who is "well-feathered" (R 9) offers only too striking a counterpoint. Even deeper in her unconscious is her motive in calling "a bug" the test detail so frequently identified as vagina [83]. Animals of unpleasant or repulsive connotation are a characteristic tactic of hers to avoid what she cannot openly face (R 12, 13, 14; compare R 24; and see notes 61 and 63). Less cryptic is the phobic motif in the "wolf" who is "stalking" (R 21; and see notes 62 and 84). The eagle, her first response to the test, requires investigation for its significance to the patient. I have found it clinically meaningful as a power bird, lordly and predatory. Nearer to consciousness are the two anatomy associations: R 20 and 23. The former is frequently enough seen in figure I to dilute its specific significance for any one individual. The vital organs of R 23 are, however, a lead to concern with health of a pathologic kind [85]. Of totally unclear significance is the reference to "throwing off emotions" [86].

Healthier thought content forms some of the repertoire of this woman's mind, and when it does, it shows her to be very much a woman. In R 11 she develops the not uncommon animal horns association into a fireplace picture, following on a "rug effect" (R 10); and she sees the "tweezers" (R 16), an object of feminine interest which recalls the speculation as to the significance of the inferiority feeling in the reflection theme (R 5). An entirely pleasant association is her "dish of ice cream," and she just about smacks her lips with relish (R 22). Still and all, these more satisfying themes are only flitting thoughts. The heavy accent in her thinking, at awareness level or below it, is on the morose. It is consistent with the painful affect which so dominates her psychic structure.

Treatment of Mrs. M. will, in a clinic, be primarily oriented around the mental health needs of the patient who was initially referred, her daughter, Lenore. Yet, the welfare of the child can only be advanced to the extent that the mother's is. Her state of mind sets up the prevailing psychologic climate in which her child's personality will flourish or wither.

Considered by herself, as an individual, some treatment assets can be detected, but the ego's losses seriously outweigh them. Change? She will resist it; her defenses are too set and her intellectual pattern too stiff; she has adopted cramped attitudes toward life and is maintaining them. Little openness to change must also be inferred in the emotional sphere: there is too little understanding of others' feelings, too little ability to imagine herself in the place of others. What her intelligence potential may be we cannot know. She shackles it too well. A moderate breadth in the associational content and some of her language and diction do suggest that more is latent than, in her constrained state, she can use. The necessary push and initiative are presently not there. Her worried and unhappy emotional mood is the too effective stifling force. It all speaks of a sense of futility, of anything but responsiveness to an invitation to change.

Searching for assets, we observe the lability in response to lively toned stimuli. Lability is the opposite of fixedness. It bespeaks fluidity, and fluidity where it counts—inwardly. To be sure, self-interest is this mother's dominant emotional set. But as affective responsivity it holds the potential for change. This patient can be moulded. Taken together with the one fantasy association, she can experience at an EA measure of 5.5. This is not much, but it is something. Whether Mrs. M. could, with psychotherapy, release some of her now repressed fantasies only a trial of therapy could determine. There is another asset in that her self-assertion trait [87] is within average adult range. This would mean that, given the impetus and the direction, she could take action, she could attempt to deal more effectively with her life's problems. She has the necessary ego stamina for such an effort. In fact, and here we return to her main handicap, it is a case of all too much ego, with resultant self-constriction under the pressure of the persistent, sensed unhappiness.

Obviously, a treatment plan on behalf of her child must start with treatment of Mrs. M. Clinical notes are available on this mother-child situation, and they are brief but enlightening concerning the child:

> She was brought to the clinic by the mother because of persistent, negativistic, uncooperative behavior, and some stealing. She always has been and is an eating problem; the mother cooks special foods for her. The girl is now overweight. School work is satisfactory. Two siblings: a brother, four years older; a sister, five years younger. As the mother states it, "The brother is quite the opposite;" "the patient fights with the younger sister." An intake note observes that, "The mother is very ambivalent in relation to the patient." The father works hard and has not much contact with the family.

Concerning the mother:

> She became very upset when discussing the child's problems. Ventilated criticism of the husband. He takes no interest in her or the child. The mother was herself the seventh of nine children; is not happy; has many problems.

We thus have a vignette of a maladjusted, symptomatically behaving child; of a mother who is unhappy and disturbed; a husband and father who pays little attention to his wife and children. In the two brush strokes concerning the father: "not much contact," "takes no interest in her or the child," we have an enlightening commentary on Lenore's Rorschach test. The longings for affectionate contact, the discouraged mood tone, possibly the "two small" people in the background and certainly the anxiety shock at father imagery, all have here their dynamic explanation: a cold parent, a cold home, and so a child out in the cold psychologically. My interpretation of Lenore's test record is subject to the criticism that it does not go far enough on this point. I could have reasoned from the descriptive data, especially her lack of spirit, and from the emotional reactions, i.e., the anxiety shocks and the flight from fantasy, to the dynamics. In limiting myself to description, I failed to carry through to the logic of the facts. The clinical note thus lights up a critical instruction value in the child's test record: the probable significant personal sources of the manifest data.

The mother is also out in the cold. She reacts with the inevitable ache and irritation and so compounds the household's noxious psychologic air. Can Mrs. M. be expected to provide psychologic sunshine while she herself is gritting her teeth over the sour grapes which is her marriage portion?

Any treatment plan must obviously envisage a therapy à trois: mother, husband, and child.

### Notes on Interpretation

[1] The shading (Y) determined responses.

[2] The patient's gratuitous questioning of the examiner, before and after R 1; excessive qualifying, e.g., in figures IV and V, and also a self-uncertainty ("I'd say ..." "Guess it would probably be ..."); the resignation attitude, figure I.

[3] The form factor is present in all the Y responses. Intensity is greatest in R 14. Here the shading element dominates over form, enough so to break down the perceptual accuracy, telling of the strength of the feeling.

[4] In R 6; the blend with a color determinant.

[5] The anxiety shock in figure IV, and see p. 45f.

[6] See note 3.

[7] Only one such, i.e., vista determined, V, association.

[8] The form element dominates; also it is F+. The unsatisfying feeling is still appraised within a realistic frame of reference.

[9] What the significance is to a patient of the mirror theme, or reflections in a mirror, is still an open question. Whichever of my two surmises in the test should prove accurate—self-admiration or the search for a blemish, the source trait would still be a feeling of inferiority. It would thus be consistent with the general psychologic indication of vista responses.

[10] See in exposition of content, p. 49; also in defenses, p. 47.

[11] Mainly represented in the test in the three chromatic figures, VIII, IX and X, although in some patients, in either figure II, as here, or in III, or both.

[12] In figure II. One of her three responses is fantasy, i.e., internalized emotion; one discloses the sense of inferiority; and one fuses the pleasurable with the passivity tones. Lambda index for this test figure alone is zero: patient responds entirely to inner experience and disregards the environment as such.

[13] The accurate, i.e., F+ perception, in each of the three responses in figure II.

[14] In two of the three responses in figure II, a shading determinant is found. An anxiety undertone is always indicated in Y (R 6); and the thoughts activated by V (R 5) are seldom pleasurable.

[15] It is the lower central red (D 3) with its connotation of blood that is disturbing, the more so owing to the vulva-like form of the detail.

[16] "Does not look like that."

[17] The slowed-up response time, the alogical approach (DW), the form inaccuracy, the pathologic theme, the failure of P, the reduced productivity: a heavy convergence of color shock signs.

[18] It is not the sheer fact of conflict that shows we are dealing with a neurosis. Many schizophrenics provide liberal evidence of conflict in their Rorschach test records. However, as this woman's personality is developed in her Rorschach test record, she is integrated. It is from the conflict in the framework of an intact personality that we reason to neurotic conflict.

[19] That is by (a) interpreting the test data according to their psychologic significance—conflict in an intact individual, and (b) following the clinical logic in these findings—neurosis, we arrive (c) at the conclusion to which Rorschach's color shock theory leads—neurosis.

[20] The CF responses in R 22, 23, 27, 28. The emotional experience dominates over the form percept.

[21] In three of the four CF responses, the F is plus.

[22] It is F− in the CF of R 23.

[23] The CF response I have found the most frequent of the color nuances in neurotics. It must correspond to the clinically known tensions in these patients.

[24] The domination by the regard for form over the feeling experience, the FC response. This woman achieves it once, R 6.

[25] In figure X. Time for the first response is again fast; productivity is liberated; the first response to the figure is a P; all form perception is accurate.

[26] The productivity in the three chromatic figures (VIII, IX and X)

as a ratio to that of the first seven; the affective ratio. For this patient it is 0.52. My working, normal, range is 0.40 to 0.60.

[27] In figures II and X. Concerning the saturation by the feelings in figure II, see note 12. In figure X the feeling is inferred from the release of associational activity, including two of the responses in which the color element is dominant.

[28] All three associations in figure II; and R 28 in figure X. None of these is at a high level of originality but some novelty is present in each, and they certainly are departures from the rut in which this woman's thinking usually courses.

[29] These preoccupations are considered in more detail in exposition of the thought content, p. 48f.

[30] R 4. It is scored W M+ H P. It is a whole response, the form element in it is accurate, a whole human is seen in movement. Taken together with the P, this formula is structurally the kind found in healthy individuals.

[31] The energy investment would not be rated above 2. Actually, it is a static fantasy, but in the belated "fighting" some activity is being projected.

[32] This conclusion is drawn from the evident fact of conflict in this patient. It is subject to the reservation that we do not know enough about fantasy living as inherited endowment. We do have statistics for M in adults. These do not follow the normal frequency curve, but they dependably indicate the frequency of M in a population of which this woman is representative. By these statistics the expectancy for M in her would be 3.

[33] Quantity: five color determined associations, for a total color value of 4.5. Thus, the decidedly extratensive experience balance. Quality: strongly feeling toned; and see note 20.

[34] The color shock in figure IX.

[35] See concerning the shading shock in the text, immediately following.

[36] Figure IV.

[37] Figure VII.

[38] As represented by the color figures in the test.

[39] The shading determinants in R 10 and R 14.

[40] The F is plus in the first three associations; the first association is P; the sequence is the methodical one in which W is followed by D.

[41] Animal content in all five responses; stereotypy is 100 per cent.

[42] The F− in R 13 and 14.

[43] The dominance of the shading determinant over the form; and see note 5.

[44] Concerning phobic thinking as a binding defense, see p. 47.

[45] F+ is 100 per cent in figures V and VI.

[46] Productivity of only two responses in each of figures V and VI is her lowest up to this point in the test. In figure V the time for the first response is very slow.

[47] Time for the first response is slowest.

[48] In R 19, on the theory that the "bugs" has an especial personal significance; and see exposition of content, p. 48f. Question of such distortion needs also to be raised with reference to R 13 and R 14.

[49] She shapes reality as her own needs dictate (if my theorizing in note 48 is correct).

[50] In this test figure as a whole; or in the upper profile details.

[51] That is, a woman of this patient's probable intelligence and integration should have no difficulty in seeing these feminine profiles here, the more so since they are one of the test's very common P percepts.

[52] Should the criticism be offered that this reasoning is not based on empiric test data, it would be sound. This patient does not refer to middle-aged women, either overtly or symbolically. The positive fact is, however, that (a) she does not see (b) the female profiles that (c) are there, since (d) they are statistically so frequently perceived there. And the psychologic principle is well established that not to see something is behavior, i.e., a positive finding. As always, however, such test interpretation is hypothesis and requires verification by nontest study of a patient.

[53] In figures III and IV. In III we are seeing the delayed effect of the emotional waves set up by figure II. The "bow" in R 8 is the most common percept for this detail and hence essential stereotypy. Concerning IV, see note 41. In figure VII too the single response, as animal content, is technically a stereotyped one. This poverty of thought content is specific for the conditions set up by these three test cards. It does not obtain for the record as a whole, as scattered trends to originality in the other test cards indicate. Another line of evidence is the distribution of animal content: in figures III, IV, and VII, it accounts for eight out of the nine associations, or a percentage of 89. For the other seven figures it is seven out of twenty, or 35 per cent.

[54] In figures V, VI, VII, IX.

[55] The time for the first response in figures V, VII, IX.

[56] See note 2.

[57] In figures I, III, V, VI. Not only is F+ at 100 per cent in each of these figures, i.e., rigid accuracy, but lambda is at the extreme, as it is also in VII, i.e., not a single response to inner experience, whether painful, pleasurable, or fantasy.

[58] The imbalance of D in the approach. This imbalance, and hence the underlying stiffness, are even more severe than indicated in the quantitative findings, since three of the W's, those in R 1, R 10, and R 15

are simple whole percepts which are less W than they are D in terms of the intellectual effort which they require. On the other hand, the patient's other three W's, those in R 3, R 4, and R 5, require a more energetic effort at synthesis, and these show that this woman can be more flexible, more adaptive in her perceptual selections.

[59] Of the aggression in R 4, and of the oral phobic animal in R 21: "face isn't so much of a wolf."

[60] The precision description throughout figure IV; also the high productivity—whistling in the dark.

[61] In R 5, the dissatisfying feeling is displaced on to the "bear." The surmise is in order that she is displacing also in R 12, 13, and 14, and the emotion here is anxiety.

[62] The "stalking wolf" in R 21, and probably the "snakes" in R 27.

[63] Unsavory animals are sometimes one, sometimes the other. An example of the binding of acute anxiety which is also a displacing is the topologic "lungs" in R 23.

[64] R 7 and R 9 can be safely set down as symbolisms, as probably can the "bug" of R 19 for the female genital, which also carries a counterphobic flavor. The proposition is tenable that phobic thoughts and displacements are communication by way of symbols. But their defensive functions differ from those of symbols proper, a difference especially emphatic in the affective loadings. A question with regard to symbolism that is anything but clear is when it is a pathogenic, and when an adaptive, defense. Definitive discrimination based on clinical data would be a valuable contribution to diagnostic thinking. I have seen it listed among the pathologic defenses, but its emergence as art and as scientific creativity points up the major role it can play as an adjustive, constructive activity (cf. pp. 236f.).

[65] The color avoidances in R 9 and R 21.

[66] See exposition of the fantasy living, pp. 43f.

[67] See above, p. 44, concerning the frequency of M in figure III. Similar content here repeats itself so much that it is prosaic in the sense of not being differentiated.

[68] See note 57 concerning the high F+ per cent and lambda.

[69] The synthesizing activity in R 4 and R 5, examples of Rorschach's *kombinatorisch Ganz*. In R 3, too, the patient organizes the white space into the percept, usually a difficult task. She synthesizes also in R 25–26, but this is not an unusual achievement here.

[70] The number of organization responses is very few. She really sees difficult relationships in only two figures: in I and in II. Concerning the limited achievement indicated in the other W's, see note 58.

[71] Accent on the common detail, D, in the approach; see note 58.

[72] The animal content percentage, 52. This is higher than would be expected from internal evidence in the test record. It is an impoverishment. See note 53.

[73] She selects not a single Dd, a deficiency the more notable in a woman since women tend to pay somewhat greater attention than men to the minute, to the fine point.

[74] The F+ per cent is very high for a record of otherwise generally mediocre quality. It reflects the high grip on reality, which has been described as a defense (see note 57).

[75] The "personal" F— in each of her three inaccurate percepts, R 13, 14 and 23. See also note 48.

[76] Nine P responses. This is above the average of the normal adult, but still not so high as to indicate a compulsive adherence to the conventional.

[77] This again is not a test datum but an interpretation of the descriptive data in this paragraph in accordance with our knowledge of human nature generally.

[78] This patient's low M score and her probable struggle against fantasy living has been described (p. 43f.); and see also the relevant notes.

[79] Anxiety stalks the patient in the pleasure-toned stimuli of the test; see p. 42f.

[80] A single FC response, R 6, tells of a reaching toward such understanding, but it is the only such one in five color-determined associations. See p. 43. Even more arresting, and critical in disclosing her inadequate interest in others, is her small total of "human" (H) content, small almost to the zero point. The low M score, too, reflects this weakness, since in a person with healthy emotional release and a healthy ego, M can be an index to his ability to understand the other by fantasying himself in the other's place.

[81] The fact of its recurring (R 3 and R 23).

[82] The intellectual retardation and disruption with which it is produced in R 23; its suppression at first, and delay to the inquiry—all these point to the dynamic, anxiety laden significance of this theme.

[83] See p. 45 concerning the anxiety shock at figure VII.

[84] The oral and phobic significance of large-mouthed, biting animals has been well enough established by clinical psychoanalysis to justify such interpretations in terms of a general rule.

[85] In a lay person, imagery of internal, vital organs will inevitably be found to stem from pathologic preoccupations.

[86] In R 4. A possible identification may be hazarded. One could range further, in other speculations, but it would be the examiner's, not

the patient's, free association. All we can be sure of as concerns the patient is that it is one of her productions, a unique one, and it tells something. But what?

[87] As judged from the percentage of white space responses: nearly seven per cent. Range for average adults is 6–12 per cent.

# CHAPTER 5

# Mrs. O.: Acute marital stress.
# Indication for deep treatment

## Response Record

### Figure I (45″)

(Very tense.)

1. D F+ Ad x   'Design-wise, resembles a butterfly' (deep sigh; D 2, wing only).

2. D M+ H   'The center structure seems to suggest outline of a female form.' (D 4. 'Robust female. Energetic, industrious, young. Purely from physical rather than cosmetic. Bovine, solid. No identity. Plodding really.')

'Other than that I don't make much out of it. Can't ... has to be spontaneous? Am I right?

'Sorry ...

'Center portion looks like a tailor's dummy.' ('Heaviness suggests it; no grace or rhythm. Perhaps a better way to be.')

'Outer looks like wings of a butterfly. I ...' (Butterfly, and inner details, 'a stolid woman. Butterfly may in a sense be pulling at the woman in two different directions. One is responsibility and obligation, and the other direction is pursuit of a [long pause] well, love, selfish but satisfying. Butterfly ... frivolity ... responsibility and obligation to others.' (W M+ A, H P 4.0).

### Figure II (40″)

3. Dd M.T− Ad   'This suggests two animals, the head, face to face.'

    3.0   (Deep sigh. Form and texture of it. 'In a kissing attitude.' Dd of D 4.) Long pause. 'Perhaps two lambs ...

4. D M− Hd, Sex   ... and this portion (D 2) with this ... suggests almost a phallic symbol, I would say.' ('Sexual intercourse would be final consummation which began with the kiss. Which is what marital status is, isn't it?' Now denies D 2.)

'This [D 2] is the vaginal tract. This [D 4] seems to be entering an area.' (Position only. 'Passion means red, is heat. In that sense, the color too.' D C.Po Sex.)

'Other than that I don't seem to be able to determine anything. I don't seem to ...'

58

*Figure III* (20″)

5. D M+ H P
   4.0

'Seems to suggest two human forms ... facing each other.' (D 1. 'Symbolically; identical; presenting two sides of a question. Myself, both myself ... one part tells me one way; another portion, a completely contradictory way.')

6. D F− Cg

'Lower portion seems to suggest almost the ... top portion of a female garment ... large sleeves.' (D 4.)

7. D CF− An

'Red in center seems to suggest ... almost in a romantic sense ... the heart.' (Color, form, and question of position. 'I wear slacks a great deal. High heeled is a feminine mode of footgear. It was all in relation to my marriage ... will it continue or won't it? ... and the conflict which the decision is presenting. This [D 4] is feminine form, and they are connected to this [D 11], the right and the left of it. Therefore, two sides. The right meaning which is right or constructive, the left which would be the destructive or the short-sighted way. The immediate impact was two figures facing each other. Both emanate from one female form and it seemed to be concerned with the romantic affair of the heart. I'm all three. This [D 9] is a figure of thought, an attitude. This [D 4] symbolized me as a flesh and blood figure—the dress with its full sleeves, therefore an extravagant affair. Seems to suggest material acquisitions ... and that's all ... economic security ... that's all.')
'That's all? ... am I ... ' (deep, deep sigh).
'I don't mean to be difficult, but, quite frankly, for the life of me I can't make anything out of it ... no ...'

*Figure IV* (1′45″)

8. D F+ Cg

'This portion seems to suggest a large boot in appearance.' (D 6. 'Essentially yes.')

9. D F+ Sex

'Upper portion seems to suggest the female vaginal structure.' (D 3; form. All painfully slow. Shakes head.) 'I'll be darned if I can make any more out of it ... ' (deep sigh). 'I just don't see anything else in it ... ' (Mouth noises. Resigned.) 'I'm reaching now ... might suggest eyes, a morose look ... a long-faced look ... male ... I don't know.' (D 1. D M− Hd.)

*Figure V* (5″)

10. W F+ A P
    1.0

'Very definitely suggests the butterfly ... antennae, wings. Bottom portion of a butterfly (W). Most possibly suggests ... legs ... assuming ... ' (Will you embellish it so I can understand you clearly?) 'a . . . a . . . semblance of a posture of an

11. D M + H

individual who was timid, shy, afraid.' (D 7. 'A child-like attitude . . . afraid of acceptance . . . ' By anyone? 'A girl . . . possibly myself. I had a tremendous sense of insecurity.')
(Very slow.)
That's all I can make out of it . . . ' (mouth noises).
(Hesitant.)

12. Dd F + Cg

'A shadow there, most possibly suggests a man's hat (Dd 30), specifically a derby, has that form and shape.' ('My husband at one time owned one . . . butt of an awful lot of humor; he laughed too. But suggested "English, if you will. To the manner born." ')

*Figure VI* (15″)

'Hm!

13. D F + Ay

'Center portion suggests a replica of a totem pole that my seven year old daughter has' (D 3).

14. D F + A P

'This over-all pattern below it (D 1) suggests to me a small white rug made of a bearskin I had a long time ago (form only). Incidentally, this rug was one of the first household possessions of mine when I was first married.' ('One of the first material things I had. We did not set up immediately.')

15. D F + Ad

'The very uppermost portion, the head, symbolizes to me, or would look like what a wide-eyed owl would look like, in some sense suggesting wisdom, but why I don't know.' (D 7. 'The cliché, wise as an owl.')
('This (Dd 31) is two heads, male and female. Attitude is hostile and angry.' Dd M − Hd. 2.5.)
'That seems to be all.' (Eyes flutter.)

*Figure VII* (30″)

16. D M + H P

'Both! Seem to represent the form of a child!' (D 2. Patient's speech is explosive.) 'Balanced very precari-ously' (deep sigh).

17. W M + H
        3.5

'These two forms below suggest two female forms, child being balanced on the forehead of the female form.' ('My head? Yes, I did think of myself. What is impor-tant to me is, it is the same only in duplicate. The form in itself seems to suggest my seven-year old to me, with her pony tail flying askew. This [D 5] is flying out, with arms here [D 3]. Vivacious, gay, the personality of my daughter. Forehead means reason, thought, re-sponsibility. All in relation to the welfare of my child

... being able to provide a stable environment. Surround her with benefits that make for security. So an anxiousness.' Deep sigh. 'That's all' (very abrupt!). 'This [Dd at D 4; inner two male heads] my husband ... both. I seem to be supporting his head| upon my shoulder. It fits into the patterns very much that I saw before. I am his emotional support. He is aware of it ...')

### Figure VIII (30″)

18. D F − Hd 'Center area seems to suggest a female form.' (D 5, with D 2. 'Shoulders, and waistline and vaginal structure. I don't know that I could ... not clothed ... I saw it as a nude ... You see, I paint, and I'm studying anatomy. I really don't know, how I pictured it. A statue? I don't know ... robust ... young.' Patient is very evasive.)

19. D F + A 'Red areas on either side seem to suggest some kind of an animal.' ('Opposum. I don't know why.') (Mumbles.)

20. Dd F − Oj, Ab 'Center seems to be superimposed and suggests tears' (deep sigh). (Dd 27, with Dd 30. 'A stain ... a tear would make ... I associate tears with unhappiness.')

21. Dd F + Hd 'Lower portion (Dd 23) again appears to suggest vaginal structure of the female form' (shakes head).
'I don't seem to see anything else ... that's all I make.' (Always looks at examiner.)

### Figure IX (55″)

22. D FY − Hd 'This area seems to suggest upper structure of female form' (D 6). ('This [D 10] neck and breast ... from a front view ... abstract idea ... young ... my age ... firm, young ... a nude figure. I thought it to myself; two white spots are the nipple. I tried to be honest with myself.')

23. D F + Hd P 'These two portions on either side seem to suggest two heads' (D 4. 'A male head, older, hair, eyes, nose, mustache, stolid and glum ... glum not proper adjective ... stolid sums it up.' Patient is painfully slow. 'Heads are resting on a female form ... my husband ... suggests weightiness, heaviness.' D M + Hd.)
'I don't seem to make anything out of these ... all I see is just design.' ('Didn't see anything that clearly delineated form. Wings of a butterfly, but I'm reaching now; perhaps antennae too.')

*Figure* X (30″)

24. W C A,Bt           'A good deal looks like God's half-acre. All kinds of
                       insect life.' (Whole. 'A garden blooming, spring, insect
                       life . . . light and gay . . . the feel to it. Purely pleasant
                       reaction to color.')
                       'Don't seem to be able to see anything in this at all . . .'
25. D CF+ A            'Green might suggest caterpillar.' (D 4; color; form.
                       'Feeding off a single leaf.' D M + A, 4.0. 'Harmonious.
                       Leaf has two stems instead of one, and each is rele-
                       gated to his half of a leaf, rather than a unified whole.'
                       Question of M.)
26. D CF+ Bt           'And the yellow, possibly flowers' (D 15; color; form).
27. D F+ A P           'The two blue designs on either side possible crabs'
                       (D 1; form only).
                            Total Time: 41′3″


Liked best:            'I had no preference really. Shall I look? I don't know
                       . . . I don't know if I really like any one. Never thought
                       of it in that light. I don't know . . . difficult to say . . .
                       completely honest about it . . .'
Liked least:           IV 'because the boots in a sense . . . heavy, sublimating
                       . . . a domineering, to be trodden under by heavy boots
                       . . . in a symbolic sense, a masculine sense.'

### Response Summary

R: 27

| | | | | | | | |
|---|---|---|---|---|---|---|---|
| W | 3 | M | 6 (−1) | H | 5 | F+ | 80% |
| D | 20 | M.T− | 1 | Hd | 5 | A | 33% |
| Dd | 4 | C | 1 | A | 6 | P | 6 |
| | 27 | CF | 3 (1−) | Ad | 3 (x,1) | S | 0 |
| | | FY− | 1 | An | 1 | Af r | 0.59 |
| Z f | 4 | F+ | 12 | Ay | 1 | L | 1.25 |
| Z sum | 11.5 | F− | 3 | Bt | 1 | T/R | 91.22 |
| Ap | (W) D Dd! | | 27 | Cg | 3 | T/first R | 37.5 |
| Seq. ? Irregular | | | | Oj | 1 | Fln R | 1.11 |
| | trend | | | Sex | 1 | Fln T/first R | 31.67 |
| | | EB | 7/4.5 | | 27 | | |
| | | EA | 11.5 | | | | |

### Interpretation

Subsurface inner living [1]* bypasses the resistance to communicating
[2]. The strong feelings with which all of Mrs. O.'s fantasies are invested
[3], as well as the psychodynamic quality in the themes [4], disclose how
urgent are the pressures seeking ventilation. Even so, the total number of

---

* Bracketed numbers refer to Notes on Interpretation, which for this chapter will
be found on pages 65–77.

responses [5] is low for this patient's probable imaginative potential; after freely producing these associations initially, she soon cuts down on them almost completely [6]. It appears that the test at first overcame her defenses but that these defenses then reasserted themselves [7]. There was a destructive shutting off of the stream of ideas [8], and this can only be very painful [9]. This pain is apparent in the ambivalent content, the opposition between the primitively erotic and the idealistic [10], in the heterosexual fantasy, in the round-about language which screens an apparently conflictual attitude (R 3 and R 4). In some instances, after first having been suppressed, the ambivalences and the mixed eroticisms fuse with what appears to be a powerful narcissism [11]. Mrs. O.'s daughter is a topic in another strongly experienced fantasy which projects her anxiety about the child's happiness (R 17), with further elaboration that suggests the patient's own narcissistic identification with the daughter. The dynamic role which this woman's fantasy plays in her mental life is more fully evaluated in the notes [12].

A severe anxiety shock at masculine (father? husband?) imagery [13] supports the inference that heterosexuality is a threat to the ego [14]. Also, it is in figure IV and in the phallic figure VI, and in no others, that paranoid traces [15] appear, suggesting a hostile attitude to masculinity [16]. Significantly, it is to the phallic figure (VI) that she associates with R 14 [17]. The anxiety threat is such as to indicate that its source is a guilt sense [18], which is confirmed by the predominantly painful mood quality of this record [19]. A recurrent lack of self-assurance, articulated in a fantasy (R 11), supports this assumption, as does one strongly dysphoric note: "tears, unhappiness" (R 20).

The passivity trend suggested in this discouraged attitude and mood is confirmed by the total absence of aggressive trends [20]. Other structural traces of passivity appear [21]. A question that must be raised here is to what degree masochism is a factor in the picture [22].

Emotional response to external, pleasure-toned stimuli is about average in quantity [23], but there is evidence that it is restricted in quality and in range for this woman's probable capacity [24]. Also, it is belated in appearance [25], suggesting that the damage is severe in this sphere too [26], and the pattern is clearly that of neurotic shock [27]. The impulse toward gratifying experience in relation to the environment arouses anxiety [28]. The responses that do emerge are labile, temperamental, typically neurotic in structure [29]. The content here, however, is dominantly pleasurable and appropriate; only rarely is it symptomatic [30]. A latent cheerful mood reaction is thus indicated [31].

Ambivalences occur throughout the record [32] and indicate the presence of a constant and pathologic struggle between urges for gratification and the demands of the superego. Intellectualization and verbal circumlocutions are frequent [33], but there are only traces of paranoid thinking [34]. There is some recourse to fantasy [35], but she defends against this [36]. The ego thus is called upon to carry the major burden of the defense effort, with the net result to the person being a pathogenic one [37].

In the main, the ego has responded with reduced rather than regressed functioning. The total productivity is seriously below what would be expected from internal evidence as to Mrs. O.'s probable mental calibre [38]. At the same time, the struggle between wishes and the superego is severe enough to produce an occasional example of pathologic thinking, a trend toward contamination or confusion [39]. These are products of her especial preoccupations [40], but are few in number [41], however. Perceptual departures also stem from her particular personal needs and also are few in number [42]. The total grip on reality is, in fact, within the healthy range [43] and, if anything, reflects the hold on herself [44]. Similarly, she has a normal respect for the conventional [45]. She responds to inner stimuli, fantasy, and other emotions in excessive fashion as compared with the norm [46].

In all [47], this is a neurosis marked by consciously held pathogenic defenses. There is absorption in highly conflictual needs but evidence also of emotional fluidity [48]. Her conflict is intense between (a) her need for security and the security of her daughter, with whom she may be identifying, and (b) some factor in her marriage which is a source of unhappiness and so may be threatening her security and generating intense anxiety [49].

The content contains associations to be explored as evidences of homosexuality [50], elaborated enough and frequent enough to open up the surmise that this is a dominant trait. A possibly more primitive erotic need is reflected in the breast associations, sometimes screened [51] and once emerging only after much delay (R 22). There is a recurrent suggestion, as in this response, of a narcissism fixated on the self [52]. At the same time, a primitive oral need is also to be considered [53]; a single feeding association emerges, after being first suppressed [54]. There is one instance of a possible devaluation of the husband [55], and one instance of an erotic urge favorable to him [56]. The recurrence of the female genital topic in the phrase "female vaginal structure" indicates her involvement over sexuality [57, 58]. Very rarely is this a healthy original response, neither in the art nor household spheres [59].

Concerning the implications for therapy, there is little question about the strength of this patient's ego [60], as can be seen not only in her integration [61] but also in her ability to recover from shocks [62], reflecting reserves on which she can continue to call in spite of the ego's being constantly in action. This ego effort is likely to be the chief obstacle to early success in treatment [63]. Yet, inner response can be activated [64], even though with effort [65], and there are unused latencies in the emotional sphere [66], suggesting that a transference can be stimulated [67]. The anguish which she suffers, as projected in the test, would be further promise that relief would be welcome [68]. The structure as a whole warrants deep treatment for this patient [69].

### Notes on Interpretation

[1] Four M responses emerge in the Inquiry to figures I, IV, VI, and IX; and possibly a fifth (Inquiry to figure X).

[2] The evidence is that this fantasy living is ready for communication, since the patient eventually does so; yet, there is resistance to it, since she only associates with this material belatedly.

[3] The energy ratings are high in a majority of the M. (See the ratings, note 12.)

[4] All the content in the M, and its very personal significance to the patient, exposing as poignantly as it does, the essence of her disturbance.

[5] Seven M, so scored for the free association.

[6] In figures I–III, Mrs. O. associates with four M; she then produces only one in figures IV, V, VI together. Mother imagery, figure VII, again stimulates two M, her final ones. The four M in seven responses in the first three test figures is evidence for this imaginative potential. She cuts this rate down to three M in 27 responses in the other seven figures, in five of which she scores no M.

[7] The reasoning is: (a) she does score M in the early cards and has thus by-passed the barriers to them; (b) she is capable of M (actually she produces eleven, and possibly twelve); hence, failure to do so is an eschewing of deeply lying but ultimately emerging unconscious needs; i.e., she finds it easier not to face these thoughts. This is psychological defense, and (c) it reasserts itself later, not only in the reduction of M but also in the five time delay of M to the Inquiry.

What is Mrs. O. defending against? She gives vivid and cumulative evidence that the interest aroused in R 2 is something from which to turn away. Within the free association she alters the human form percept into an inanimate one, "a tailor's dummy." Here is denial. Then, too, the patient repeatedly loads devaluing adjectives on the at first "robust female," making her "bovine, solid, no identity, plodding; no grace or rhythm." This also is the language of denial. Secondly, the speculation is warranted that she is defending against the strong emotions attached to her fantasies, i.e., the high energy with which she invests so much of her M (see note 12: energy ratings). Psychological economy (Freud's concept) is thus being achieved.

Another line of evidence is the content of the avoided (Inquiry) fantasies. It always deals with needs of distressing personal import. In the Inquiry to VII, in what is possibly this patient's most highly energized M, the theme is her daughter, with what explicitly is a healthy wish. The conflictual forces are only too clearly communicated in the Inquiry to figure I, forces which have been contending in the patient to the degree that the strain has been too much and she finds herself in the hospital. Although the overt energy is less strong in IV (Inquiry), the personal significance is acute, as inferred from its paranoid quality. Similarly, in figure VI, energy rating is low, but the theme, hostility between a male and female, connotes strong feeling. She saves for the Inquiry, figure II, the full development of the most intimate of desires: "sexual intercourse." In the free association she had screened it in animal content; i.e., dream structured fantasy. The stronger the wish, the more she avoids it.

[8] "Destructive" since it impedes the free exercise of an ability, particularly because it is the ability indicated in M, i.e., creative imagination. It could be argued that Mrs. O. is using this ability to live out in her imagination her frustrated or conflictual needs, i.e., not creatively but symptomatically. Hence, is she not better served in cutting it off? However, inhibiting fantasies does not dissolve them; it simply drives them underground. The repression is then more severe than when feelings are converted into and acted out as fantasy, even if of a sick quality.

[9] The pain is inferred from the sheer fact of setting up a dam against an ideation that permits relief. Against the seduction of fantasy that will alleviate the stress, there is resistance which is motivated by value forces with their emotional charges, i.e., by ego. Tensions that counter each other are pulling in opposite directions, and the net experience can only be pain.

[10] See the lengthy elaborations in the Inquiry to figure III; the rejection in figure I of what was at first an attractive female form; the woman being pulled in opposite directions (Inquiry, figure I) in which the ambivalence becomes manifest; the motifs both of displeasure at and tenderness concerning the husband ("head resting") percept in figure IX.

[11] The "passion" motif in the Inquiry to II, as well as the "romantic ... heart" in III. It should be stressed here that these motifs are leads opened up by the test which should be explored in the therapeutic sessions for their full significance to the patient.

[12] Over-all survey of the fantasy living: structurally, the M in the free associations are, in the main, sound; the forms, with two exceptions, are +; and the content is whole humans. Regressive ideas do appear, however, in the themes; in the immaturities of the M in Hd (one in the free association, three in the Inquiry) and in the retreat to dream work

in the M with animal content in figure I (Inquiry), in II, and in X (Inquiry). Viewed within the framework of this woman's present neurotic adjustment, we must find a serious discrepancy between this quality of her fantasy living and her total inadequate imaginative achievement in life.

The stance in Mrs. O.'s fantasies provides a lead to the structure of her neurosis. It is markedly extensor twice; in figure I, Inquiry, and in VII, the elaboration concerning her daughter. It is clearly flexor four times: R 3, II, the Inquiry to VI and to X (the caterpillar, feeding). In R 2, it is static, and in the others no judgment can be made. What is clear is that (a) the dominant inner pose is submissive and feminine but that (b) there are also strong urges to self-assertion of a masculine quality. The result is: opposed sexualities conflicting at unconscious levels. The further lead, to be pursued in direct exploration with the patient, is the role of masculinity in this woman's homosexual needs, which are reflected in the content. The affective quality of the fantasying is, judged from its explicit content, pleasurable. But in view of the tensions in this woman, one must wonder whether the pleasure is not the more painful one of day-dreams supplying gratification for which she yearns with actual frustration. The eroticisms in some of the content in the fantasy too clearly uncover primitively powerful desires. The service of her fantasy living to Mrs. O. is that of a vent for otherwise trapped feelings. It is a withdrawal recourse, but with strong, even anguishing, affects.

My ratings for the amount of activity, based on the Levy Scale, is as follows:

| Area | Response | Rating |
|---|---|---|
| R 2 | "energetic, industrious" | 4 |
| Inq. I | "butterfly . . . pulling" | 6–7 |
| R 3–4 | "kissing . . . intercourse" | 7 |
| Inq. IV | "morose . . . long-faced, look" | 1–2 |
| R 11 | "posture . . . timid, shy" | 1–2 |
| Inq. VI | "attitude is hostile, angry" | 2–3 |
| R 16 with Inq. | "balanced precariously . . . pony-tail flying askew" | 7 |
| R 17 | (the heads on which) "child is being balanced" | 3–4 |
| Inq. VII | "my husband . . . supporting his head" | 3–4 |
| Inq. IX | "heads on female form . . . husband . . . heaviness" | 3–4 |
| Inq. X | "caterpillar feeding" (question of M) | 1 |

[13] Figure IV. The very slow time for the first response is the obvious indication, but not the only one. Retardation within the card is reported by the examiner, and the patient herself articulates inhibition ("I'll be darned," etc.). The hesitations reflect an avoidance of her percepts. The emotions betray themselves in motor signs: deep sighing and mouth noises. How troubling these emotions are is attested to in her language at

the close of the test when she picks this test figure as the one she likes least: "a domineering, to be trodden under by heavy boots, in a symbolic, a masculine sense," disclosing her painfully phobic state of mind at the imagery which this figure stirs up.

[14] Whether the anxiety shock in a married woman at figure IV stems from an older attitude to the father or from a current one to the husband can usually not be known from the test alone. What the shock does tell is that her heterosexual pattern is the source of anxiety. It is, thus, the defensive threat described by the psychoanalysts. The patient cannot reconcile her actual attitude with her standards as to what she ought to be in her marital role. The attitude is ego-alien.

[15] The M in the Inquiry, in figure IV, and in figure VI.

[16] The *test* projects this, not the patient, using "project" not in the clinical sense but in its more literal one, i.e., in the sense of throwing an image on a screen, the only sense in which the term "projective" is warranted for the psychological tests so classified. However, as paranoid ideation, these responses are projections, clinically speaking, since the patient is imputing her own hostile attitudes, unpalatable to her, as if they were in the object of her hostility.

[17] A nostalgic note with its mingling of the painful and the pleasurable is here related to two themes deeply rooted in femininity: the early days of this patient's married life and a household article in which she took a woman's pride. A possible third note, of a remembered deprivation, appears: "We did not set up immediately."

[18] Shock is most violent in IV, the figure producing the severest retardation in the first response and the other findings already described above. Probable shock is to be noted in VII, which is absorbed by introversion (both responses are M); it is betrayed in motor symptoms, the explosiveness of her first association (R 16), and in the abrupt way in which she returns the test card. Emotional reaction in varying degrees is thus aroused by two of the test cards known to stir up disturbing thoughts about parental figures, with the attendant depressive mood tone. The paranoid motif in IV and in VI has been noted. In figure VI, however, as also in V, she masters her feelings, with apparent adaptivity. A question of shock is also raised by the pattern of figure I (the first response is one of her three most delayed ones; she fails to associate with the simple P; and the x response tells of constricted vision). Still, it is figure IV, that evokes a state of free anxiety. The inference is that this shock must be due to the principal dynamic in her current illness: the unhappiness which her thoughts about the male are causing her. They are thoughts at variance with ideals; the ego suffers under chafing from her superego. The anxiety

is a warning to this woman that she has wishes for which she cannot hold herself blameless.

It is from our clinical knowledge, and, in fact, from our larger knowledge of human life, that we derive the interpretation as to this woman's specific present illness, namely, that it is a collision between her attitudes toward her husband and her ideas as to what she ought to be as wife. An inference from the general to the particular is, however, not proof in the field of human personality, whether the pathologic or normal personality. The variables are many, and the particular person under study may be the exceptional one in his group. The interpretation always needs to be confirmed by exploration in the individual under observation. The Rorschach test interpretation, until confirmed, is hypothetical.

[19] The self-effacing language ("I don't make much out of it ... don't seem to be able to ... can't"), the resignation formulae ("that's all; don't seem to see anything else"), the apologetics and uncertainties ("sorry, am I right?") and the excessive qualification of her responses reflect the mood tone of this record. These I have found so regularly in depressed persons and in some anxiety states as to look on them as typical products of unhappy mood conditions. Deep sighing is reported by the examiner at various points. Although such observations are not structural in the sense of being scorable associations, they always add critical information. Our patient more directly confirms these mood findings in the content: in R 16, "balanced very precariously," with its insecurity motifs; the explicit self-identification in the fantasy of the shy and fearful girl (R 11); possibly in the "shadow" in R 12; and in R 20, the "tears."

This mood tone is, paradoxically, a benign finding. In accenting the unhappy affect, as well as in its reactive features (the shock phenomena above, etc.), the test contraindicates a more malignant disorder, e.g., a possibly schizophrenic pattern. Not that this test record is clear of all malignancy. The contamination in the Inquiry to figure I is a serious thinking dysfunction, a retreat to a dereistic mode of thought, and other regressions of varying depths are in evidence (see below). But with the dysphoric mood so influencing the condition as a whole, the intellectual deviations become understandable as a measure of the severity of the agitation. They are not the intellectual fragmentation that follows on a primary disorder of the ego.

[20] The white space count is 0. Parenthetically, "oppositional" would be a better word than "aggressive" in referring to space responses since certain content themes are necessary before postulating the aggression urges.

[21] Traces are found in the shading determined response (R 22), as well as in the use of this determinant for identifying the detail selected

in R 12. However, in the latter the shading element does not actually influence the percept. The patient thus shows much ability to shuffle off the
passivity and the dysphoric experience. The shading determinant is also
secondary in both R 14 and R 22, and the form element is primary; ego
forces are dominant over the emotional, even though there are signs of a
struggle (the F— in R 22). In all, whether in the small number of the
shading determined associations or in the degree of the saturation with
shading (neither Y or YF), this woman does not score to the degree seen
in depression. This observation would influence the over-all judgment of
the severity of the illness, and hence has implications as to therapy.

[22] This (masochism) is one of those stabs at interpretation in which
one reasons from Rorschach test logic to known clinical logic even though
the data from which to infer this psychologic trait, masochism, is not
available in the test protocol. A problem in making a report to the clinical
practitioner, a report which he can find immediately helpful in understanding his patient, is whether the test report should note what is a
product of reasoning but not a test observation. By the latter criterion,
the interpretation "masochism" was not warranted here. Yet, would a report for purposes of *clinical* information have been complete without it?

[23] The number of color-determined responses is four; and the weighted
color value is 4.5. If anything, this value is slightly high (average for
normal adults is 3.11). This weighted total is high in relation to the total
productivity (a point to which I shall return).

[24] The quality restriction is seen in the affective nuances which this
patient shows in her color structures: CF in three of these responses,
while the fourth, unmodulated C even more strongly accents this excitement tone, as does the similar color response which was at first suppressed
in figure II (Inquiry). The restriction of range refers technically to the
absence of FC responses. Psychologically, it is a narrow emotional range
which we see—an inability of Mrs. O. in her present state to let her feelings reach out to and understand those most essential data of her environment, other persons. She reacts in a limited, egocentric range, but a probable capacity for broader, more allocentric experience emerges in the
content (see below).

[25] She produces three color responses in figure X, none in the two other
all-color figures (VIII and IX). The color association in figure III was
the final one of five associations in figures II and III, and, as we have
seen, one other in II was fully delayed until the Inquiry.

[26] It is damage since, for one thing, this patient's emotional living is
now less whole (narrow range) or free (delayed) than it could be (as
indicated in the liberation of strong feelings); she is prevented from enjoying contacts and relations that are within her potential. More posi-

tively, she suffers from being under pressure from the strong and primitive feelings represented in the C and CF responses.

[27] The intellectual dysfunction in figure III betrays the disruption; it is a shock which set in, and persisted, from figure II. Although the stresses are cushioned in II by introversion—the two M—the disturbance is severe: the slow time for the first response, the irregular sequence, and the form inaccuracy in both M, all of which is further proof, if that were necessary, of the deeply regressive source of these associations, also indicated in their content. In VIII and IX the shock effects are severe: the F— in VIII, in which test figure alone we find two of the three F— in the entire test; and the altered selective attention represented in the Ap, as two of the four Dd make their appearance here. She fails the very common P, and, on the other hand, releases one of her most individualized thoughts (tears) evidence of the degree to which her emotions have upset her. In IX, time for the first response is the next to the slowest in the test, and an F— in her first association is shaped by a deeply regressive need (R 22). All this is manifestation of a free anxiety, the patient's ego control lapsing, similar to her reaction under shading shock.

However, recovery is possible. She concludes her associations to figure IX with a P, a recovery which forecasts the one more fully achieved in X in which all the forms are of sound structure, and a healthy affect dominates in the content (see especially R 24, 26).

The pattern in figures VIII–X is typical neurotic shock: disturbance or disruption of ego control, followed by the regaining of self-possession.

[28] The color-toned response is an index to the out-going emotion, a reaching to the other. Whether egocentrically or as a shared experience, it is pleasurable to the person so reacting. The shock in the color figures is the work of the anxiety. Hence, the inference that the urge to be in a pleasurable relationship carries with it a threat. This woman is so structured psychologically that promise of having what she wants frightens or disorganizes her. Strong affects whether painful (shading shock) or pleasurable (color shock) generate anxiety.

[29] Lability, the quick sensitivity of "temperament" are the indications in CF. This is the most frequent color determinant in neurotics. However, this interpretation in the original report inadequately stated the facts. The pure C reactions tell that the patient is liable also to uninhibited impulsivity. In addition, the total of weighted color response is, relative to the productivity, high. So the mobilization of the emotions and their strong role in the whole reaction pattern are pointed up, together with the unstable forms in which they will emerge.

[30] R 24 is articulately healthy in tone and in theme, in fact, to the point of elation. The "caterpillar" and the "flower," as nature topics—

unless the patient gives explicit evidence of pathologic interest—I evaluate as healthy, presumably reflecting an appropriate response to nature. The "heart" of R 7 is of symptomatic significance, and the latent "passion ... heat" (R 4) is even more deeply so.

[31] In R 24, 25, 26. Content in the color associations frequently reflects the patient's mood state, and it may be the main test index to it. The coincidence of a wish-fulfilling theme (God's half-acre) with undiluted color indicates a high-keyed affect and has the quality of the manic's happiness.

[32] More correct would be the observation that Mrs. O. is in a constant state of ambivalence, pulled by gratification urges (as described in the color figures and in some of the fantasy living) and at the same time threatened by self-accusations (see note 18). We thus see an ego in, in Fenichel's description, typical alert on two fronts: now against id, now against superego.

[33] The avoidances are especially numerous and in instances are extended into delays which are essential suppression. Note the round-about phrasing "a female form" (R 2), which followed an evasion effort by way of excessive ("seems to ... suggest ... outline of ...") qualifying. The more usual association here in persons not overly sensitive to an aroused idea is "shape of a woman" or some simple variation of this percept.

Other examples of avoidance are the "kissing attitude" (R 4) and the manner of associating throughout figure III: hesitation, much qualifying and the delay until the Inquiry of the primary motif. Suppression is clearcut, although the tactic is technically screening, in R 6. The interest is in the breast, an inference which is supported in R 22 where it is also shunted off, becoming articulate only in the Inquiry. The circumlocutory language will be noted in both these associations. The delaying tactics or suppressions are evident also in fantasies of critical import, those that emerge only in the Inquiry in figures I, IV, VI, IX, and possibly X.

Denials appear twice and possibly a third time. In R 18, the obviously amoral thought, "nude," to be explained as a homosexual theme, is made into "a statue." In R 24 she neutralizes her first response, whose very pleasurable tone is inconsistent with her morose mood, by completely rejecting the card. The third instance is in figure I: she transforms the, at first obviously attractive to her, lively young female into an inanimate "tailor's dummy," and with apparent aversion. What is essentially dynamic in all this is that the ego is separating itself from ideas alien to its sense of the proper.

Among verbalist behaviors is "embellish," which is out of context (figure V), and the unnecessary emphasis on formal language, e.g., "structure," as well as the ponderings with philosophic flavor around abstract, symbolic topics (figures II, III, VII).

[34] The two Inquiry M in figures IV and VI raise a question of pathologic expedient. But, at worst, these are traces only. So far as this Rorschach test shows, this woman is not systematically trying to get out from under by projecting her unpalatable wishes onto others.

[35] Fantasy is a defense that permits a detour on coming upon psychologic terrain too difficult or painful for the ego to negotiate. It relieves the strain on the ego. It is thus a psychologic economy that minimizes the weariness or exhaustion resulting from conscious struggle.

[36] The delays or suppressions above observed (notes 1 and 33).

[37] Some more adaptive defenses are in evidence, to be sure: the search for symbolisms and the sublimation indicated in Mrs. O.'s art avocation (figure VIII). Such, also, is her apparent ability to maintain a strict hold on reality, albeit in phases, i.e., throughout test cards IV–VII. But what the cost of this is in the coin of spontaneous functioning is a question to be asked in the light of the low response total (and see below). Direct evidence of inhibition is seen in the slow response tempo within figure IV, as well as in the slow time for first response (30 seconds to 105 seconds) in seven of the test cards. The term "pathologic" is still somewhat too strong for appraisal of this patient's defenses as a whole. More accurately, her defenses are constriction and withdrawal.

[38] A person with this patient's vocabulary and her familiarity with topics requiring advanced education would, in a healthy state, produce a record of fifty or more scorable associations. Her total of 27 responses is actually below the mean of an average adult sample (32.65).* The x (Rorschach's Do) response is extremely rare in the healthy, whether of average or superior intelligence. It mirrors a narrowed-in field of vision. The narrowing shows up also in the content range, centering as it does around her symptomatic needs, and so depriving her of a more adaptive variability of interests. This reduction, in quantity and in breadth, is the serious loss which her illness is costing her.

[39] Contamination in R 2, Inquiry; the primitive elaboration after R 7—"two figures emanate from one female form;" and even a trend to condensation in relating this percept to the "romantic affairs of the heart." These are regressions, essentially a retreat to more immature, de-differentiated, intellectual behavior patterns. Fortuitous, tangential processes appear in the thinking: Po associations in figure II, Inquiry; and possibly

---

* A synopsis of all statistical norms, for children and adult, healthy and pathologic, will be found in ref. 15 in the bibliography. For report of the research which established the adults' norms, see ref. 12; the children's norms, ref. 68.

in R 21; these are regressive behaviors. Confusion, although less serious, and some fragmentation of ideas are apparent in II and in VIII.

[40] The preoccupations are seen in the themes. They are consistent with what emerges as the nucleus of this patient's illness. However, the severity of the disruption can be discounted since essentially all the individualized thinking can easily be understood for the personal significance it has to her; in other words, it lacks the perplexing, dream quality of schizophrenia. The relationship is clear between most of her thought content and her conflictual personal desires, and her verbalizations show that she is herself cognizant of the forces with which she is contending.

[41] "Few" refers to the deeper regressions and thinking relapses. Examples are "butterfly pulling the woman" (I), and "two figures emanate out of the one female" (III).

[42] All three of her F− are "personal": R 6, 18, 20. The role of her needs in impairing these percepts is clear. The observation also holds for those form inaccuracies in which the scoring formula includes a non-F element (the "extended F−"; Schafer): R 3, 7, and 22. "Personal F−" are found in various disorders, including schizophrenia, but they are especially characteristic of the neurotically disturbed. These latter, at the same time, commit fewer "impersonal" perceptual errors, a kind of inaccuracy more characteristically found in patients with brain pathology and in the feebleminded. The schizophrenic's test record may be dominated by either the personal or impersonal error, or by both.

[43] F+ per cent for the record as a whole, 80, is breaking through the high end of the neurotic range, which I am dependably finding to be 60 to 75. In view of the acute distresses which this patient is enduring, this percentage is evidence of a major personality reserve in her: an ego strongly enough rooted in regard for recognized values to hold to them in spite of emotional storms.

[44] The hold is on reality rather than on the self, and is one of Mrs. O.'s adaptive defense measures (note 37). The accent on D in her Ap shows a pattern of overattention to the conspicuous, which is defensive, but deleterious to adaptive intellectual functioning: for one thing, there is the element of the inflexible in it; for another, she is prevented from free use of her intelligence in achieving larger, more extended percepts and values. Hence, she cannot fully grasp her own situation in its fullness. This disability is manifest in her Z score, 11.5, very low for her probable ability (note 38).

The animal content per cent, 33, is another indication of constraint on her intellect, a loss of originality. It is higher than would be expected for her intelligence. Again, a loss of resilience is reflected. The reverse effect is seen in her narrowed breadth of interest: the actual count of richly original content not symptomatically channelized is small.

[45] The P count is six. The normal range is five to eight.

[46] This is seen in the lambda index. She scores low: 1.25. The normal range is about 1.50 to 2.50. Thus, the pull of the inner forces, whether pleasurable feelings or painful, introverted or expressed—those responses in the test having a C, Y, T, or M component—is so strong as to permit her fewer than the expected number of associations that are solely form-determined, i.e., dominated by environmental stimuli.

[47] A summary diagnostic description is: serious impairment of efficiency in a woman of probably above average to superior intellectual endowment; her thinking is now dominated by mobilized affect of persistent, unresolvable conflicts that are seriously interfering with her ability to engage in the normal pleasures of life. Unique thoughts and attitudes emerge. The self is badly devalued and a painful mood tone is prominent. The total picture: a neurosis, and as stated in the original report.

[48] The pattern of response to the color stimuli of the test (above).

[49] These topics are the principal foci of her anxiety and of her conflictual stress, as is obvious from much of the content. Two major concerns are in interplay in figure III and explicit (my marriage, will it continue? ... material conditions, economic security). The latter is the center of her thoughts in R 16–17; there is an insecurity theme emanating from deep (fantasy) sources in the personality. The language in these free associations speaks for itself. For her articulate statement of the consummation in married life see R 4. How much these overtly recognized issues are interwoven with related ones, some from more unconscious sources in the personality, is highlighted by the content, both as shown in the fantasy material above and in other associations.

[50] In R 2, R 18, R 22 (see note 52 for more concerning this response); possibly in R 3.

[51] Screened in R 6, and the patient skirmishes around the percept and avoids it in R 18; then removes the screening curtain and fully articulates it in R 22.

[52] I.e., in R 22. For other associations to be explored for their derivation from what would be a normal feminine narcissism but is, in this patient's illness, overstressed, see R 5, R 6; possibly also R 18. At the same time, a strong concern over her daughter raises the question of identification, which would disclose a potential for a healthy narcissism.

[53] How much the "breast" associations stem back to primitive orality and are a statement of reunion urges, only direct therapeutic exploration can establish.

[54] In figure X, the "caterpillar," belatedly.

[55] Actually two such responses: 12 and 23.

[56] In the Inquiry following R 17.

[57] These will be found in figures II, IV, VIII.

[58] A lead in another direction is given by the "owl wisdom" theme in R 15. The owl is a bird with old symbolic connotation. What it means to this woman would have to be threshed out in therapeutic sessions, but one can speculate that she looks to wisdom as the equivalent of strength and as providing the security which would shore up her personality structure where she senses it as weakest. Whether there is significance in the fact that she so associates to the phallic figure is another question. The content is here corroborating the dysphoric and passive mood findings. It will be noted that she knows that she is thinking in symbolism. Also, she recognizes the "cliche," i.e., her group's language, and so shows herself in social contact, which helps rule out serious pathology.

[59] The art interest in R 18 and the household motif in the "rug" of R 14. This latter is a very common association, in fact, a P. Yet, in this patient it excites all the intense wishes related to the household of a woman in the early phases of her marriage. My interpretation "healthy" was here an understatement. This wish is an absorbing one and uncovers what, in favorable conditions, can be a richly wholesome relationship.

[60] A first point of interest in appraising treatability is necessarily the state of the ego. How much wish does the patient show to hold on to established values? And to direct herself by them as a central, piloting set of dictates? This woman's occasional deep regressions may generate therapeutic pessimism, intensified by the picture of the storms which rock her. Yet, the very severity of the struggle is evidence of an urge to be rid of trends alien to her central values (see note 19) of the wish to be whole psychologically and in consonance with her milieu. As such the acute agitation is paradoxically, a healthy sign. Where there is ego, there is hope.

[61] See the notes above (43–45) for evidence of the ego's reserve stamina.

[62] Described above (note 27).

[63] This looks like another paradox. Yet, it refers to a not uncommon dynamic in treatment. The ego is strong but under pressure from defensive needs, and it limits its sights to those needs. The insecurity of the individual, as he sees it in his illness, urgently commands those defenses. Should they break, the anxiety and terror go out of bounds. Hence the sometimes desperate sticking to the defense pattern and the frightened resistance of any insight that disturbs or breaches them.

[64] Referring first to the fantasy living (M associations), but this tells only part of the story. The externalized emotions also have their

source in the inner life (note 66). See in this connection Rorschach's post-humous paper,[58] an exposition of a patient's actual emotional life as com-municated in both M and C. The EA (Chapter 2) is the test's gauge to a person's inner resources. In the present case they are extensive: EA, 11.5.

[65] See note 63. The effort will need to be exerted by both patient—a prerequisite always—and therapist. But the word (effort) was, in the re-port, intended as information for the latter: the ego's narrowed-in need to defend and to resist will set up roadblocks.

[66] The reaction pattern to the color cards is, of course, equally im-portant with the fantasy production in indicating the personality's liques-ence emotionally. The picture in this connection is developed in notes 23–31.

[67] Concerning transference, see Chapter 16. This protocol is replete with Mrs. O.'s acute anxiety over a conflictual imago; her generally fluid emotional state, including not only the EA findings, but also the dys-phoric mood; and traces of the devaluing of others (note 55; also R 2). But a more vigorous hostility and the self-assertion which is an essential dynamic in transference are not yet in evidence.

[68] The psychologic anguish suffered by Mrs. O. has received full exposition. Its importance in appraising her treatability cannot be over-estimated. Her neurosis is a cry for help.

[69] What manner of treatment, finally, do all these Rorschach test findings and their logic indicate? The considerations here, as always, are two: (a) how seriously ill is the patient? and (b) how capable of respond-ing is she—to what level of probing and with what related insight? The answer to the first question has already been seen: an acute neurotic disruption. The illness is severe both in its emotional intensities and its impairing intellectual effects. The answers to the second question have also emerged: ego reserves, emotional fluidity, release of deeper needs out of the unconscious, signs of transference potential, and probable resources of high intelligence. These are structural components of the kind that promise results in deep psychoanalytic therapy. A principal contraindica-tion is this woman's need to cling to her defenses and the likelihood that for a time she will hold to them fearfully. The therapist's main problem will be to direct her toward a slackening in these mechanisms and toward facing her seeming impasse clear-headedly. Treatment less than deep can, of course, serve to relieve the oppressive emotional load, and it can tem-porarily palliate her conflicted state. But it would remain palliative. It would not cure. The pain within will continue to fester and periodically must break out in symptoms of varying acuteness. There can be healing in this case, but it will take the radical reconstruction effort of deep therapy.

## Clinical Note

This woman was referred by a psychiatrist from his private practice for evaluation as to her ego strength, with special reference to her present treatability. She had been in treatment with another psychoanalyst up to about a year prior to the referral for this Rorschach test. She described this earlier therapeutic experience as "unfortunate." In the meantime, she had been having "a trying time; under physical and emotional strain."

This fragment of history was not known to me at the time I wrote the interpretation of this test protocol. It will serve the patient and the referring psychiatrist better for the psychologist to know the referring problem. However, the exigencies of referral conditions frequently preclude any communication. Willy-nilly, the Rorschach test situation, in these instances, is an experiment the more compounded.

# CHAPTER 6

# Mrs. L.: A woman suicide

## Response Record

*Figure I* (45″)

'Frankly speaking, I don't know what it is; just a design.

1. W F+ A P
   1.0

'Would it be a butterfly?' ('It looks like a butterfly, the entire thing, the general outline.')
'I can't . . . it is some sort of insect, don't know exactly.' ('Some kind of flying insect.')

2. D F+ Hdx

'Two hands protruding on the top.' (D 1. 'It is not; if it was more fingers, it would be.') 'My mind was so foggy this morning, I had to take a dexedrine. I am not very well acquainted on pictures of insects. Can you see the two hands—is that correct—and the insect?

3. D F+ H

'Now I see it almost like a person (D 4) in here with the feet that way; could be, only I can't see any head. Suppose this would be a flyer dressed in a flyer's dress.' ('The shape of a person, like a flyer dressed in a heavy coat, a belt around the waist; you can see the waist. The only thing I saw first was the feet.')
'Like wing, not of a plane.

4. D F+ Tr

'Almost like an airplane.' ('The flyer in front of an airplane. When I saw these two points, D 8, I thought of wings and that is why I thought of a flyer. There is no plane.')
'This could be so many things. That is about all I can see. This whole thing looks like an animal of some kind.' (Insect, as above.)

*Figure II* (5″)

5. W M.CF+ H P
   4.5

'Two people sitting, holding hands together; most like clowns.' (W. 'Dressed with red hats and red stockings. Like children play with their hands. That is why they are clowns.')

6. D FC− Fi, Hh

'What else could it be? Could it be a light, torchlight? The top of it looks like it.' ('Flame of a candle looks like that, not exactly that shape if the candle is not held straight up, the flames get that shape; no, perhaps it is the color too, the red color.')
'It is something more too, except people.

7. Ds F+ Hh  'Could the entire thing be sort of a light? It could be;
I don't think it is, I don't.' ('Here it is [Ds 5]; these
in here; is here for some reason. It is brought out so
prominently, so it is a reason for that; the story lies in
that.') 'A chandelier hanging down from the ceiling, the
shape of it.' (Ds 5. 'Could be a light; no, it is not. Just
a white globe chandelier.') 'What else? Better seen this
way. These two things [D 2], no, it is nothing.')

8. D F— Pr  'This is a chain (Dd 25) hanging down from the neck,
a piece of jewelry.' (D 3. 'Just the form, not the color.
Can you see the chain? And the jewelry?')

### Figure III (73″)

  ∨ ∧ ∨ 'I don't know what it is. Gets me real . . . I
don't know.

9. D F+ A  ∨ 'Two birds (D 12) resting on
10. D F— Bt  'Branches (D 6) and yet I know it is not.' ('The birds?
  3.0  I said it could be. Resting on branches. They look like
birds; the form; like pins one can see in stores. The beak
[top of Dd 21], the eye, white spot, standing on something [Dd 30], wings.')
  'I can't make out anything. ∧ ∨ ∧
11. D F+ Hd  ∨ 'There is the face of a colored person (D 4), yet I
know it is something else.' ('A child or an old person. A
real old man's face.' Why colored? 'You can see the
protruding chin and mouth. Oh, wait a minute; two
heads of two birds of some kind; there is their eyes.
Yes, these are two animals.')

12. Dd F+ Ad  ∧ ∨ 'Oh, it looks like a face of a mouse or a rat.' (Dd
21. 'The only thing is, it looks a little more the shape of
a beak.')
  'It is about all I can make out of it.
13. D F+ Ad  'Would you say it is a fish? (D 5) And yet it does not.
Just this part of it looks like it. ∧ It has double meaning, different things, upside down. This represents
something (D 8) and these spots (D 2) but I can't make
it out.
  'That is all.' ('The head of the fish is most like it, not the
other part; that has not the shape of it. No, I don't
know. This [D 3] could be the shape of a bow-tie.')

### Figure IV (45″)

14. Dd M+ Ad  ∨ 'Hm . . . two eyes.' ('The eyes of an owl, big and expressive, just the eyes nothing more' [in D 1].)

15. W F+ A  ∧ ∨ 'Almost like a bat and yet I know it is not.
  2.0  ∧ Hm. ∨ No, I cannot make this out. From the first
glance I would say it is an animal.

16. W F— A       'It is not a butterfly; yet it is almost the shape of one. ∨ ∧ ∨ I really can't make this out. ∧ No, I can't do more. It could be an insect of some sort.' ('The whole thing, but it is not good. Just the eyes make me think of a bat, but it is not. Looks like it, outline. The whole thing; shape, almost. Bat or butterfly. The whole thing could be an ornament, a pin; just the form, the dark whole only.')

### Figure V (52″)

∨ ∧ 'Getting more difficult as we go along.

17. D F+ Ad      ∨ 'Would you say it was heads of two bulls.' (D 4 with the horns, i.e., D 10) 'yet ...
'I know it must be something else; neck to neck.' ('I have seen them and the matadors in movies. Almost neck to neck, the face is not good, just the horns. In Art Institute you can see heads standing out from the wall.')

18. W F+ A P     ∧ 'Could be, you know, bird with wings open or a bat;
    1.0          no, not a bat; something in bird's family this way. ∧ ∨ ∧ 'All I can find here. It could be so many things. ∨ ∧ ∨ 'No; when I look more closely it is not the head of two bulls; was just the first glance.' (W. 'The two wings open, the little head. What kind I don't know, eagle or something. No, it is not. Outline of bat but not the head of a bat.')

### Figure VI (43″)

∨ ∧ ∨ 'No, I can't see ...

19. D F+ Oj,Hh   ∧ 'This is a pole (D 2) of some kind. ∨ ∧ I can't place this thing at all. ∧ Almost like a leg of a furniture in here, carved. I don't know what it is. No, I just can't. The leg of a chair or table all I can see in this picture.

20. Dds Y Hh     ∨ 'Could be a lighting picture, the globe, but it has no
    6.5          flat base ∧ or this could be the base.' ('The light of a torchier. The light is thrown up in the ceiling from this globe.' [Dds 30; with surrounding light grey; light because of its light color.] 'Not that color but that shape; I have it at home.')

### Figure VII (57″)

∨ ∧ 'This is absolutely nothing.' ('I just can't see anything in this picture; just a puzzle.')

21. Dd F+ Cg     ∨ ∧ 'Part of a zipper (Dd 27) but I know it is not'. ('Looks just like the end of a zipper, I say just looks like, I have one in my bag. Just the way they are made.') 'Hm, I cannot, ∧ ∨ just can't. Just does not look like anything; yet, it must be. I can't make out.' ('These

could be dolls made out of felt, I saw some in a store; lying in bed, looking out in the dark I can see everything. In traveling through the West I saw the rocks in Grand Canyon. You can see these as rock' [D 3 and D 10].)

*Figure VIII* (38″)

22. D F+ A P

'First glance, two animals standing here. Sort of thick head; these do look like two little legs.' (D 1. 'Just looking out of the window I saw a chipmunk. But these are not animals.')

23. D F+ Cg

'Fur cape (D 5) if I was not looking too closely, fur cape over the shoulders; no head, just shoulders with fur scarf over it; you see the shape? I know it is something else too. This is hanging just from a ceiling. What is it?' ('I was looking in a magazine last night and saw fur capes for the winter; just exactly this shape. Just the form I saw. This runs all the way down, I just don't know. No, it is not in this picture. Assuming this [D5] is the shoulders of a person, it is very possibly the neck; and [Dd 27] a chain' [not seen until now].) ∨ ∧ 'When they are turned, they get quite a different meaning, ∨ something else entirely. I don't know. These (D 1) are not like animals this way. About all I can make out of that. I saw a chipmunk climbing right outside my window this morning, that's the reason why I thought of animals. Very misleading; must be something else; I don't know.'

*Figure IX*

24. Ds F+ Hh

∨ ∧ ∨ 'Could be a vase' (Ds 8).

25. D CF+ Bt
            5.0

'With flowers (D 6); maybe I am a little hasty.' ('I don't think it is a vase, because a vase is not round in the base. First I saw the plumes; I have seen different colored plumes in this color and shape, not the shape of a vase; color most important in flowers.')

26. Ds Y Fi
            5.0

'One could make . . . assuming . . . a picture of a light hanging.
'These are not animals, that I am sure of. The different colors must represent something or they would not be here. ∧ ∨ ∧
∨ 'Too close to the forest to see the trees, that is what I feel about this (holds card at arm's length). I can't make anything out of it except I have seen vases of

this shape and plumes coming out; yet, I know it is not.' ('Just the first glance; a white light in globe hanging [i.e., by D 5] down from this [D 6]. I don't say that [D 6] is the ceiling. The globe down here [the part of Ds 8 above D 5]. The rest does not say anything. I like red and dislike green. I cannot find an animal in this picture as I did in the others.')

27. W CF+ Fe
    5.5

'The whole is like a pretty pin, an ornament with different colors, chandelier, jewelry.' (W. 'Pretty pins like we have today; the form and the colors; ornaments generally come in colors. Pretty pin, a locket or lavaliere, usual now in different shapes and colors. It is first the colors that struck me.')

*Figure X* (51″)

∨ ∧ 'No . . . I can't.

28. W CF+ Art, Hh
    5.5

∨ 'All of these pictures just look like wallpaper pattern.' (W. ∨ ∧ 'Just don't know, make me quite . . . No. Not at all. This is quite . . . I am ashamed. I just can't. Some of them have too many colors. No, the colors. No, the colors I think are important. Could be a cover of a book too, colored.')

29. DsW FY+ Hh,
    Art

∨ 'Just a sort of ornament. Just can't make anything out of that at all.' ('An ornament bracket, some in this pattern I have seen. Lighting fixtures out of a wall. The part that is against the wall [Dds 29] the part that is against the wall could be just anything. It looks like a bracket-light. This [D 11] is the metal part, a white globe; it is burning.')

### Response Summary

R: 29

| | | | | | | | |
|---|---|---|---|---|---|---|---|
| W | 7 | M | 1 | H | 2 | F+ | 85 |
| DsW | 1 | M.CF | 1 | Hd | 2 (x,1) | A | 34% |
| D | 17 (s,3) | CF | 3 | A | 6 | S | 17% |
| Dd | 4 (s,1) | FC− | 1 | Ad | 4 | P | 4 |
| | 29 | Y | 2 | Art | 1 | Af r | 0.38 |
| | | FY | 1 | Bt | 2 | L | 2.22 |
| Z f 10 | | F+ | 17 | Cg | 2 | T/R not recorded | |
| Z sum 39.0 | | F− | 3 | Fe | 1 | T/first R 40.9 (nine cards) | |
| Ap. Normal trend | | | 29 | Fi | 2 | F1nR | 1.11 |
| Seq. Irregular | | | | Hh | 4 | F1n T/first R 24.7 (not recorded in fig. IX.) | |
| | | | | Oj | 1 | | |
| | | | | Pr | 1 | | |
| | | | | Tr | 1 | | |
| | | EB 2/4.5 | | | 29 | | |
| | | EA | 6.5 | | | | |

## Interpretation

The incessant self-disparagement and a related distressed mood tone so dominate this woman as to be an immediate lead to the psychologic tensions fermenting in her. She tells of this state of mind, and also her devalued perception of herself, in her very first reaction [1],* and she persists in this vein throughout the response record [2]. At times the attitude heavily saturates her associations [3]. The stress is stirring up heavy waves of emotion, and even when these subside the agitation is still manifest [4]. Mrs. L. discloses her state of mind arrestingly in her language and in nonscorable productions that unmistakably reveal her lost self-esteem. She does not know; she asks rather than tells the examiner what she sees; she is painfully certain of her inability; she lacks faith in her own percepts to a degree beyond that which healthy persons display; she rejects what she does see ("It is not") or negates the percept even while reporting it ("It is not a butterfly") [5]. Her verbal behaviors, in sum, exemplify those observed in depressed and very anxious persons: complaints of inability or of ignorance, a questioning or negative form of response, excessive self-qualifying, and rejection trends.

All this is the overt expression of an oppressed state of the mind. In addition, the patient lays open to view in the test's technical data certain psychologic processes that are the source traits for these emotions [6]. The pain in these emotions is likely to be of unrelieved intensity [7]. Only rarely can she soften it through understanding [8]. Whatever the intensity gradation, its affective quality is an apprehension flavored with dejection and resignation which is pervasive in the character structure.

Further accenting the evidence of unhappy mood content are certain shock reactions, the clinical implication of which is malignant. These are her behavior in the test figures that are especially effective at stirring up ideas bothersome to the conscience [9]. They arouse that anxiety which has its taproots in one's ideas of self-worth. What shocks the person is not any sensing of a current emotional interest in something or somebody outside himself, not some impulse to a relationship which might be sensed as a temptation or which is for any reason unpalatable to his standard of conduct. Rather, the shock is an entirely self-starting mechanism. The feeling generates spontaneously. The person is appalled at the thought: "What have I done?" This is in a pathologic sense of feeling he has violated values he wants to conserve. The very fact that the individual holds values is the energy source for the attack on himself, and for not only expecting but inciting punishment commensurate to the violation, i.e.,

Bracketed numbers refer to Notes on Interpretation, which for this chapter will be found on pages 90–95.

extreme punishment. The victim is scourged by an accuser he can never escape, for his superego accompanies him wherever he goes. Gretchen's thoughts and misery in the Cathedral scene in Goethe's *Faust* are a sample of the abysmal depth to which guilt can agitate: "The celestial countenances are turned away from you . . . The hands of the guiltless shudder to reach to you."

Our patient, in the test's language, shows herself unable to tolerate the ideas that stir when she is faced by guilt-arousing imagery [10], more especially when it is a "father image" [11]. The thoughts are too disturbing; the ego cannot bear them. The anxiety is here relatively free.

The ability to blunt the keen edge of sorrow by absorbing it inward in the world of the imagination is little available to Mrs. L. [12]. Whether she fears the figments of her inner world and defensively flees them, or whether the dysphoric mood state is dulling this aspect of mental life, or whether she was never endowed with such ability, the test finding is that she is not now capable of diluting her pain by wish-satisfying imaginative activity. Of the two fantasies which she does produce, one (R 5) reflects a pleasurable mood moment, that whimsy which the adult indulges himself in in a clown scene. Its structure follows in all respects the associations here elicited from most healthy adults of average or high intelligence [13]. To this extent at least, she has the usual vision of the person in sound spirits. At the same time, however, she betrays in it a submissive attitude [14], and so supports the evidence for a mood of resignation in the findings and adds the further information that the trait is deep-set in the personality [15]. The other communication out of the patient's inner world (R 14) bears no features of healthy stamp; on the contrary, it is autistic both in structure and in content [16]. A motif of dream variety, it has bypassed the ego. The theme in it is of paranoid flavor [17]. We see her here reacting to some unwelcome thought [18] by a regressive expedient. However, by the time she has converted into fantasy living the wish (R 5) or fear (R 14) in these themes, they have lost most of their feeling intensity [19]. The lowered mental tonus consequent on the emotional flight is here reflected. Support of this reasoning is available in another finding: she does not bring to life the little humans of figure III, the most common of all the fantasy responses elicited by the test. Yet, she must be capable of this feat since she succeeds in it in figure II, where it is somewhat less frequent [20]. One of two influences explaining the failure in III may be inferred: (a) neurotic shock in which anxiety, i.e., an inhibiting force, is implicit, or (b) the retarding effect of the depressive feelings.

Meanwhile, Mrs. L. is living through feeling pressures from another, and urgent, source. She is sensitive to, notably stirred up by, her environment, i.e., by the events and the *dramatis personae* in it [21]. Plunged into situations which are especially exciting [22], she follows one of two courses: she responds almost entirely to her mobilized feelings [23], or succumbs to anxiety [24]. The quality of these feeling processes may vary from that of unhappiness to spontaneous outward reaching [25]. In either event, she is so wholly responsive to her emotions as to ignore the world's realities and values not colored by her own affects. She is almost wholly swayed by them. The discomposing effect of the anxiety makes itself known as her self-mastery weakens and she has difficulty in regaining efficient control [26]. The efficiency with which she can carry on intellectually is lowered [27], her imagination is deadened (figure III; see note 20), and she is prey to erratic judgments [28]. Since she so reacts when responding emotionally to persons and events outside herself [29], it follows that such response, and the relationships involved, arouse anxiety in her. She is sensitive (the process) to the ideas (whatever may be their content).

Sensitivity is the clue to unsettled personal issues, i.e., to conflict, a finding which, in turn, tells us that the patient's basic reaction pattern is not depression but neurosis. Her predominantly hypersensitive, unstable but not infantile, impulsive level of feeling reaction [30] is the emotional nuance most characteristic of neurotics in the test. As she maintains herself at this mild level of excitement, her ego is adequate to keep a restraining grip on her feelings [31]. Then, too, the content in these emotion-toned responses tells of healthy interests: clowns or children; flowers in a vase; a pretty pin, jewelry; wallpaper; interior decoration for a home. Nearly all of these are concerns high on a woman's agenda. Also, she likes red [32], a warm color, a trait found in persons with a love for life, and she dislikes green [32]; Rorschach reports a valence for cold colors in depressed persons. In this dislike, is our patient showing the opposite side of that coin which is her love for red? Or is she betraying her attraction to the cold tone, and also the discomfort it breeds, and defensively rejecting it? One other test datum adds to the evidence of a depressive picture: in pleasure-arousing situations she is relatively less free in responding [33]. She does so at a level that begins to characterize persons under dysphoric mood influence. For all her more pleasurable wishes [34], even spontaneous moments, she remains weighted down under her worry.

Mrs. L. can be resistive. The trait plays a major role in her character [35]. Yet, the test findings yield no evidence of resistance *thinking* [36]. Here is a case of process—she can be in opposition—but process without content. What then happens to this opposition? The clue in the test is that it is directed against her environment [37]. How it became redirected and rerouted in a closed circuit, to attack its own source, the patient herself, is an unanswered question. The present Rorschach test reaction pattern does not clear up the riddle, which is also the general mystery of suicide.

Why had this patient not developed defenses? For ego resources were available to her, as we shall see presently, and defenses are an ego product. Why was her defense organization inadequate to stave off the tragic consummation? Concerning her defensive processes, they operate chiefly by way of constricting her mental life [38], but a question must also be raised of more pathogenic expedients (paranoid trends?) [39]. A more adjustive mechanism is apparent in the possible symbolisms [40], or perhaps sublimative interests [41]. Her major defense strategy is, however, also her most pathogenic: her self-effacement in the face of painful affect—which, as final events showed, was ominous.

The critical question now becomes: what can be known from this Rorschach test about the ego stamina of this woman, its strength relative to the tugs upon it, and her ability to overcome the destructive forces? The intellectual processes are our first lead here, and the evidence about them is mixed. She is realistic, well within normal range [42]; language and direction are for the most part orderly; she normally distributes her ideas among concrete and abstract concepts [43]; she can synthesize her percepts into meaningful relationships [44]. Yet, this latter ability is one she exercises unevenly and inefficiently [45]; her intellectual method is at times lax, or the procedure can blunder [46]. It is in her thinking, in fact, that she permits herself sporadic slips and deviations which tell that, beneath the realistic exterior, she is anything but calm. There is some circumstantial reasoning [47], confused talk [48], and, in fact, she can become discursive to the point of rambling [49]. A question of whether there is interference with her thinking is raised by the perplexities through which she muddles [50]. There is evidence of great retardation [51]. Tensions too great for the ego's usual mastery occasionally find motor outlet [52].

Such are the inadequate intellectual behaviors in our patient which attest to the ego's weak points. What about the strengths and the personality resources on which her ego can call? Intelligence is one, at least of high average, if not superior [53], caliber. She can, when not carried away by emotional tumult, attend to her environment [54]. And, as we have seen, she is realistic. But the inference is also in order that her grip on reality is a two-edged instrument. So sharply does she carve out reality as to highlight the excessive guarding forced on her by the apprehensive mood state, thus showing us the picture of an ego taking losses because it is too stiffly set [55]. In the winds of her emotions the ego is a brittle structure, has too little "give." A violent enough storm must topple it.

Whether the total adjustment—the balance of ego, defenses, stresses, and resources—is such that the catastrophic denouement could have been prevented is the critical question. One lead is her asocial way of seeing things, her disregard of obvious social values [56], amounting not only to withdrawal from her world but also, in the light of her opposition trait [35], to her rejecting that world. Her deviation from the norm is great enough, in a nonschizophrenic, so that perhaps I might have detected the danger of extremely unconventional solutions on her part. She withdraws from her world, although she does have the emotional need to be of it; she is capable of enjoying it, responds to it with some warmth [57], in fact, with intensity; yet, she can know the needs of others emotionally [58]. She becomes anxious at such interrelations [59] and cannot even enjoy herself by way of the imagination [60]; we have already speculated that repression may be at work here [38]. Meanwhile, a considerable degree of self-will is operating within her [35], directed by an alert ego [61]. The result is a collision between psychologic stresses: the persistent, insoluble conflict and the attendant acute pain. It is acute enough to have produced the gloom that is coloring and blurring what she sees when she looks at herself; hence, the all-dominating self-devaluation. Within this setting we find also scattered instances of thinking anomalies (note 47 ff.); the ego is capable of actual regressions [62], and it lacks inner flexibility [63]. What the personality dynamics were that provided the soil for the bitter fruit she is tasting is a question to which this test record does not afford unequivocal clues. Nor does the patient verbalize in her associations (except for one faint possibility in figure VII) those particular themes that usually make their appearance in the test records of patients with suicidal trends and of those who have eventually taken this exit.

Her content themes are, nevertheless, points of departure for some searching questions. In one recurrent percept the patient displays normal feminine narcissism (R 8, 10, 23, 27). Closely related is an apparent interest in the home and household affairs (R 19, 20, 24–25, 28–29). Why does a woman who will so soon end her own life have in the forefront of her mind thoughts about jewelry, pins, a fur cape, a vase with flowers? And what is the significance to her of the candle, torchier, and the related topics (R 6, 7, 20, 26, 29)? Symbolism is likely here, but the meaning of a symbol to any one patient must be elucidated by that patient. A surmise on the meaning here is hazarded below. Then, too, there are the less healthy ideas: the bulls and horns (R 17); what is the meaning of their being "neck to neck" and what is the meaning of the matadors? The four responses of "eyes" are a paranoid motif; in two instances she elaborates with comments ("a double meaning," R 13; and "must mean something else," R 23) that have a similar flavor. Then there is the strange complex of association and comment to figure VII, which usually evokes markedly feminine or specifically mother-like imagery: she sees "a zipper," a unique association to the vagina-form detail, and she fails to see the human profiles (very commonly seen even by torpid patients and by some feeble-minded) seeing, instead, dolls—one way of avoiding the live human—and, finally, the elaboration, "lying in bed, looking out in the dark, I can see everything." There are ominous overtones in this, the nearest approach to a specifically suicidal thought. In the light of her emotional burden and of her self-devaluation, perhaps this thinking should have been adequate reason for setting out the caution signals against suicide.

One teaching value in this Rorschach test record is the aid it may be in helping us to detect the scent of a suicide hazard in a patient who does not betray the danger by specifically suicidal thinking. It is a potential which we can apprehend from the test data only in the light of certain clinical, non-Rorschach data, however. The reasoning is: this woman is under unremitting pressure from a need to devalue herself; she suffers acute pain; manifests disturbance, which is the effect of anxiety, at the guilt-awakening stimuli in the test—most arrestingly, at the father imagery; and in scattered instances the ego shows itself fragile. Since her history tells us that she had been resentfully caring for an invalid father who had recently died, the question now becomes is the ego vulnerable enough so that, under the shock incident to his death, the emotions will dissipate her self-mastery and good judgment, with culmination in the tragedy of self-destruction?

In this chain of reasoning, two items are strictly clinical and non-Rorschach: her resentful care for her father, and his death. Clinically, we see a patient in a forced position in relation to her father, the wish to be freed from this situation, the unhappiness it caused her, the hostility with which she unconsciously reacted, and the guilt which the hostility bred—all this was an impasse, with no exit apparent. In the light of this clinical fact, the data of extreme pain, emotional lability, and of an ego susceptible to moments of fragility are ominous.

The clinical data alone, however, is not enough. It does not assay the intensity of the pain nor penetrate to the ego's weak spots. Insofar as the test has done this strictly by its own reference points, i.e., "blind," it has provided findings that can give critical significance to the clinical material. Certain inferences follow as to treatment measures to be undertaken, measures that must be strenuous, if not heroic. What is to be learned from this Rorschach test is how very important it is for the therapist to have both clinical and psychological test information before him and to evaluate each in the frame of reference provided by the other. In this way, he has a perspective on the patient that puts him in as advantageous a position as possible to be of aid in clinical decisions concerning the patient.

What, then, "might have been," according to the test's findings? Viewed in retrospect, they show us a woman possessing the two major resources necessary for treatment: ego and emotional flexibiity; and also a third which, in the proportion that the patient is endowed with it, contributes to the success of the treatment effort: intelligence. Our patient is not only endowed with a probably high level of intelligence but she is also still free enough in her everyday attention to her affairs to be able to vary her tactics adaptively as varying conditions make it necessary [43]. The ability to change is the *sine qua non* of treatment. Also, she is keen in her perceptions [42], can distinguish the accurate from the erroneous, can estimate values. Furthermore, she is capable of that larger intellectual grasp which sees the meanings of happenings in relation to the entire situation and so enables the making of sound judgments [44]. All this takes ego, and this woman had ego.

Emotionally, we have seen that she is hypersensitive [30] and able to be in tune with the feelings of others [34, 58]. The ability to know how the other person feels is a prerequisite to living with others, i.e., to being in social good health. It is psychologic equipment most essential to adaptive response to the conditions of life. "Know the world by heart, Or never know it," is the poet's (MacLeish) version.

Then, too, she channelizes her feelings and her interests into pathways that preoccupy a healthy woman [64]. Helped to rise out of her impasse, to emerge out of her gloom, she would attend to, devote her energies to, the activities normal for her social role.

Finally, she is in conflict. This too is a treatment asset. Paradox? It is resolved in the fact that conflict as struggle for values is ego. This patient would have collaborated with the therapist. The great problem would have been in helping her come out of the impasse into which events and her emotions had wedged her. The logic from these test findings is that this liberation could have been achieved. It might have been.

But, as I have noted, I am analyzing in retrospect. The fact is that I did not detect the suicide potential in this patient. The sole value of such retrospective thinking is, of course, in the guide lines it provides for the interpretation of future similar records.

## Notes on Interpretation

[1] "Frankly speaking," and the expression of inability.

[2] It subsides moderately in the color figures, VIII, IX, X, although

here, too, she qualifies her responses excessively and strongly doubts the correctness of her associations.

[3] Exemplified in figures IV and VII, and also figure III.

[4] As in the color figures, above noted. It is also moderate in figure II.

[5] Associations in question form: R 1, 6, 13; not to mention the questions she asks about her associations after giving them. For negated response, see R 2, 9–10, 11, 15, and others.

[6] The shading-determined responses and evidence of shading shock in figures IV–VII, and see notes 9 and those that immediately follow.

[7] Two of the three shading-determined responses are without modulation by a form percept.

[8] A form element is present in the shading-determined associations, and it is more influential (FY) than the shading (R 29).

[9] Figures IV–VII principally; sometimes also figure I.

[10] The patient here deviates from her customary attention (Ap) habit and selects three of her four Dd. Here, too, she more severely constricts her already constricted mental productivity, with an average R of 2.00 in figures IV–VII as against 3.50 in the six others.

[11] In figure IV, there is a notable loss of intellectual efficiency. Whereas up to now her attention was adaptively adequate, she now disregards the obvious (D) and focuses on a minute matter (Dd). She seriously deviates from the usual norm in respect to orderliness (Seq), a deviation especially notable in that it gives the Dd priority over the W. This is one of the figures in which she perceives inaccurately (R 16), although it is an impersonal error, i.e., not a distortion of reality but a disregard of it, due to uncritical perceiving because of a momentary lapse in attention. The figure evokes one of her two fantasies; moreover, this is a regressed one, uncovering a paranoid idea (R 14, and see note 16). The ego's grip has weakened.

[12] Only two M responses in the entire test record.

[13] The form perception is accurate, hence M+; content is an entire human, H; and the theme is one of high frequency, P; an organization into meaningful relationships, Z, and, in fact, one which embraces the entire figure, W. Also consistent with findings in adults of healthy spirit, she enriches the fantasy experience with emotional vibrancy, CF.

[14] The bent pose of the human figures, and the centripetal direction of the movement.

[15] "Deep-set" in accordance with the theory that M associations, representing unconscious ideas, have their foundations in the deeper layers of the personality.

[16] Autistic in structure, i.e., an M in a Dd and in an Ad. A very small portion of the test figure is selected, and vitalized, with a human emotion,

which is ascribed to an animal. Children freely fantasy with a structure of this kind; as do also adults in some state of regression, neurotic or otherwise. Autistic in content: "eyes" are suspect as a paranoid motif; the term "big and expressive," whatever the personal source trait in the patient, expresses a human attitude of especial significance to this woman (it being unique), and to the degree to which she can so displace her attitude, this M is "autistic," i.e., serves only her own ends.

[17] The owl is a bird about which a variety of myths and beliefs have accumulated. Projections as such myths are, they carry affect-laden ideas.

[18] Whatever it is that Mrs. L. is projecting in her paranoid thinking is displaced onto an animal in this M.

[19] The energy, as measured by the Levy Scale, which she invests in these M is low, not more than 2 to 3 in R 5, and 1 to 2 in R 14.

[20] The "clowns" in some kind of action is also a very common response. Still, it is the little humans in figure III that are most easily seen in some activity, the test's paradigm M.

[21] The reaction pattern in the color figures (and see the notes immediately following), together with the fact that five of her associations are color-dictated, i.e., spontaneous feelings have been released. Five color-dictated associations is an above average quantity, especially for a response total of only 29.

[22] In the Rorschach test, the color figures, with special reference to VIII, IX, and X. The two other figures with color, II and III, do not have the stimulus value that the all-color figures do.

[23] The lambda in figures IX and X. It is zero in X, and almost that in IX. The patient is here so responsive to her feelings that she attends inadequately to the objective environmental stimuli.

[24] The shading dictated (Y) associations, R 26 and 29. Their minor key significance has already been noted (in notes 6 ff.). They take on an additional significance when produced in the color figures (VIII, IX, or X), pain within the setting of a pleasure-toned excitement, a mingling of feelings the identifying flavor of which is irritation, unhappiness.

[25] The five responses that are color-determined: R 5, 6, 25, 27, 28.

[26] The intellectual disturbances, or the reduction of function, in figures II, III, and VIII; and see notes 27, 28, 29. It may not be technically accurate to call our patient's response pattern in these figures the result of neurotic shock since her functioning is either perturbed or constricted throughout. Yet, for purposes of clinical judgment what we call it is not so essential as the finding that these lively stimuli are further stirring up waters already troubled by the patient's unhappiness.

[27] She fails altogether to synthesize her perceptions meaningfully

in figure VIII, and does so in only very low amount for her high productivity in III. Also, P fails in three of the four color figures (III, IX, X).

[28] The F− in figures II and III.

[29] Such, by Rorschach test theory, being the significance of the color-determined associations; and see note 21.

[30] She responds more frequently with CF than with FC, and not at all with unmixed C. The one FC− also tells of a process such as that in CF.

[31] The F element with which she moderates all her color associations.

[32] In the inquiry in figure IX.

[33] Her affective ratio is at 0.38, below the low point for findings in the normal range.

[34] As indicated in the content of the color-dictated associations; with the exception of R 6, they show her as being animated by topics of interest to most healthy women, i.e., R 5, and more especially R 25, 27, 28. These are the ideas about which her strong feelings are playing. It is possible that R 6 also belongs here, but its possible symbolism gives it a more idiosyncratic tinge. The truly spontaneous moments are rare; R 27 is the one clear-cut example: "a pretty pin."

[35] The white space count is high, whether in terms of percentage (17%) or simple number of such responses (5).

[36] No aggression themes in the content.

[37] Indicated in a high white space finding when EB is one in which the sum of color values is clearly greater than the number of M.

[38] The total productivity is low for the breadth which Mrs. L. shows in her content, as well as the achievement potential indicated in her synthesizing ability. The low number of human form responses (H) speaks of a constriction consequent on avoidance; and the self-doubt and rejection trends, as denial, are a like mechanism.

[39] The paranoid motif in R 14 has been noted; it is supported in the doubly accentuated "eyes." The expression "double meaning" (R 13) also has a paranoid (suspiciousness) flavor.

[40] Responses to be explored for symbolisms are: R 6, 14 (the owl), 17, 21.

[41] The feminine, personal and household, interests, i.e., those reflected in R 7, 8, 10 (the pin), 23, 24–25, 27, 28. Whether the themes in R 20, 26, and 29 are symbolic expressions of personal needs or whether they also uncover the channels for sublimation of her wishes, only direct exploration in the patient could have determined.

[42] The F+ per cent of 85.

[43] The distribution of W, D, Dd (Ap) is about what would be expected for the response total.

[44] Her Z score of 39.0, while not at the level of some intellectual heavy-weights to whom I have given the test, is still within the range of the superior group.

[45] Her Z score is high in four figures (II, VI, IX, X), low in the six others, in two of which (VII and VIII) she builds no meaningful relationships.

[46] The sequence is disorderly in IV, irregular in V. She is alogical, sufficiently so to permit scoring, in one response (R 29) and shows such a trend in another (a question of DsW in figure II, R 7).

[47] She sees "a flyer" because of the circumstance that she had previously seen "wings of a plane" (R 4). Tangential, too, is her reasoning (R 5) that the "two people" are "clowns" because their hands are together and "children play with their hands."

[48] See, for example, the meandering elaborations following R 7, R 10, R 16, R 21, R 29.

[49] One example will be found in R 23, another in R 26. The elaborations referred to in note 47 also exemplify this rambling behavior.

[50] Very frequently, throughout the test: in figure I, for one sample; in figure III, (R 13) for another; in figure VIII following R 23, in which the memory of a chipmunk seen earlier that day is an intruding factor.

[51] The time for first response is very slow, except in figure II. It is unknown for figure IX, having not been recorded through an error.

[52] In the card turnings, which are found at scattered points only. These are never excessive, but, when appearing, they are frequent enough to arrest the attention, indicating as they do the unsettlement underneath.

[53] Seen in her high synthesizing ability, including some of the difficult W's (see also note 43), as well as in the breadth of her interests. The total productivity is sharply lower than would be expected from the intelligence indicated in the Z, the W, and in the breadth; and we see here more evidence of interference by the depressive mood.

[54] Her lambda index is at 2.22 (normal range 1.50–2.50). When she is under strong pressure from feelings, this index approaches, or is, zero (figures IX, X), i.e., this finding is lowered under the special conditions induced by exciting (color) stimuli. It would otherwise be notably higher than the present over-all rating of 2.22. In fact, if we were to calculate the lambda index for figures I–VIII alone, it would come to 4.75, an excessive attention to the environment at the price of inadequate response to feelings, i.e., inadequate flexibility; thus disclosing more of the constrictive defenses (see also note 33).

[55] The constrictive defense organization is the basis of the reasoning here, since defense is the work of the ego. Another line of evidence is the F+ per cent at 85. This is higher than is usually found in persons

suffering this woman's stresses and it reflects her effort to keep an iron grip on herself. It should be noted too that her three perceptual departures (R 8, 10, 16) are well within normal and neurotic range in both quantity and quality. The stiff ego is also reflected in the animal percentage, which is higher than expectancy for a person of above average endowment and discloses an impoverishing process.

[56] The P count is low. The number of human associations is very small.

[57] The ability to use the colors as determinants and to turn her feelings to interests appropriately feminine (see also notes 21 ff.). Also, the evidence for some emotional spontaneity (see note 34).

[58] The dominance of CF, valued in the light of her warmth (note 57). CF can be selfish pursuit of pleasure, in an infantile form. It can be, in an otherwise mature individual, an excitement that derives intense gratification from identification with another, such as seen in adolescents and in some neurotics. The test here exemplifies the axiom that a finding has the meaning which the entire personality gives to it.

[59] The shock at the color figures (see also notes 26 ff.).

[60] The pleasure-toned fantasy (see note 12).

[61] See notes 42 ff.

[62] The structure and content of the fantasy in R 14 (see note 16).

[63] The small total of fantasy associations, i.e., a lack of the shock absorption made possible by recourse to an imaginative solution. Also, the constricted defenses (note 38); see also concerning ego rigidity (notes 54, 55).

[64] See in the *Interpretation* concerning this woman's normal feminine narcissism.

### Clinical Note

When this 48 year old woman was admitted to the psychiatric unit of a general hospital, the referral reason was stated as: acute anxiety with depression symptoms. Her father had been an invalid for many years, and the other children had shuffled the burden of caring for him onto the patient. She was married, and her husband, a kindly man, was helpful and shared the burden with her. The patient resented, although without conscious insight, the injustice to her but she continued to care for her father until the breakdown which precipitated her admission to the hospital.

Her father died while she was in the hospital. The patient had improved to the extent that when she asked permission to go to the funeral, the psychiatrist granted it. From the funeral she returned to her own home. When late that afternoon the head nurse telephoned to ask why the patient had not returned to the hospital, the husband informed her that the patient was sleeping and had been for some hours. The head nurse telephoned the psychiatrist in his office, and, without asking any further questions, he sent an ambulance directly to the home. The patient was brought to the hospital comatose, having swallowed the entire supply of seconol in her possession. She never regained consciousness, and died three days later.

The psychodynamics as clinically formulated were: (a) Mrs. L. suffered guilt from not wanting to care for her father, but at the same time she (b) had a great need to be with him and cared for him in order to be with him; (c) by her illness she had abandoned him; hence (d) the unbearable guilt, and the suicide.

# CHAPTER 7

# Mrs. E.: Incipient brain pathology in a woman of 47

## Response Record

### Figure I (2″)

1. W F+ A P
   1.0
'Looks like a bat. That all right?' (W. 'Shape of it looks like a bat, but what reminds me of it, I couldn't say. My brother-in-law was a poor sport. We used to go on camping trips a lot and used to kid him about being a poor sport. But once when we were on a trip, we had a picnic and there were lots of mosquitoes; my sandwich was all covered with them and I couldn't eat it.')

2. D F+ Ls
'These things look like mountains. Is that all right?' (D 5. 'They just look like mountains ... they just did. Three years ago, we drove a car for an agency up to Alaska. Only place we stayed was like a flophouse. Door to our room had a great crack under it and you could hear drunks coming back and forth all night long.')

3. D FY− Cl
'Oh, you might say these are clouds down here. Is that enough? That's all I can see.' ('Just like it ... the way it's shaped ... coloring too, I guess. O.K.?')

### Figure II (50″)

'I don't know what that looks like ... the red ink on it. Can't tell you.

4. DW F− A
'Looks like a bug and I couldn't tell you what kind.' ('Whole thing. This looks like a head ... made me think of it. All right?')

5. D F− Cl
'That's all I can see except the sides look like clouds.' (D 1. 'Just looks like it ... shape of 'em.')

### Figure III (1″)

6. D F− A
∨ 'That looks like a frog.' ('Whole thing except those red blotches. [D 2]. The face [D 8] made me think of a frog. Looks like a frog.')

7. D F+ Bt
'Looks like some tree limbs.' (D 5. 'This part here. O.K.? Just the shape of 'em, O.K.?')

8. D F+ A
'Looks like a butterfly in middle.' (D 3. 'Way it's shaped.')

97

*Figure IV* (10″)

9. W F+ A P
    2.0

'Looks like animal skin, a bearskin, O.K.?' ('Whole thing. I don't know ... Just looks like one ... sorry ... shape reminded me.')

10. W F+ A

∨ 'Some kind of bug, but I couldn't tell you what kind.' ('Whole thing reminded me. Here's face ... Just looks like one ... face reminded me ... face and little eyes, cute?' Excludes D 4; Dd in D 1 are eyes.)

11. W YF+ Cl
     2.0

< 'Looks like a bunch of clouds again. My little grandson ...' ('Whole thing. Dark colors and shape.')

*Figure V* (5″)

12. W F+ A P
     2.5

'Looks like another bat. O.K.?' (W. 'Shape ... little tails and headpiece.')

13. D FY− Cl

'And a bunch of clouds. That's all.' (D 4. 'Coloring and shape. More the shape. Looks like tornadoes. We were on a motor trip ... almost got caught in tornadoes; they were all around us.')

*Figure VI* (4″)

14. W F+ A P
     2.5

'That looks like a skin again ... Those dogs they keep barkin' all the time ... keep me awake.
'I don't see anything more and I don't know what to call what I do see.' ('Whole thing ... way it's laid out and modeling.')

*Figure VII* (2″)

15. W YF+ Cl
     2.5

'That looks like a bunch of clouds. That's all ... Doesn't look like any animal. You're writin' down what I say?' (Exr: Yes.) 'That's cute.' ('All of it ... They just look like it, and they look almost like rain clouds, they're so black, and shape. What is your name? Do you work here? My sister is a teacher ...')

*Figure VIII* (4″)

'I don't know what that looks like.

16. D F− A

'It looks like a bug and ...

17. D F− Cl

'It looks like a bunch of clouds.
'Should I say it looks like a butterfly?' ('Whole thing ... More the inside than those two little things on outside.' W, excluding D 1. 'I have to go to the toilet.' (Exr. took her back to the ward and waited). 'I just had to piddle,' she confided on returning to testing room, 'but thought I might burst if I waited until we got through.' Butterfly was alternative for bug.)

*Figure IX* (6″)

18. W F − A          'Looks like some kind of bug. But I couldn't tell you
      5.5          what kind . . .
19. D F − Cl          'And a bunch of clouds' (D's, indiscriminately).
                'I must be stupid . . . I see colors, pink, green. I can't
                see anything more. Sorry. Are you a doctor? Oh, you're
                going to be a psychologist! That must be nice. My
                sister and I . . .' ('Whole thing was a bug. I don't know;
                just looks like one . . . They just do . . . the whole thing
                . . . the print.')

*Figure X* (2″)

20. D F + A P          'I see a coupla things that looks like crabs.' (D 1.
                'Here, these blue ones . . . the legs and feelers made me
                think of it.')
21. D F − Cl          'Then it looks like a bunch of clouds.' ('The whole thing
                here . . . don't know what made me think of it . . . Just
                did . . . Just looks like clouds.'
               Total Time: 10′42″

### Response Summary

R: 21

| W | 8 | YF+ | 2 | A | 11 | F+ | 53% |
|---|---|-----|---|---|----|----|-----|
| DW | 1 | FY− | 2 | Bt | 1 | A | 52% |
| D | 12 | F+ | 9 | Cl | 8 | P | 5 |
|  | 21 | F− | 8 | Ls | 1 | S | 0. |
|  |  |  | 21 |  | 21 | Af r | 0.40 |

Z f 7                                                   L    4.25
Z sum 18.0          EB 0/0                       T/R   30.6
Ap. W! D          EA 0.                          T/first R   8.6
Seq. Methodical                              Fln R   0.55
                                            Fln T/first R   13.6

## Interpretation

The data in the intellectual sphere in this record delineate a woman whose mental life is losing its sap, is becoming dehydrated. The emotional picture is of very meager affectivity and accents the drying up of this woman's spirits. The Rorschach test pattern quickly opens up the question of whether this is a person showing the effects of brain pathology.

A first pointer to this condition appears in the content of the associations, not thematically but structurally. It is lean—an example of Rorschach's stereotypy in the extreme. Two categories account for nearly all of Mrs. E.'s interests [1].* A severely narrowed interest scope is being

* Bracketed numbers refer to Notes on Interpretation, which for this chapter will be found on pages 108–112.

reflected, as of a person looking at her world through a narrow aperture and able to see only what its limits permit. She is unable, except very rarely, to embellish or in the slightest elaborate on her associations [2]. Her first percept is her sole one and awakens no related ideas or overtones. There is a bone-dry quality to the thought processes, the skeleton of imagery without the enlivening color of flesh. To speculate in terms of brain activity: the connecting pathways between cortex and thalamus and the radiations within the cortex, with their enriching effects, are not being set in motion.

Attention habits are defective. The patient inefficiently distributes her attention over the data before her, is bound by holistic views of her percepts, or at best by their larger components, and she remains insensitive to the minor, less obvious elements [3]. As a way of manipulating her problems, this pattern is inadequate; it lacks flexibility. She does not shift her focus from whole to parts, nor effectively in the reverse direction. She thus misses possible meanings and interrelations in her data, meanings whose significance could be essential to her life situation.

The total blindness to the finer point is as much a defect as the excessive binding by the global situation. Too much is being missed. An experiment with the "graphic Rorschach" method developed by Grassi yielded such findings for the brain-damaged generally. "The entire organic group displays certain common characteristics. Productions of organic patients are dictated largely or entirely by the immediate situation, so that they are unable to discriminate between the essential and nonessential. Their naming of a blot represents conceptual thinking only superficially...."[24]

Mrs. E.'s intellectual pattern is pedestrian and unvarying, and hence not adaptive to life's changing circumstances [4]. She shows another attention fault in permitting the repeated incursion of topics far afield from the one at hand. The connections are there but they are circumstantial and tenuous. From a "bat" the leap is an easy one for her to the camping trip, the picnic, the mosquitoes all over her sandwich, the brother-in-law who was a poor sport (R 1). Similarly the mountains (R 2) open up the memory of an Alaskan trip, with vivid details concerning some drunks [5]. A slackening of the attention's grip is here disclosed, that failure of criticism which in the healthy speedily shuts out what is not appropriate to a thought complex. A weakening of the ego can thus be inferred, something more positive than stereotypy or restricted mental range. It is more than a reduction in function, which is a loss, to be sure, but not a break. Here it is positive dysfunction, a more serious symptom.

Perseverations are numerous, and these further highlight the ego's asthenia. When perseverating, a person is not responding to a current stimulus but to a former one which continues to occupy him and has more force than the one now being presented. Four of this patient's "clouds," R 5, 17, 19, 21, I take to be preseverations. None of these is an accurate percept for the detail to which the patient is attending [6]; nor is there evidence in these associations that they are the expressions of some affect [7]. They are perseverations of "clouds" seen earlier [8]. Thus, our patient's thinking is not manipulating her environment; rather, the environment as a perseverating memory picture is manipulating her. It is a weakness of function, as inadequate will, which may well be reflecting the declining vigor in the tissue. Bleuler reports perseveration as frequent in patients with brain damage [9]. He attaches to this symptom the term *aboulia*, i.e., loss of will power. The term can well refer to the perseverative process in whatever clinical condition it is found.

The subject's perception is too frequently uncritical, and on occasions seriously so. Mrs. E.'s over-all percentage of accuracy is notably below that which I have found a dependable minimal margin for persons in the normal range [10]. The extent to which she deviates from the norm can be gauged also from the number of her F− percepts, the converse of perceptual accuracy. Eight is a large number of errors, particularly when the total productivity is as low as it is here. A peculiarity common to all her inaccuracies [11] is their impersonal quality: there is no indication in them of a personal need to see what she does see. She simply makes a mistake, uncritically gives a response that has vague, if any, resemblance to the stimulus. She is violating Rorschach's third rule for F+ perceptions [12]. She is here disregarding reality, and in at least one instance, R 18, the inaccuracy very seriously ignores [13] the given outlines. Here, again, one may speculate about her brain tissue losing its resilience. In any event, the ego is losing its toughness. It is satisfied with an easy judgment, without concern as to whether it will receive the approbation of others.

This loosening control makes itself known also in Mrs. E.'s language production, her wandering from the topic at hand. It takes the form of a loquacity long identified with aging or debility: the conjuring up of old experiences (R 1, 2, 13); the inappropriate relating of herself to the examiner (figures VII, IX); the irrelevant bringing in of her grandson and her sister (figures IV, IX). In R 1 and 2 she becomes completely channelized in the tangential thoughts and the connection with the appropriate one is entirely broken. Once again, we see an inability to hold fast to an idea, an infirmity such as is due to diminishing of the mental firmness. Fixed phrases also dot the record, the seemingly automatic "looks like," and this is another effect of mental inelasticity. An additional adventitious chord, characteristic of mental declining, is complaining. This occurs in figure VI. Rorschach notes querulous grumbling as among the traits of brain-damaged patients [14].

The patient is herself sensing her ego's ebbing strength, whether or not she is clearly aware of the fact. She demonstrates this in her recurring need for the examiner's approval. "That all right?" "O.K.?" "Is that enough?" recur throughout the record. She is perplexed sporadically: "I don't know" (figures II, IV, VI, VII), and expresses inability (Piotrowski's "impotence;" figure II). She explicitly devalues herself, "I must be stupid" (figure IX). A contraction of the ego's boundaries is inferred from this behavioral data, especially in the turning to the examiner for support, i.e., dependency behavior. Her own ego does not provide a solid enough foundation of confidence in her.

In the formal structure, still other evidence converges to depict an in-adequate ego. The total productivity is seriously below the mean of the healthy average person; it is nearer that of the feebleminded [15]. Is she perhaps feebleminded, and are we seeing not a person who has *lost* ability but one who has never had it? A negative answer to this question is given by her apparent synthesizing ability, an ability in which she does seem efficient and scores within the average range [16]. However, her score for this variable is deceptive, since it is incidental to her holistic perception [17]. Inspection of her W responses show them to be, without exception, neither the additive (Rorschach's *kombinatorisch*) nor the qualitative rich (*simultan*) groups. Far from disclosing intellectual drive, they betray a sluggish inability to break the stimulus down into its components and to resynthesize these components. In no instance does she meaningfully relate any part within the test figures to another. This Rorschach test behavior characterizes many feebleminded. Another equivocal finding is the limitation of the visual field [18]. This time, however, the data are not such as obtain in brain pathology: our patient only restricts her vision in the Inquiry; the feebleminded do so in their free associations [19]. In focusing on isolated portions, usually minute ones, in the Inquiry the patient is justifying her free associations. This need to explain and justify is a trait again characteristic of the brain-damaged, conscious as they are of their failings. Then there is this woman's trend to alogical thinking, blundering analogies in which from the meaning of parts she jumps to conclusions about larger areas or to wholes [20], again a faulty thinking form, which will be found in various clinical pictures.

We are now back at the question as to why the test findings point to a decline from a healthier status rather than a mind always feeble. The answer is found only partially in the test, namely, in the findings reported above and those still to be discussed that are characteristically those of brain damage. Once we have such an indication, then new data, the significance of which we are uncertain of, can be fitted in with this diagnosis, i.e., brain pathology. For example, another positive observation in the present test record, although qualitative to be sure, is Mrs. E.'s vocabulary. A modest intelligence, at the low end of the average range, is to be surmised. Were she as feebleminded as would be required by some of the doubtful signs, language would be inferior to what it is and much less integrated. Finally, i.e., after we have concluded the interpretation, extra-test evidence will make it clear that this woman has not been mentally deficient through most of her life. However, that is something we cannot introduce here while we are using the test experimentally and interpreting strictly from its data.

Of the mental sprightliness that is expressed in imaginative living, Mrs. E. shows none. She does not make even a remote approach to a fantasy response [21]. In figures II, III, VII, and IX, which most freely evoke this kind of associating, her percepts are static and are of either "animal" content or "clouds"—one of her two stereotyped categories. None of the animal forms connotes the movement forms of the human. An unimaginative, and in this respect dull, mentality is therefore being projected here.

Emotionally the picture is more mixed. Not once do lively feeling tones contribute toward determining an association [22]. In the four instances when she notices them, in figures II, III, IX, X, she is unaffected by them [23]. Thus, she actually manages no externalized response to these stimuli, and with the monotone quality of her record gives the impression of living sluggishly in an unchanging emotional state. Of similar quality is the inappropriate affect in her comment, "cute" (figure VII), referring to the examiner's writing down the associations. Yet, other evidence in the whole reaction pattern does tell of sensitivity, of feelings still being activated. One is the color shock in figure II, with probably shock also in figures VIII and IX [24]. Here is a segment of neurotic behavior; how this reconciles with the picture of brain pathology is a question we can postpone for the moment. One other behavioral sign of inner unrest may be noted meanwhile: the garrulity, (especially in figures I, VII, and IX) and the fretting (in figure VI) over a recalled external (non-test) stimulus, i.e., one not active at the time. Mrs. E. discloses here a poorly controlled feeling distribution. In all, then, the test's indications are that this woman's responsivity to external, pleasurably exciting events is reduced. The surmise is warranted that she has lost much emotional richness, but there is also evidence that she is still touchy and can still be roused inwardly.

In that other modality of emotional experience, that having a painful quality, the patient is in fact frequently sensitive, and at times intensely so [25]. Her ego twice attempts to hold the feeling under restraint [26] but the affect is strong and its effect is seen in impairment of perceptual accuracy [27]. Characteristic of these reactions is a passivity need which is flavored with anxiety. Some resignation formulae ("That's all I can see," R 3, 5), and the giving up trends ("I don't know ... don't see ... couldn't," at various points) smack of the depressive. How painful the emotion can be is seen in her themes: "tornadoes" (R 13)—the recalled incident still communicates the tinge of panic, "almost got caught in tornadoes, they were all around us"—and in R 15 with its heavy accent on the dysphoric quality. Both these reactions were evoked by gray-toned stimuli, which stir up feelings out of inner stores of anxiety (from super-ego sources). But this patient can be anxious also under other conditions, as seen in the already reported color shock [28], i.e., a disturbance set going by lively mood reactions. The anxiety has its roots in a current urge which is also sensed as a temptation. From whichever of the two directions, inner or external, it is set off, it is free anxiety [29]. In sum, in this sphere of the painful affects the patient does react and strongly.

What about the defenses in a patient whose ego is weakening, since it is the ego that is the architect of the defense structure? A first critical fact in this connection is that this woman has need of defense effort. Her anxieties make it necessary, the more so since they can be intense and since she cannot bind them. She does defend, but maladaptively: her passivity and resignation (above), her apologetics ("sorry," R 9, 19, and the expressions of inability), her self-devaluation (R 18). In all these tactics the mechanism is withdrawal. A more emphatic but still constrictive tactic is the affect rejection (R 6: "except those red blotches"). Even more pathologic because of the paranoid trace in it is her questioning the examiner (figure VII) about "writing down what I say," a kind of behavior which I have observed in patients suffering from suspicious apprehension.

And now a new differential diagnostic problem arises. Defenses are primarily a neurotic manifestation. How then do these defense activities fit into the Rorschach test picture of a woman with brain damage? Before turning to this question, I want only to note that the cross-currents of trends emerging in the test replicated the confused clinical course that made this woman the perplexing diagnostic problem she was. Certain symptoms of a more strictly psychologic nature obscured those resulting from the brain pathology and made the picture a deceptive one.

The review of Mrs. E.'s mental life shows that her thinking, although reduced in level, is coherent; her language productions are for the most part orderly. She uses one word not likely to be employed except by the above average: "modeling" (in figure VI)—one word only but it helps place her functioning level and tells of language she can still use. Her motor functions, as judged by the tempo of her associational processes, show her operating within normal range in one respect; in another, at the beginning of retardation. She is alert enough to react speedily to environmental events when she first faces them, but after such a first recognition, she is slow in the usual elaboration of nuances and in perceiving any differentiated content [30]. On the question of whether she has the drive to initiate activities and whether she is motivated by the spark of ambition the evidence is again ambiguous. But we must postulate some residual capacity for grasping larger possibilities and some itch still to "do things" [31]. She is in a borderline phase in respect to awareness of surface amenities; she can "do the right thing" in most of her day-to-day relations but there are signs too that she may slip up occasionally [32]. In all, she is still integrated insofar as her overt behavior discloses. Here is the solution to the puzzle which she was to the clinical staff. Viewed with the naked clinical eye, she was not wanting in integration.

Certain findings in the test meanwhile necessitated questioning her ability to function effectively. Even if she can still recognize the gross conventions, how frequently will her sharper discriminating powers fail and her judgment be faulty [33]? Her debatable achievement potential screens a heavy-footed intelligence; her productive energy is meager [34]. The narrowed and impoverished thought content reflecting a restriction of interest also indicates a dull, unoriginal, nondifferentiated type of functioning. She is handicapped in respect to the ability to vary her method so as to adjust to life's ever-changing details [35], a disability which is reinforced by another, i.e., her excessive adherence to raw objectiveness unenriched by emotional tones from within [36]. Enough intellectual fragility is uncovered by the test to indicate that the patient's faulty judgments and discriminations are premonitory of worse things to come: unrealistic planning and goal-seeking, unsound expectations from others, and progressive decline in the effective handling of her life's problems, waning ability to care for herself. This is not her condition now. It is the test's forecast. Rorschach's generalization is recalled: his test does not describe the person as he does live but as he *can* live. The premonitory findings here recall Lear's follies in the first act of the Shakespearean tragedy: his gullibility to the scheming flattery of Goneril and Regan, his obtuseness concerning Cordelia's austere honesty. Lear in the fourth and fifth acts is in senile psychosis. Act I foreshadows this disintegration in the erratic judgments: how Lear *could* be, and eventually was.

How our patient can be emotionally is also portended in the test findings: her potential for pleasure dried up, no longer responding to the cheerful events of human life, experiencing few needs, and seeking no gratifications. She will fail to relate to others socially, since this requires emotion. The condition is not one in which the person is withdrawing emotionally; rather, the patient just does not experience the feelings essential toward making social contact.

Yet, the facts are that this woman is still sensitive to social values, as are so many patients in the early stages of decline. We have seen that she still suffers color shock (see note 24), a trait characterizing the neurotic. That is, she experiences anxiety in moments when pleasurable or exciting feelings are stirring. Anxiety at such times is a defense—pathogenic, to be sure, because neurotic—but as defense it is symptom of an ego that is stirring, and for the ego to be stirring, it must be responding to something the person senses. Assuming the soundness of Rorschach test theory [37], this woman is sensing an impulse, i.e., having an emotional experience. This would be manifest overtly and so would steer the clinical observer, and correctly, to think of a functional disorder. The test is, in this way, sensitive to trends not openly manifest: this woman's actual inability to live an emotion that has body to it. Only a spark stirs, faintly. Again we are seeing how the person *can* be, psychologically.

How severely she is deprived inwardly is conclusively highlighted by yet another finding: the inability even to fantasy a gratification (see note 21, and p. 103). Her inner total existence is indicated as complete aridity. This is the significance of her *Erlebnistypus*, or Experience Balance. It adds up to an Experience Actual of zero [38]. This is what she is heading for, how she will live, "sans taste, sans everything."

But Mrs. E. is not yet "sans everything" psychologically. Her associational content shows her with some memories that arouse an affect, that of irritation. Some of these are at the same time clues to the needs that stir her up personally. She is unkind and, we may infer, hostile in her derogatory reference to the brother-in-law, can recall only an unsavory detail (the drunks and the flop-house flavor) of the trip to Alaska, and only the frustrations (mosquitoes and their spoiling the sandwich) on a camping trip (all in figure I). The querulous complaining over a common incidental noise (the barking dogs, figure VI), usually disregarded by the healthy, is a trait that emerges even more extensively than in the present patient in more advanced states of brain pathology. Again, then, we have evidence both for such pathology and its mild degree. A vividly fresh memory from one motor trip is that of the tornadoes (figure V); and in one of her numerous "cloud" associations she is impressed by the threatening ("black" and "rain") qualities. How personal are the many "cloud" percepts? To what extent do they refer to a psychologically significant theme? The perseveration responsible for some of them has been noted (see pp. 100–101; also notes 6, 8, and 9). But why did the *cloud* theme rather than another perseverate? The inferential question is: does this theme arouse affect in the patient? Even as perseveration, it is a clinical lead to a focus of disturbance [39].

The response of "mountains" is of interest in this connection. The percept is a frequent one in test records with "cloud" associations, and it is not unusual for the two to enter into the same response. It has the connotation of loneliness. Caution is dictated, however, by the fact of only a single "mountains" percept. Two other themes that also appear only once each have a painful emotional loading, with the scent of even more serious pathology: the "frog" (figure III) and the "eyes" (figure IV). The former brings to mind the repulsive; the latter may be the revealing footprint of paranoid thinking. Only a single association for each of these two possible trends makes, to be sure, for a very faint scent; yet, it is not a far psychologic step from sensing the repulsive to paranoid thinking (it is the other fellow "who smells to high heaven"), i.e., the two associations reinforce each other. Also, they have support in the above-noted trait of hostile irritation.

A pleasant tinge too must attach to memories such as those of picnics and automobile trips. Healthy spirits are being awakened around lively topics relating to the enjoyment of life. This patient will still respond to ideas about, and perhaps invitations to, recreation. Warmth, in fact, emanates from her in relation to "my little grandson" (figure IV) in which the diminutive bespeaks affection, and there is apparent family pride in "my sister is a teacher" (figure VII), the more revealing in that it emerges in connection with the examiner's vocation (both in figures VII and IX). The prestige of teaching as a vocation to some extent rubs off on the patient ("my sister and I"). Her family thus appears to carry a favorable valence and to provide her with some impetus toward self-extension. As will be seen in the clinical notes, one observer wondered about a manic trend, and the test findings provide the logic justifying that observation— an occasional overflow of the feelings—at the same time that it also enables us to evaluate the limits of its significance. It is of interest to examine this record here for Piotrowski's ten Rorschach test signs of brain pathology.[56] Six are clearly present: slow time per response, low M score, color naming, perseveration, the low F+ per cent, and the low P count (40). Strong evidence for "perplexity" and for "impotence," which are really overlapping behaviors, and a trend toward "automatic phrases" can also be made out. The only "sign" clearly lacking is a low total number of responses. A frequent characteristic of these patients, which might be added to Piotrowski's well-known list, is the garrulity and wandering from the point that I have described above (p. 101).

Her emotional outflow, even if of a weak current, is a bright spot in this now barren personality. It is information to the therapist that he can fall back on an old philosophy of treatment: let nature do the work. Mrs. E. still has the ability to be affectionate to others, i.e., to give, and giving is the essence of mental health. Of that other prime resource for treatment, ego, she lacks too much. All that is available is ego as integrator. It is defective [41] as criticizing agent. She lacks the important traits of drive and of differentiated interests. The flame of prestige ambition flares up weakly, but even this little heat is borrowed (from the sister). Her own energy is weak (see p. 105; and notes 31 and 34) and her thought content is drying up [1].

Are there ingredients in her that make for learning, for adaptive change? For this is what treatment is. The reality which the therapist must accept is that this patient possesses none. The fact is that her condition is a process, and not one that can be arrested. Nor are any new ego resources likely to be uncovered. The treatment design, therefore, must have a goal within this woman's reach, one utilizing such ego as she does have. Treatment must be centered about the interests which are live ones to her, principally her tie to, and probably affection for, her sister and grandson. Her ego is intact enough to warrant expecting, for a time at least, that reality grasp and judgment will be adequate and appropriate. The relatively deep (because of the biological ties) interest may activate her sense of responsibility in the treatment process; if so, she would make that much greater effort to be psychologically well. The feedback to her would be toward neutralizing her ideas of impotence, burying old anxieties, and reestablishing self-confidence, at least to the limits which her brain tissue imposes. In turn, this would feedback to the ego and keep it bestirring itself to utilize the patient's abilities. The circle can thus be a benign one. Treatment would be principally under social work direction. As to transference [42]?

## Notes on Interpretation

[1] Animal forms and "clouds" account for 91 per cent of her percepts. "Clouds" is here an instance of individualized stereotypy, a kind found in some persons with limited or impoverished minds. Although the topic may vary from patient to patient, it still bespeaks that poverty of thought content, that single mindedness, which is more usually disclosed by the per cent of animal forms.

[2] For example, the "mountains" of R 2, which "Just look like mountains. They just did." "Looks like a bug, (R 4) made me think of it." "Looks like clouds, (R 5) just looks like it." This imprecise style will be observed in most of the responses.

[3] The Ap is W! D. The patient is overattending to the whole at the expense of the major detail and with total disregard of the minor one. The

intellectual drive which would be inferred from the large number of associations to the wholes is more apparent than real. Actually, Mrs. E. is perceiving her environment as massive, conglomerate data, for she lacks the energy to break her stimuli down and attend to their component elements. The intellectual processes in these W's is thus actually a defective one.

[4] Sequence is rigidly methodical. This is another manifestation of an invariant, inflexible method in the handling of one's problems.

[5] Other examples will be found in R 11, 13, 15, 18.

[6] Perseverations are usually, although not necessarily, F−, inaccurate percepts, since the patient is only vaguely seeing what he is looking at and the former image is still in his consciousness. It may chance that the perseverated image is accurate for the new stimulus, as when a feebleminded child sees figure I as a "bird" and also calls as many as seven other of the test figures "bird." The scoring would be F− for figure II, III, IV, and F+ for V.

[7] An affect-laden association cannot be a perseveration. The very fact that it is arousing emotion I take as evidence that the patient is reacting to the current imagery. See also pp. 105–7.

[8] R 5 perseverating from R 3; and R 17, 19, 21 perseverating from R 15. The Y factor in R 3, 11, 13, 15 is an indication of the minor key mood tone in them, while the content in R 13 and 15 also tells of threat feelings specifically.

[9] See Bleuler.[20]

[10] An F+ per cent of 60. This patient's F+ per cent is 53. I should add that while an otherwise integrated and emotionally not unstable person can "get by" with the minimum of 60, well-functioning individuals rate in the high 70's, 80's or the low 90's.

[11] Referring here to the F− in the responses other than R3 and R 13. These two include a Y factor, and concerning these, see notes 26 and 27.

[12] She is unable to perceive clear images. See Rorschach, ref. 57, pp. 23–53.

[13] As judged from known associations to figure IX by mentally well persons.

[14] See Rorschach.[57]

[15] Mean for normal adults is 32.65, SD 17.68.[17] For the feebleminded it is 17.4, 21.4, 24.4 for the low, medium, and high levels.[5]

[16] The mean for the normal adult is 22.48.[17] Patient's Z score is 18.0. Our normal adult sample was broken down into four subgroups, viz, I: executives; II: skilled; III: semi-skilled; IV: unskilled. The respective Z means are: 28.60, 24.70, 20.60, 16.20. Our patient's intellectual achievement as measured by Z is then nearest the mean of the unskilled person

in the population at large. As a reading of the clinical notes will show, this is consistent with her history, and she has therefore maintained her effectiveness at this level.

[17] The fact is that all her Z scores are for W responses, and as the text states, these are of poor quality and are an index rather to the low level intellectual functioning.

[18] The trend to x responses. The best examples are the "face and little eyes" of R 10; the "little tails and headpiece" of R 12; the "legs and feelers" of R 20, and we see also the "head" of R 4, and "face" of R 6.

[19] This is not to say that only the feebleminded do so. Patients with brain damage frequently so react, as do the anxious, especially children, who are physically intact; in fact, this response will be found in patients in most clinical groups. The healthy adult of superior intelligence is a clear-cut exception. Only once in my experience has an x association cropped up in such a patient.

[20] The DW (R 4). In other trends to DW they never become clear-cut as such responses. In R4 the patient is reasoning from "head" to "bug." In R 6 the language is more convincing: "the face made me think of a frog." The other examples are in R 10: "the face reminded me," and in R 20: "the legs and feelers," in which we have a Dd with meaning as part of the "crab" and the entire detail is interpreted from the meaning seen in the part. This is really a DdD, analogous to a DW.

[21] M score is 0.

[22] C score is 0.

[23] Simple color naming in figures II, IX, X.

[24] The very retarded response time in figure II is the most positive indication of the shock, a temporary halting of the associational processes. It will be noted that the patient explicitly verbalizes her impairment. The disturbed perception, F− in both responses, may be questioned as color shock evidence on the ground that since this patient is chronically impaired, this weakness is not differentiating for figure II. Yet the difference is clear in respect to F− and to time for first response to figure II as compared with both figures I and III. The facts are similar in figures VIII and IX in respect to F−. All her responses to these two cards are F−, in contrast to the plus perception in figures IV to VII; while recuperability is shown too in the F+ and the P structures of her first association to figure X. Finally, we cannot help but be impressed by the fact that all of her eight F− percepts are in cards with color stimuli in them.

[25] The shading-toned associations; four is a high quantity, and the shading factor is strongly dominant over the form element twice.

[26] In R 3 and 13, where the F dominates over the Y.

[27] The form quality is poor, F− in both.

[28] On the theory that all shock, whether in reaction to color or to shading, is an anxiety reaction. They differ in respect to what triggers off the emotion. In color shock it starts with an external stimulus which is a temptation to gratification in relation to an object in the environment, i.e., anxiety in which the ego is struggling against id (Fenichel). In shading shock the source is an idea and related attitude within, i.e., the ego is struggling against the superego.

[29] Free as judged from the acute onset, the very retarded reaction time in figure II, and the acute intellectual dysfunction (see note 24).

[30] Average time for first response, at 8.6 seconds, is well within the normal range; if anything, it is nearer to the fast end. The average time for all her responses, however, is just about at or beyond the slow end of the normal range, although it does not show a severe sluggishness as yet.

[31] The W score, which is an index to the drive for achievement— Rorschach's *Leistungsehrgeiz*. The doubtful significance of this patient's W's as reflecting organizing effort has been noted (p. 102) and I shall comment on it again below. Yet, the sheer fact of eight W's cannot be ignored, and one of these is to figure IX, which rarely calls forth a whole percept. Although this latter is more of a global, unanalytic reaction than a vigorously intellectual one, the fact remains that relatively few persons, including many in better mental health than this patient, can grasp figure IX in its entirety. Patients with advanced brain impairment are not able to see wholes, except the easiest ones (figures V, IV, and I). The flame of intellectual life is then, even if diminishing, still glowing in Mrs. E.

[32] Her P count of 5 is just within the normal range, i.e., at the lower level.

[33] An F+ per cent of 53 is low, critically so. It must breed strong suspicion of weakening intellectual stamina as judged by all four of Rorschach's rules for the meaning of F+.

[34] The total productivity of 21 is well below expectancy for a well-functioning adult (mean R: 32.65). Concerning the Z score, see note 16. Concerning the quality of her W's, see note 3, also note 31. The fact remains that they are for the most part the dull W's.

[35] See note 2.

[36] As shown in the high lambda index, 4.25. My point of reference for the healthy group (as empirically observed) is 1.50 to 2.50.

[37] The theory is that the chromatic figures of the test awaken lively feelings, those derived from the psychoanalytic id, whatever the objects to which these feelings may attach or the forms in which they may emerge, as love or aggression, for example.

[38] M = 0: C = 0. This adds up to an EB of 0/0. This is Rorschach's fully coarcted EB. Its EA equivalent is 0 + 0, i.e., exactly zero.

[39] A distinction is to be made among perseverations, between those of stimulus and those of content. In the former it is the image of the inkblot figure, or some portion of it, which perseverates, and it is impersonal, since it has no personal significance to the patient. In the latter, it is the valence of the thought content to the patient which is effecting the perseveration. This distinction is hypothetical, my surmise from empirical observations in using the test. Perseverations of stimulus are more frequent in the brain-damaged, those of theme in the neurotics. Both kinds are found among schizophrenics.

[40] Piotrowski's sign[56] is a low P per cent. This sign is here lacking, since the P percentage for this record would be 24, above Piotrowski's cut-off point. For reasons I have detailed elsewhere, I still look on per cent as a fallacious criterion for P, and I use the actual count. By this standard, this woman comes very close to showing this one of the ten "signs."

[41] See note 1 and the following notes, and the relevant text.

[42] The question of transference need hardly enter into consideration, since the problem is not that of treating for a neurosis (see also pp. 242ff.).

## Clinical Note

Mrs. E. entered the hospital as an in-patient for observation "as a favor to her husband and her sister." Some four months earlier, at the age of forty-seven, she had manifested the following symptoms: She was "jittery," giggled and grinned inappropriately, laughed without good reason, was sloppy in dress and person, lost interest in her surroundings, neglected her work moderately and acted silly. The symptoms began about the time when her married daughter moved away. It was about this time too that the patient had closed a small business which had been her father's and which was losing money. Relations between herself and her husband were described as fine, and the specifically sexual relations as satisfactory. Patient is the eldest of four children. The next sibling, a brother two years younger, was her father's "favorite." She never got along with her mother, admired her father because he was kind to her. She graduated from high school and, after working as a telephone operator, married at the age of eighteen and a half. Her husband was then twenty-five. She describes herself as always active and a leader of a Girl Scout troop.

The psychiatric notes described her as restless, reticent about herself. She drank much water, a tactic she employed whenever the interviewer shifted the conversation to her personally. Happy on the surface, she nevertheless showed anxiety about herself, and was restless and agitated. Intellectually she gave the impression of being intact; memory (psychiatric examination) was not impaired. Insight, however, seemed poor. It was noted too that she evoked little sympathetic response from the examiner.

The diagnostic thinking was cautious. The questions raised were: an anxiety state; schizophrenia, because of the inappropriate affect; atypical involutional reaction.

The Rorschach test was obtained by another psychologist and referred to me for interpretation. My reasoning in concluding that it is the record of a patient with brain pathology is detailed above and in the notes. After so concluding, I studied the clinical chart, from which the above clinical note was excerpted. I then reported to the hospital staff that the test gave evidence of organic involvement, mild in degree, not specific in variety, and probably related to presenile deterioration.

A pneumoencephalogram was ordered shortly thereafter. The report ten days later was: clear evidence of cerebral atrophy, frontal and occipital.

The instructive questions that this case raises are: since this woman showed no gross neurologic signs nor intellectual loss to a degree that could be detected in the psychiatric investigation, how can these negative findings be reconciled with the brain pathology pattern in the Rorschach test and the cerebral atrophy which the pneumoencephalogram traced? These discrepancies are, of course, not as dramatic as they appear at first glance. Since the damage is frontal and occipital, it would not involve the temporal and parietal areas in which those intellectual abilities for which the psychiatrist was exploring are located. The patient had suffered no gross intellectual impairment and so there were no findings within the psychiatrist's sphere of observation. The psychiatrist accurately noted certain symptomatic behaviors, both intellectual and affective. But these remained fragments. It is the task of such a test as the Rorschach, exploring as it does along the several dimensions of the personality at one time, to reveal these fragments in their interrelations, and it is the task of the examiner to translate the Rorschach test logic into clinical logic, to grasp this person in her entirety, and extrapolate to the clinical logic for all her behavior.

# CHAPTER 8

# Mr. C.: A case of nonpsychotic schizophrenia

## Response Record

### Figure I (8″)

1. W F + A P
1.0

'Looks like a bat.' ('Whole. Hard to say. I suppose way it branches out here. I guess the whole appearance. Hard to remember. No, not for sure.')

2. D M+ H
4.0

'Well in appearance, no ... but in thought. That's pretty filthy ... looks like intercourse.' (D 4. 'Feet, more imagination, two protrusions right here. Sort of resemble figures.')

3. D F+ A

'Or it could be a crab.' ('Center, claws at top.' D 1. 'I suppose pincers at top, and shape down here.')

4. Dd YF − An

'Looks something like an x-ray too in the middle.' ('Shaded spot in here [D 3]. Darker in middle and light on sides. I think maybe a chest x-ray. Just a little the shape.')

### Figure II (3″)

5. D F+ A P
3.0

'Two teddy bears, nose to nose.' (D 1. 'Shape of head and body. Looks like ears. Color made it more outstanding, but ... no.')

6. D F− Cg

'Woman's slippers on top.' (D 2. 'Just the shape.')

7. D F+ A P

'Butterfly at the bottom.' ('The shape.' D 3. 'No. Well, color might have added to it. Of course, it made it more distinctive, being red.')

8. D F+ Im

'Looks like sort of arrowheads, spears.' ('The appearance.' D 4. 'Shape.')

### Figure III (7″)

9. D F+ A

'Couple of monkeys.' ('Head and tail. Just the shape.' D 2)

10. D F+ A

'Butterfly in middle.' ('Just shape.' D 3)

11. D M+ H P
3.0

'People ... couple of dancers or something.' ('Shape. Just shape.' D 1)

12. Dd F+ Hd, Sex

'Now, I'll tell you, I have a tendency to go into sex things ... might as well tell you and get it over with.' ('Breasts [Dd 27] and penis [Dd 26]. After ... mind sometimes goes that way. Shape, or also where they're at.' Same as above.)
('They still look like men to me.' D 1).

*Figure IV* (4″)

13. W FT+ A
    2.0

'I would say this looks like a bat . . . sort of a fur-covered bat.' (W. 'Well, the appearance. Fur-covered, darkness, dark areas made me think of fur.' Appearance, shape.)

14. D F+ Ad

'Dog's head.' (D 2. Shape only.)

15. D F+ Ad

'Couple of goose, hanging heads.' (D 3. 'Just the shape. As if they were dead.')

*Figure V* (4″)

16. W M+ H, Sex
    2.5

'Two ladies lounging with big tits. That's about all.' (W. 'Legs and the rest. Just shape.')

17. W F+ A P
    1.0

'Or the word bat comes to mind; I don't know.' (W. The shape? 'No.')

*Figure VI* (9″)

18. D F+ Hh P

'In a way, a rug, I guess. That's about it.' ('Took me a while on this one. Beats me . . . guess I haven't got the imagination I used to have. Appearance. Looks laid out flat, arms and legs . . . bear rug. Two heads actually. No, that didn't strike me.')

19. D YF− An

'Could be an x-ray at top again.' (D 3. 'Light and dark. No. I imagine the shape a bit.')

20. D F+ Ad

'Snakes' heads at top. Remind me in a way.' (D 7. 'Just the shape.')

*Figure VII* (5″)

21. D F+ HP

'Couple of kids, girls with pony tails, arms sticking back.' (D 1. 'Just the shape. Pony tail flopped up, but didn't strike me as being in any kind of activity.')

22. D F+ Hd
    1.0

'Couple of boys with dunce caps.' (D 3. 'Just the shape of it . . . head.')

23. D FY+ A

'Sort of a butterfly at bottom.' (D 10. 'The shape . . . and the darker in the middle accentuates it.')

*Figure VIII* (4″)

24. D F+ A P

'Couple of animals on side . . .' (D 1. 'Ground hogs. Shape.')

25. D F− A

'An ox or broadhorn skull here.' (D 5. 'Just the shape.')

26. D F+ A

'That's about it. Maybe a butterfly again.' (D 4. 'Just the shape.')

*Figure IX* (5″)

27. D F+ H P

'Couple of witches.' (D 3. 'I remember the hats. Shape, just shape.')

28. D CF.Y + H          'In a way, reminds you of unborn babies at bottom.
                        'Just say that's it.' (D 6. 'The pink and the light around
                        it. Shape in a way, head, body.')

29. D FC − Hd           'Couple of fellows with whiskers.' (D 2. 'Whiskers, chin,
                        head. Shape, and maybe coloring had something to do
                        with it.')

*Figure X (2″)*

30. D F+ A P            'Two crabs.' (D 1. 'Just the shape.')
31. D M+ H              'This is imagination, couple of old guys with arms up
                        in air.' (D 8. 'Not too distinct. The shape. Just jumping
                        up in the air.')

32. D M − H             'Couple of little kids sucking on something here. Of
4.0                     course, what came to mind was tits, but I didn't see
                        them.' (Outer edge below Dd 25 and D 7; shape.)
                        Total Time: 11 minutes.

### Response Summary

R: 32

| | | | | | | | |
|---|---|---|---|---|---|---|---|
| W | 4 | M | 5 (1−) | H | 7 | F+ | 91% |
| D | 26 | CF.Y | 1 | Hd | 4 | A | 50% |
| Dd | 2 | FC− | 1 | A | 13 | P | 9 |
| | $\overline{32}$ | YF− | 2 | Ad | 3 | S | 0 |
| | | FY | 1 | An | 2 | Af r | 0.39 |
| Z f 8 | | FT | 1 | Cg | 1 | L | 1.91 |
| Z sum 21.5 | | F+ | 19 | Hh | 1 | T/R | 20.6″ |
| Ap. (W) D! Dd | | F− | 2 | Im | 1 | T/first R | 5.1″ |
| | | | $\overline{32}$ | | $\overline{32}$ | Fln R | 0.33 |
| | | | | | | Fln T/first R | 2.78 |

Seq. Methodical

EB 5/1.5
EA 6.5

## Interpretation

Judged by the formal tabulations of the Rorschach test findings, this man
should be a paradigm of normality. This would be the inference from the
level of his productivity [1]*, and from his regard both for reality [2] and
for the conventional amenities [3]. He appears broadly capable of interest
in his fellow humans [4], which may be a most important trait, reflecting
his healthy contact with the social environment. Other individual features
in this test pattern, taken by themselves, can be the basis for a clean bill of
mental health.

How deceptive these outer features are can be detected in R 2, 12, 16, 32,

* Bracketed numbers refer to Notes on Interpretation, which for this chapter will be
found on pages 127–132.

with supporting indications in R 28. A crude sexuality, mirrored in a most primitive imagery, is breaking through into the conscious thinking of this superficially controlled and proper man. These thoughts stand out in sharp contrast to the, for the most part, socially appropriate mental life. They are ideas not predictable from his other responses and not consistent with the rest of the personality structure. They are not conscious goal ideas; they simply emerge, without being under any direction from his self. As he naively tells us, "I have a tendency to go into sex things," and how bland he is about it also leaks out in, "Might as well tell you and get it over with." He is not a scoundrel planfully using his intelligence for a villainous design, as, say, Tarquin did in his rape of Lucrece. Rather, he is a weakling, suffering a debility of the will—Bleuler's "aboulia." Thoughts emerge which are an unforeseen change of ideation. Their sexual content speaks of infantile traits in the personality, inclinations that have persisted unaltered alongside the man's adult ability to know reality and the proprieties. Process-wise, too, the arbitrary shift in content is a lead which speaks of a schizophrenic way of life. It uncovers an undeveloped ego, one that has never grown beyond the sapling stage, and we see it here blown about by the winds of chance thoughts. The outward integration has screened the pathology. The essential question really becomes, what manner of schizophrenia is this that is so highly characterized by apparent integration?

The pattern of emotional expression both supports the inference as to schizophrenia and helps answer the question as to specific form. Quantitatively there are few outward signs of feeling: only two such reactions [5] by a person living at a tempo of production which is normal. The deficit is more obvious in the volume of expressed feeling [6]. Events which draw out affective response from the healthy leave this patient relatively under-reactive [7]; they arouse in him neither pleasurable enthusiasm nor self-indulgent excitement. It is a bland condition that the test projects, one with few of the variations that make up the full tonal range of normal day-to-day living.

Yet, there are some variations. The quality in the two emotion-toned responses which do break through uncovers a degree of reactivity in sharp contrast to his placidity. When he lets himself go, he is impatient and irritable. The feeling push can be moderated by a regard for reality, but even so the impatience sticks out, and the man's total emotional tone is nearer the quality of a callow selfishness [8]. Agitation complicates some of this excitement with a painful, anxiety-toned chord [9]. Thus, he usually manifests no feeling and presents a dead-pan exterior, but he can also be peevish and bad-tempered. He is capable of a few emotional displays but no affective fluidity.

The malignity in this pattern is softened by signs of anxious upset. The word *signs* requires emphasis. All we can really speak of is a *question* of anxiety rather than convincing evidence of it. Nearly all the usual marks of such disturbance are lacking. Yet, there is a trace of sensitivity in him [10] which must argue for the ego's concern about emotion-toned events. Since *ego* sense carries with it consciousness of *alter*, the patient to this extent shows himself less detached from his world. Still and all, it is a weak flare-up of anxiety, not only lacking the quantitative data but also the qualitatively observed affect; the patient vents none of the utterances of surprise, elation, displeasure, or rejection that characterize the true neurotic. We are looking at a neurotic reaction that lacks the feeling tensions of neurosis.

We have seen how discrepant with this affectless status is the irritability in his momentary emotional flashes. The content in one of these, the "unborn babies" of R 28, helps explain the anomaly: a preoccupation with a topic of regressive vintage. Questions of a rebirth idea animating him are raised here. Support of this lead is afforded by the crude language of the oral reunion fantasy in R 32. The ego's armor is being penetrated by developmentally primitive character needs which persist in this man as an adult. These thoughts and their attendant emotions reach levels more distant from conscious thinking than would be expected in a neurotic structure.

The inadequate, and, in fact, shallow, affect shows up also in the qualitative elements of this test record in its entirety. The patient produces his associations in dull fashion, with no variation in interest and with lackadaisical explanations: "I suppose the way it branches out here," or, "I guess," or, "Just say that's it." His is an invariant tone, and this trait appears also in such measurable data as the fluctuations of his response tempo [11]. In his one other association which is in part a product of his feelings (R 29), he gives no evidence of being personally involved. His impatience is a detached one; it is about nothing in particular. Again, in R 5 and R 7 the patient dispassionately observes the presence of the feeling determinant: "Color made it more outstanding . . . more distinctive." But he is not influenced by it, not in what he sees nor with any sign of healthy warmth, and not even in an unhealthy neurotic fashion. He neither avoids nor rejects the color; it is just there [12]. In sum, this man outwardly has very little affect. To the usual piquancies of life, he is unresponsive or, at best, lukewarm. He is distant from others, barely touching them emotionally. This is his most characteristic condition, but it can be punctuated, although rarely, by outbursts. What forms these may take, i.e, as fears or rages or unique interests, is a question about which the test findings add some information (see below).

Fantasy living is, as a rule, scarce to lacking in personality pictures such as has so far been postulated for this man. These persons are sterile in imagination, just as they are in overflow of feelings. Our patient appears to be violating this rule in his quantitatively high imagination [13]. Yet, there is poverty within this apparent plenty. The poverty is manifest in his failure to fantasy where others do. This omission stands out because it is discrepant with the fact of his apparently above average ability to do so [14]. Discrepancies have their uses in opening up trails to some source trait that produces them. So with the present one. The content of his fantasy is autistic and symptomatic. Very immature fantasies have persisted into the patient's adult life, and these he now airs. He has not grown to the point of living the wishes or fears of most healthy adults.

The energy estimate in these associations also tells this story. His imaginative push is very meager [15]. For three of the five fantasies the estimate by the Levy scale is minimal; for one it approaches, but is below, the midpoint. Only in one does it clearly speak for a high degree of activity. In psychologic terms, only once does the patient invest any intensity in the wish which he has introverted (R 31). The others, even though the themes arise in primitive cravings of the personality, are weakly experienced.

What these cravings are is obvious in R 16 and R 32: the yearning for the breast. In R 2 he conjures up the idea of sexual intercourse. What the latent meanings of his most energetic fantasy: "couple of old guys . . . with arms up . . . jumping up" (R 31), is not clear and must be left to be determined in therapeutic sessions. The fantasy is unique, differentiating, and is screening some urgent personal trend. His one fantasy within a normal frame of reference and with pleasurable flavor is the "dancers" of R 11. It is weak in intensity and ordinary in quality. He is thus off course both in what he achieves and what he misses [16], and he is living a morbid sexuality of a kind that other writers have noted in these patients.[37]

Of central significance concerning any person's character is the question: how self-assertive or submissive is he? These alternatives correspond to the masculinity-femininity poles in the unconscious. For the present patient, a male, the finding is an adverse one. Only once, R 31, does he manifest a trace of the action [17] that speaks of self-assertiveness. In the others, including even the "intercourse" (R 2) fantasy, he is either static or altogether supine—"lounging" (R 16)—or he projects the most infantile dependency—"kids sucking" (R 32). This grown man is not only far from self-assertive; he is very near to a listless inactivity.

Some of the language in which he tells this is also diagnostically illuminating. He is uncouth in the "tits" epithet: the usual conventions are not encrusted on him, the social civilities are not stamped into his character. Ego as sensitivity for the regard which others hold of oneself, is not part of him. The early personality state is operative. Just as themes in the fantasies disclose him thirsting for the baby's nurturance, so his language for this is primitive; he uses the unadorned word for the source of these boons. The fixation sticks out in one dereistic fantasy. In it, reality is ignored and wishful living shapes the imagery, a characteristic dream process in which ego censorship has been removed [18]. The gratifying ideas in the other fantasies also have the flavor of dream work. We must conclude that his imaginings do not serve as escape from painful or anxious ruminations but that they are ego-syntonic. They are, to this weak personality, an autistic way of obtaining primitive erotic pleasures.

The persistence of such infantile traits into adult life is essential schizophrenia. The apparent overt integration offers no serious difficulty to this diagnostic thinking. The concept of pseudoneurotic schizophrenia[37] rationalizes it, as does the S-3 pattern in Molish's and my previously published results.[52] What may be of especial theoretic significance is the very fact that this patient is both consciously very correct and at the same time liberates deeply unconscious material. Bychowski[25] in a paper on latent psychosis refers to increased communication among the mental systems and concomitant baring of the repressed unconscious. The present test pattern appears to be one in which the patient's conscious is in communication with his unconscious. He may be departing from Bychowski's observation in that his infantile eroticisms may never have been truly repressed. The shallow affect with which he can carry on this communication is a schizophrenic trait. To the healthy or neurotic, the eruption of old infantile wishes, their parading before consciousness, is accompanied by acute pain and anxiety. This patient's manner of resolving the anxiety triggered at shock points has interesting theoretic implications for this kind of schizophrenia. The patient disposes of the pain in these anxiety reactions by being without shock. The barely perceptible psychologic tremor described above (p. 117) is essentially none in comparison to the disturbing upsets that actively conflicted neurotics experience.[19] This man responds at these points with his usual speed and is as freely productive as usual. He sees most of the conventional forms, follows an orderly procedure, and, except for the two deviations from good perception [20], sees things accurately. He enjoys this immunity to shock whether the events that set it off originate in external sources or internally, i.e., out of thoughts and emotions being bred within [21]. Assuming that his passive disturbances [22] are the result of shock, he is going through them without substantial anxiety. On the other hand, he can be anxious without more notable shock effect [23]. One may speculate that he has thoughts which should be accompanied by fear but he does not have the fear. Be it fear, rage, or love—those three primary emotions as Watson isolated them—this patient knows them never, or hardly ever.

The "hardly ever" qualification is prompted by the signs of the painful affect. In two of his associations (R 4, 19) the psychologic process stems from painful mood [24] and the themes in these speak of anxious preoccupations about health [25]. This process enters also into a third response (R 28) and ruffles the emotional waters (see again notes 9 and 22). His self-percept carries a disagreeable taste. He devalues and condemns his own thinking (R 2), apologizes for it as for a fault (R 12), and at another point (figure VI) devalues himself, qualifies much, and employs the resignation formula. All in all, he reveals more emotion at this than at other points in his test. He gives no lead, however, to any personal dynamic as a source of this feeling [26], other than may be present specifically in R 19. One other thematic indication of an unhappy moment is the "dead" association (R 15), which is presumably of dysphoric quality. Yet, neither here nor at the other points (except for the painful undertone in figure VI) does Mr. C. show signs of strong feeling. The exclamations, sighs, rejecting language, phobic or counterphobic attacks that characterize the neurotic and many healthy at these test stress points [27] are not part of him. Even when he has the thoughts, when an undercurrent of disturbing emotion stirs him, he does not vary his reaction pattern. He has "moments" [28] and these are in fact related to his unsatisfying percept of himself, and so to his sensed interpersonal relations. But whatever goes on inside of him, he does nothing.

Another kind of emotion to be explored for painful elements is that produced by erotic hunger [29]. Only once is an association so structured, which is not enough times to be convincing. Nevertheless, it excites our interest. Mr. C.'s identification of the "bat" by his fur is unique, and so differentiates his thought content. His emphasis on the darkness points up the moody influence. More decisive is the indication (in his thought content) of an infantile erotic thirst in this patient (see p. 125). In a person having these yearnings, the presumption of a hunger for body contact (in the texture determinant) is a lead that cannot be ignored. It is a lead only, not proof. The pain in it would be that which goes with a sensed lack, a want unsatisfied. Mr. C.'s test pattern shows him totally lacking in overt aggressiveness, with not so much as a single indication of the trait structurally [30]. One weapon theme (R 8) and one possible latent hostile caricaturing (R 22) are thoughts that he has in this sphere, but they are without the character force to implement them. The fight is not there. An arresting theoretic question here is: does his devalued self-perception serve to prevent his self-assertion? Is it the dynamic behind the lack of fight? Fitting into the picture of nonaggression is the submissive inner stance (p. 119). It all adds up to a weak will. Taken together with the shallow affect (notes 5, 6, 7, and the text) and some other findings in his intellectual behavior (notes 39, 40, 42) this weakness is a nuclear one in this man's personality. Such defect in volition is typical of this nosologic condition.

This weakness is also the architect of this man's defenses. In his protestations of difficulty (R 1), self-accusation (R 2, 12), self-qualifying with devaluations, including denial of his imagination, he is taking the easy way out. By making himself less worthwhile, he is less a target of punishment [31]. The death feint is the extreme form of this strategy. It is an expedient of the immature and timorous. Also immature is the probable displacement or avoidance of sexual interest in the "woman's slippers" (R 6). This directs attention again to his other eroticisms, in the fantasy and in the more conscious thinking (R 12). By providing daydream gratification and thus softening the pain due to the deprivation, the inner world serves his as an emollient, i.e., defensively. Its undeveloped stage (the content) helps us identify the time in which he was experiencing the conflictual impulses as being very early in his growth. The simpler regressive character attitudes, Fenichel points out (op. cit., p. 523–24) in discussing certain defensive mechanisms, are the more archaic ones. Assuming my reasoning is verified by the clinical history, this patient reacted to his conflictual infantile sexual needs by fixating his imagination on the body part and the fixation has persisted. The test has performed the archaeologic job of digging it up.

However, Mr. C. is also using defenses of which only a more mature ego is capable. The almost invariant accuracy testifies to a stringent hold on reality. The caricature theme, "dunce caps" in R 22, smells of hostility with its source in resentment and so marks out an ego trail. If the "snakes' heads" (R 20) is symbolism, it is an even more maturely adaptive defense. Still, the dominant picture is a constrictive one: content is stereotyped, interest is narrowed, attention is contracted [32]. The rigid hold on reality has the damaging effect of confining the man, intellectually, within very narrow limits. This is the defensive solution which he has achieved. What does it mean in terms of his over-all adjustment to the ins and outs of daily life and in terms of his major character course?

Described only from the quantitative response summary, Mr. C. appears well able to test reality (see note 2), can readily recognize the obvious stimulus [33], knows surface conventionalities too well (note 3), and attends to the objective fact as compared with the subjectively toned one [34] about as much as is to be expected of him. His mental output is just at expectancy (see note 1). He seems to be interested in human beings at a healthy level [35]. His procedure, intellectually, looks orderly enough [36], if, indeed, he varies it at all, something he does much too inadequately [37] in his reaction pattern generally. His approach to his problems by way of the over-all view, or by the more immediate concrete datum is, on first glance, close enough to normal [38]. Scrutiny of his method, however, shows that such overviews as he manages are the equivalents of simple and modest achievements. His perception and thinking are nearly all essentially in concrete terms [39]. It is an invariant pattern and reflects a weakness which he glaringly betrays in other of his test behaviors. One is the just-about-wooden tempo of his mental activity [40]. The changing stimuli to which life subjects us all do not ruffle his dispassionate exterior. He is underreactive in an externalized, motor sense. This, in turn, would tell of inadequate initiative. Taken together with the single prevailing affect, it all patterns out into an ineffective and inadequate person. He is a man unable to launch himself into a difficult effort, without the aspiration to prod him into it [41]. His devalued view of himself (see p. 122; and note 31) must sap what little ambition may flare up and eat away at the weak morale he has. His interests as reflected in his thought content disclose a similar dull state, within which, however, some true signs of richness can still sparkle on occasion (R 25; also 6, 8), although his symptomatic needs [42] narrow his range and confine his possibilities for an effective richness. His crude language discloses this limitation at two spots: R 16 and R 32. He notoriously ignores the conventional aesthetic amenities with which sexual organs are screened in everyday conversation. To this extent he is asocial, does not look for a good name in the sight of others. He lacks ego.

In the light of this confined horizon and stunted ego, the almost unerring sticking to reality loses much of its apparent high asset value. He sees what is unquestionable in his field of vision, and stops there. It is an unadventurous brush with his environment, one that is safe, and it prevents any expansion of the ego's boundary.[30] Having no urge to push into new intellectual territory, he makes next to no errors. It is a safe course, but a solution achieved by the least effort, in fact, by noneffort. The patient does adapt to reality, in his unexciting way; he actually over-adapts (see note 3). Provided nothing of too personal import happens and nothing forceful enough to move him out of his inertia, he can stay in this safe and conforming pattern. He will be appropriate in what he expects of others and in what they can, usually, expect of him. But all this is a facade.

An easy susceptibility to deviant thought is also part of him and points to the underlying psychologic frailty. His thinking has in it an element of the circumstantial [43] at one point. Of interest also is the language in R 17, in which the word appears to be equated to its referent. Healthy people, neurotics, and even patients with more severe pathology associate "a bat" to the animal itself. To our patient it is the "word bat." This resembles, I believe, the "literalness" which Benjamin[17] reports, a kind of language oddity noted by Cameron,[26] and a "stilted, artificial manneristic denotation" listed by Ruesch.[59] These writers report all these communication peculiarities as occurring in schizophrenics. Circumstantial thinking is also peculiar to schizophrenics. Other thinking defects in this Rorschach are a contaminated flavor in the "fur-covered bat" (R 13) and the uncritical relating of differing sexual percepts (R 12). An inability to make smooth transitions in his thought processes is a more deep-seated failing. This is inferred from the wooden, invariant, and stereotyped pattern described above, which is his chronic condition. Channelized in it, he cannot shift his thinking.

But at times he does, and then it is more than a shift. It is a jerk. Of this order is the incursion of the severely regressive ideas into his overtly realistic way of life. The sexuality of R 2, 12; the oral reunion fantasies of R 16, 32; the crude language; the archaic theme, out of context, in R 28; all these are bizarre flashes in the otherwise dull stodginess. They are unpredictable deviations from his general course. Uneven, too, is his sporadic self-qualifying and devaluing. Most frequently, he associates without qualifying his responses, an uncritical procedure more characteristic of the young child, as is the fast initial response time, which is also found in the present test record [44]. In the shifts of attitude to the self and in the shifts of ideas the test discloses the possibility of behaviors unforeseen by the patient himself. The test is a reflection of planless changes of conduct in life's arena. The ego lacks directive stamina. Under the cover of later, learned habits of knowing reality, this patient is nourishing his infantile ego needs. He can adapt to external demands unless, and until, this early ego is activated. Then it takes the field and, even if only temporarily, these regressive ideas and whims toy with him. It is the pattern of pseudoneurotic schizophrenia, or S-3.

This man's ego weakness discloses itself also in his small ability to enjoy life, something we know from his emotional state (see p. 117). And even when he does express himself with lively feelings, it is not to reach out for something that gives him pleasure. This we may judge from the topics in which he does liberate some feelings [45]. These topics tell of uniquely personalized absorptions. Since the emotional life is structurally immature, another defect in this man's character is his inability to know others by sharing their joys, by making affective closure with them. He relates to others only for what there is in it for him [46]. This trait he manifests also in his day-dreaming: here the content is pleasurable but infantile. It is a day-dreaming which he cannot weave constructively into a social context.

The gap in emotional contact with others is, in fact, the core of this man's psychologic structure and the nucleus of his maladjustment. In the midst of his environment he is detached from and affectively bland about it; his realism is skin-deep and remote from the underlying, affectively toned, more essential realities; he is not in communication with his world. When thinking about other persons, his is likely to be a self-serving idea [47]. His interests show too little differentiation, and some of his thought processes are of an order apart from customary forms (see p. 123). The weak and dubious neurotic shock (p. 118) now can be characterized as pseudoshock, just as the entire pattern is a pseudoneurosis. The pattern resembles neurosis in the usually orderly language and in the thinking that is as a rule coherent, i.e., there is an outwardly intact personality. This is what he may look like indefinitely to the naked clinical eye. What the test penetrates to is the arbitrary incursions of thinking dysfunction, the baby's ego still flourishing under the cover of the adult's, the ease with which this archaic ego and the grown one can interpenetrate (p. 120), the sometimes uncontrolled affect, and the lack of sustained purpose. All this is schizophrenia, S-3.

Some human wants which stir in this psychologically disabled person can be read in the thematic content. They are (a) infantile oral erotic needs and an immature sexuality, as we have already seen (p. 124); the fantasy activity is especially significant as revealing very deep-seated wants; (b) the "breast" and the "penis" of R 12 speak for themselves but arouse further interest in being details of the two sexes in a single association— an undeveloped sexual imagery of a kind observed with homosexuality. This lead has support in (c) the proximity of two persons of the same sex and "lounging" (R 16). A further clue in this direction is given in R 29 in the emphasis on the "whiskers." Still immature, yet an advance, is (d) the "woman's slippers" (R 6); this reflects voyeurism, and hence a blocked heterosexual wish. This trend needs to be considered in the patient's emphasis on the female genital-like detail, "the darker in the middle" in R 23. What (e) the "unborn babies" of R 28 may mean is too much a matter of surmise. A different kind of interest is (f) the "arrowheads . . . spears" association of R 8 with its connotation of aggression. It could be a nucleus for maladjustment, but in Mr. C., it need not be taken seriously (note 30 and text). The "dunce cap" theme of R 22, caricaturing behavior, is a transparent screen for hostility. What connection there may be between these thoughts or urges and (g) the "dead" geese of R 15 becomes again a subject for surmise. Is it a dysphoric note, his pained reaction to his own hostility? The "dead" motif, while not unique as an association to this detail, may be emanating from "that within which passeth show." More convincing evidence of an anxious mood tone are the (h) two anatomy topics. In a nonmedical person they betray a preoccupation with health, and they have been observed in anxious and depressed persons with especial frequency. (i) The "ears" of R 5 may mean nothing, being the only instance in the record, or its implication may be paranoid ideas, but confirmation of this trend in the test record is lacking.

So much for the pathologic thought content. Some of healthy variety is also brought to the surface. In the important fantasy sphere, there is the "dancers" theme of R 11, a weak one but, as fantasy, discloses a wish. It is one of his rare signs of a pleasurable pursuit. Cheerful in flavor although not transmuted into an innerly lived wish is the well-developed imagery of the "kids, girls with pony tails" (R 21). Whether or not this screens sexual need, he comes as near as he ever does here to sharing in what would be enjoyable activity in others. He strikes a cheerful note too in the recreational topic "teddy bears" (R 5). In the "broad-horn skull" he uses a term that is probably peculiar to some locality, and in any event original. Here is one, rare sign of intellectual liberation.

It is of interest now to inspect this man's reaction pattern by reference to the conceptual scheme I have outlined for schizophrenia (ref. 15; p. 132). The S-3 personality components are:

> Defenses: constricted
> Intellectual functioning: orderly
> Fantasy: little or none
> Emotional state: lability, or fixed tone
> Social adjustment: self-deprivation

In one of the traits listed in this schema, our patient does not follow a strict S-3 pattern. He uses too much fantasy (but see p. 119). In respect to total social adjustment, he shows some of the behaviors characterizing the self-absorbed but he is dominantly S-3 in his propensity for self-deprivation. For the rest he consistently follows the S-3 design.

The treatment outlook for this kind of patient is not good. Such patients change little. S-3 is a protected position to which the afflicted person has moved from a more disturbing one. Mr. C. presents the signs of cramped, inflexible intellectual habits (see p. 122f., and note 32) and of constrictive defense. The restriction on his ability to enjoy himself also argues against that fluid state which facilitates response to a treatment experience.

Yet, the man is not totally without substance intellectually. The sheer fact of his high accuracy presupposes the brain tissue wherewith to discriminate and judge. A feebleminded person can be emotionally bland but not highly accurate, not certainly at a nearly one hundred per cent level. Nor can he develop as much imagination as this patient does (note 13), sick as it is. It will be a very rare feebleminded person too who will demonstrate the intellectual energy available to Mr. C. [48]. Here is latent ability, but it has never come to fruition.

The findings concerning inner living lend color to the pessimistic view. In his Experience Balance (EB) this patient is decidedly turned inward. In a mentally sick person this is unfavorable to treatment. Such persons do not change readily. They too easily turn into their inner worlds as an avenue of escape, and the unpleasant facts about themselves with which the therapeutic process confronts them are just something else for them to escape. Also, introversive persons characteristically are set in their ways. The other element in his EB, the patient's outwardly expressed feelings, is, as we have seen, of immature quality and self-serving. Moreover, these responses are too few in number and he reacts with minimal freedom to stimuli that evoke these reactions (note 7). Emotional fluidity is thus lacking. Viewed from either side of the EB picture, this patient lacks the flexibility necessary for change. The EA of 6.5 looks better than it is. It has apparent breadth but is made up of fantasies that are regressive or weak, or both, and of feeling reactions that are immature and self-serving. In both spheres, healthy responses are lacking.

There can be no question, as judged from this test record, of a transference relationship. The total picture is too little neurotic or conflictual. The patient shows no anxiety around any image, father or mother. He articulates only traces of hostile thinking. His opposition trait is at the zero point. Why this failure of human resources? The associational content suggests a conflict with which this person had to cope in his earliest years, one which in his then immaturity he solved by way of the only avenue open to him, a fixation around that infantile eroticism. In the absence of the good fortune to have experienced a relationship or an education that would have built a strong character, and in the absence of treatment the infantile solutions have remained fixed. How this squares with the data of the patient's life can be seen from the social history notes.

### Notes on Interpretation

[1] The number of responses, 32, is exactly at the mean of our normal sample, 32.65.

[2] The F+ per cent, 91, is above the mean of 79.25 found for this population sample.

[3] His P score of 10 is very high. Mean for this sample is 7.0, SD 2.47.

[4] As seen in the H associations; mean for the population is 4.02.

[5] Two responses determined, in any degree, by color.

[6] As indicated in the sum of his color-determined associations, which is 1.5. The mean for the normal group is 3.11.

[7] The number of scored responses in figures VIII to X yields an affective ratio of 0.39. This is not only far below the mean of 0.60 found in the normal sample but also short of the 0.40, the mark which, on the basis of empiric observation, I have been finding as the critical minimum for the healthy.

[8] The FC— and the CF. Feeling is subdued when there is an FC determinant (R 29). But the F— betrays the weak control and hence the relative dominance by the feelings. The psychologic significance of FC— is one that stands nearer to the green-stick feelings represented by CF than to the matured emotion in FC+.

[9] This is the significance of the shading determinant. Y, when blending with a color-determined association, as here with the CF of R 28.

[10] The two F—'s in the two color shock figures, II and VIII; these are the only F— in this record.

[11] See below, note 40. Also in the text, p. 123.

[12] Compare this patient's pattern with that of Mrs. O.

[13] 5 M is a high quantity for an average adult (mean is 3.50) and is far above expectation for this impoverished and unoriginal record.

[14] The misses are those in figures, II, VII, and IX, which readily elicit M associations in persons capable of them. They certainly should have done so in a person producing five other M. The failures of M are the more flagrant in R 21 and 27 where the patient can and does perceive the human forms which, when perceived, are almost without exception imbued with life. He rejects M. Some doubt is in order with regard to the scoring of R 21. But in view of the evidence in the inquiry I take the term "sticking" to be descriptive of the detail rather than perception of movement. This kind of description is a mode of expression not uncommon in persons whose intellectual functioning is limited or, as in this patient, impoverished.

[15] By the Levy Movement Scale the energy ratings would be:

R  2 ........................ 2
R 11 ........................ 2
R 16 ........................ 1
R 31 ........................ 5
R 32 ........................ 1

[16] He produces two M in figure X and one in V. Both these test cards are among the least effective in eliciting fantasy. His missing the M associations in figures II, VII, and IX, therefore, stands out in greater contrast.

[17] The direction of the action in R 31, while not extensor in ac-

cordance with Rorschach's strict description of such movement, i.e., away from the center axis of the inkblot configuration, still has something in it of *"streck-kinesthesie,"* a pull outward. In this response the arms are "up in the air" and the jumping is "up in the air." A trace at least of the extensor activity is here present, and this is the test's indicator of independence-seeking (see the Rorschach-Oberholzer paper[58]).

[18] The M— in R 32. This is a fantasy in which the form percept is inaccurate, a distortion of a kind that is produced by dream work. It is a kind of M found characteristically in persons in severe disturbance or in disruption.

[19] See, for example, the color shock pattern in Mrs. O., pp. 63, 71.

[20] A touch of color shock. See note 10.

[21] This patient is immune to both color shock and to shading shock.

[22] I.e., those manifest in the inaccuracies in figures II and VIII; also, the F— element in R 29. Again, in figures I and VI he shows what are still minimal effects of anxiety, this time due to shading shock, in the F— elements of R 4 and R 19. But none of the disorganizing effects of shock appear in any of these figures.

[23] See the exposition concerning figure VI in the paragraph in the text immediately following.

[24] The Y determinants in R 4 and 19. It will be noted that in both these associations the Y, i.e., the affective component, dominates over the intellectual one scored by the F, and this dominance is further reflected in the fact of F—, i.e., the F— is strong enough to vitiate the control.

[25] The anatomy content in both R 4 and R 19.

[26] The phallic significance, frequent in figure VI, is not here a factor. One is tempted to see phallic symbolism in the snakes' head, but this percept is common here; it is produced by many individuals who give no evidence that the response is symbolic. The present percept must, therefore, be looked at as a function of the stimulus and not of the patient.

[27] See, for example, the protocols of Mrs. O. and Mrs. L.

[28] These painful moments are inferred from the self-percept as mirrored in the expressed self-disparagement, which has a possibly dysphoric motif (R 15, and see p. 125). Another datum of painful mood tone consists of the shading determinants. The patient's "sensed interpersonal relations" is an inference drawn entirely from known clinical logic, which, however, rests on these empiric data. The test tells us in this data that this man is suffering psychologic pain, and from established clinical theory we reason that he feels this way because of his relations with others.

[29] Indicated in the texture determinant, T (R 13).

[30] The white space, s, is 0. In fact, the patient does not so much as notice any of the white spaces and he does not attend to them in the Inquiry.

[31] Being self-effacing and self-demeaning is, of course, a well-known defensive strategy, a way of seeking sympathy from the other. One may escape condemnation from himself and from others in this way.

[32] The animal percentage, 50, is no worse, but no better, than the mean (46.65) of the normals, i.e., it bespeaks a mediocre mind. The apparent breadth in the eleven H and Hd is an *ignis fatuus*, or, in good American slang, a false alarm. Of the nine associations with human motifs in them, all but two and possibly a third tell of preoccupation by this man with symptomatic ideas. The two are R 11 and R 21, while the possible third is R 22. What we are seeing here is a "personal stereotype" (see fuller description of this trait, p. 213). The narrowed interest is reflected by the same concentration on so small a number of topics: in his total of 32 associations, 29 fall within three content groupings: animals, humans, and anatomy. The hemmed-in attention we know from the Ap, with its over-emphasis on D.

[33] Referring again to the animal percentage, since animal forms are the most frequent ones seen.

[34] The lambda index, which is 1.91. The normal range is 1.50 to 2.50 (see pp. 79, 92). A ratio of the associations determined strictly by form (whether F+ or F− and uninfluenced by any of the other determinants) to all his other associations, it is a measure of the patient's response to environmental data, as contrasted with associations in which he is responding to any inner stimulus, i.e., associations influenced by any emotional nuance.

[35] Such would be the inference from eight H, i.e., whole human associations. How deceptive this finding is in this man has been noted in note 32.

[36] Seq. is generally methodical. However, it can be judged only in two figures, I and III, these being the only ones in which he varies at all as between W, D, and Dd.

[37] Concerning the fluctuations, see p. 123; also, note 40.

[38] The Ap, while accenting D at the expense of W, does so moderately and is not unlike findings in many individuals in the neurotic and even in the normal range.

[39] His four W's, the apparent overviews in his intellectual grasp, are in figures I, IV, and V. His percepts in three of these are the very common and easiest holistic ones and are actually equivalent to D's. Once, however, he does break up the entire card and resynthesize it meaningfully as a larger scene (in R 16). Hence, the qualification "nearly" in the text.

[40] The fluctuations in the productivity and in the time for first response from one test figure to the next are extremely small: 0.33 for the former; 2.78 for the latter. For the normal adult the means are: 1.35 for fluctuation in productivity from test card to test card. SD 0.89; and 23.36 for initial response time, SD 18.75. This patient even deviates significantly from schizophrenic adults. Their mean fluctuation in productivity from card to card is 1.36, SD 0.92; and their mean time for first response is 18.78, SD 14.30.[15]

[41] As seen in the low W score, which is an index both to the weak ambition and the low achievement. Actually (compare note 39), only one of his W's shows him carrying through to meaningful achievement, R 16. That this is a character weakness and not a constitutional disability we know from other evidence in the test (see concerning Z, in note 48), and the patient's history confirms this indication.

[42] See note 32. It may be added here that while this patient's animal percentage of 50 is not too far from the normal adult mean of 46.65, SD 13.12, it is also not too far from the mean of the feebleminded group (55.4, SD 20.8[5]). What all these figures point up is that (a), with respect to dead-level mediocrity, the persons at the lower end of the normal range function at about where the higher level feebleminded do; and that (b) our patient in his present sluggish mental state shows up with a limitation at some point between the means of the two groups.

[43] The position element in determining his sex association in R 12: "where they're at."

[44] His average time for first response, 5.1", is at the fast end of the scale, even by the standards for children.

[45] The content in his two color-determined associations, R 28 and 29. In neither is it of healthy connotation. Judged from his performance with the color stimuli alone, we could in fact speak of a total inability on the part of this man to get any pleasure out of life. But he does give signs that thoughts emanating from the pleasure principle do flit across his mind, as the exposition of the content more generally shows, p. 125f.

[46] He lacks FC+ responses, and also color-determined associations in which the themes are socially healthful. See note 8, and the relevant text.

[47] In note 32 it was observed that the themes in his H content were channelized into symptomatic thinking. More specifically, four of these H associations (R 2, 16, 28, 32) consist of infantile erotic or even more primitive thinking. So also does one of the Hd (R 12). The personal significance to the patient of R 31 is unclear but suspect. The possible latent hostile attitude in the Hd of R 22 has also been commented on (p. 122).

[48] Inspection of the individual associations in which the patient is

credited with a Z shows him repeatedly achieving at levels beyond the easiest, even in instances of some difficulty. For example, he must break down and resynthesize the stimulus meaningfully in R 2 and R 16. In R 11 he integrates the leg detail with the rest of the human form, separated though they are by white space (see Rorschach, ref. 57, p. 26, concerning the achievement process here involved). In R 32 he organizes two details that are quite disparate under pressure from his regressive need (the "sucking" association). His simplest and most weakly organized association is in R 5 in which he sees a simple relationship between two adjacent details. The ability to grasp relationships meaningfully corresponds directly with active intelligence. In this generally arid Rorschach test picture, one that must be discouraging to the clinician searching for a therapeutic opening, here is some latent potential which may offer leverage.

## Clinical Note

This thirty-five year old white male entered the hospital as an inpatient, on self-referral. This was his second of two admissions, the first, also to this hospital, was eight and a half years earlier. The complaint then included headaches, "not as pain, but as nervousness," some inappropriate and foolish behavior, a sense of dread, an unwillingness to "face anything real," the feeling that he was apart from others and that people were staring at him. He was discharged in the care of his parents. Diagnostic statement at the time of the first admission includes: "a lonely, shy, ineffectual young adult who is unable to establish relationships with other people and who has become increasingly tense in the last year with acute periods of panic and depression. Some evidence of an imminent paranoic schizophrenic breakdown in his recent attempts to be aggressive. He has little with which to endure his present crisis."

The patient had been raised as an only child. He had graduated from public school at fourteen, and from high school at eighteen. His hobby in high school was surveying, and he had made some instruments himself. He was also interested during this time in music and in radio mechanics. He did not dance until after he was out of high school, because he was shy. Beginning at age fifteen, he had sexual thoughts about his mother, about a physician in relation to his nurse, and also some centering around religious figures. A very inadequate sexual history is reported for his early adult years. Mr. C. was holding a factory job at a semiskilled level at the time of his first admission.

Following this first discharge he had made an overtly quiet adjustment. His job carried responsibility of a modest degree. Following his transfer to more ordinary work in the factory, symptoms set in anew. Complaints at the time of the second admission were: he cannot think well; feels depressed; cannot mix with people; failing vision; a tendency to panic; cannot make decisions; does not know what to say to people. It was during his second stay at the hospital that the present Rorschach test was obtained. An early diagnostic formulation during this period states: "The patient protects himself from psychologic trauma by withdrawal and fantasy. He has handled conflicts with defensive mechanisms that are inadequate but which tap almost every neurotic outlet conceivable. Personality development emerged in terms of highly schizoid defenses, and under the force of the environmental stress, these are seen to break down. Schizophrenic reaction, undifferentiated, in a schizoid personality; a pseudoneurotic schizophrenia."

Diagnostic notes after two more weeks of observation: depressive reaction, schizoid personality. A final diagnostic note, six months later, in the course of which the psychiatrist had seen the patient: schizophrenic reaction, schizoaffective type.

# CHAPTER 9

# Harry: Anxiety cripples a bright boy of six

## Response Record

### Figure I (6″)

'I don't know.

1. D F+ Hd   'Something without a head.

'A shadow.

2. W FY+ Hd, My   'Could be a ghost, people without a head.' (W. Form and
    4.0   shadings. 'Yeah, missing head and neck, could be a
ghost; two men ghosts, and one lady in the middle,
can't think, bad ghosts, could be from Mars.' Shape
only.)

### Figure II (25″)

'Now what!

'Colors, do I have to think of colors!

'Red and black, orange.

3. D F+ Cg   'Half of a hat, I can't think, now what?' (Each D 2.
'Could be half of a face, half clothes; black; can't
think.' Form only. 'Colors are too hard.')

4. W YF+ H P   'A shadow and a ghost and people.' (W. Shading and
    4.5   form.)

'I can't think of anything else. I don't know.'

### Figure III (5″)

5. D F+ Cg P   'That's a tie in the middle.' (D 3. Form only. 'A bow
tie.')

6. Ds Y Na   'A shadow with a part cut out in here and a hole in
both.' (D 11 with Dds; shading only.)

7. D F+ H P   'A shadow, people. (I could say just a shadow, women,
    3.0   high-heeled shoes; bad; I don't know. This one is hard.')

### Figure IV (1″)

8. W Y.M+ H   'A giant shadow, my only answer with this one.' (W.
    2.0   Shading and form. 'A giant from Mars, a bad one, all
giants are bad; it's black, only black ones are bad; he
has a whole bunch of giant ghosts.')

'A shadow of a giant. A ghost and that's all. Nothin'.
Color is black.'

*Figure V* (1″)

9. W F+ A P
1.0

'That's easy, a butterfly.' (W. Form only. 'Leave me alone! That's it!')
'A butterfly shadow.' ('Could be the shadow of the butterfly.')

10. W Y My

'A butterfly ghost.' (W. Shading only.) 'And that's all. A shadow of some kind of animal from Mars. And that's all. I don't know. What is it? I don't know.'

*Figure VI*

'That's too hard. I can't think (and repeats). A hard one certainly (deep sigh). I can't guess of anything.' ('I don't know. I could say never mind! I said, "Stop that business."' (Patient cries bitterly.)

*Figure VII* (7″)

11. D F+ H P

'Still too hard.
'Now, I get it, an Indian!' (D 2. Form only; only a feather of an Indian, can't find the whole thing.)
'A shadow of Indians.' ('Nothing.')
'Nothing.' ('Could be a design of an Indian, girls, unfriendly.')

*Figure VIII*

'All it can resemble is color: orange and pink, and blue and grey.
'I don't know. Too hard. Can't think of anything for that. It's real hard.' ('My mind! I'm getting all mixed up on this one. I notice the colors, nothing else.' He is very agitated.)

*Figure IX* (7″)

'Another hard one. Now, I get it.

12. W C Fi

'It is supposed to be fire.' (W. Color only. 'Fire, colored stuff. Logs make different colors, red, green, orange. Once in a while it burns that way.')
'That's all I get from this one. Colors! And shadows of them.
'Stop that business!' (Very irritable; hostile.)

*Figure X* (45″)

'Too much colors! The hardest one of all! A matter of fact too hard. (Encouraged.) You mean my brother! He is smarter than me!'

13. W C Art                  'Some kind of an Indian design.' ('The whole thing,
                             colors, just the colors.')
                             'Some kind of a shadow, an Indian shadow.' ('I still
                             meant the shadow of colors really.' W. Color only.)
                             (D 2: 'a boot'; D 5: 'pants'; D 1: 'I don't know'; D 9:
                             'very hard'; D 6: 'something, but I can't guess what.')
                          Total Time: 10 minutes, 7 seconds.
Likes best: X, because of the colors.
Likes least: I, because it is black.

### Response Summary

R: 13

| W | 7 | Y.M | 1 | H | 4 | F+ | 100% |
|---|---|---|---|---|---|---|---|
| D | 6 (s:1) | C | 2 | Hd | 2 | A | 8% |
| — | | Y | 2 | A | 1 | P | 5 |
| | 13 | YF | 1 | Art | 1 | S | 1, 8% |
| | | FY | 1 | Cg | 2 | Af r | 0.18 |
| Z f 5 | | F+ | 6 | Fi | 1 | L | 0.86 |
| Z sum 14.5 | | — | | Na | 1 | T/R | 46.78″ |
| Ap. W!! (D) | | | 13 | My | 1 | T/first R | 12.1″ |
| Seq. Irregular | | | | — | | Fln R | 0.72 |
| | | EB 1/3 | | | 13 | Fln T/first R | 12.43 |
| | | EA 4.0 | | | | | |

### Interpretation

A devastating anxiety characterizes this young child's entire mental life
and cripples all facets of his personality. Its effect is seen in the reduced
productivity, the withdrawal from both outward and emotional stimuli, and
in the monotopical content (ghosts and shadows), evidence of the painful
solution of his unbearable life situation. This anxiety-laden withdrawal
is already very extensive and gives an ominous tone to the entire problem
[1].*

The boy's intellectual life suffers especially: it is very constricted [2],
limited in range [3], and is essentially devoted to shutting out his surroundings [4]. This is the more serious in the light of his rich endowment (psychometric findings) [5]. While there is no serious disorder within his narrow
range (in the sense of pathologic thinking processes) [6], the entire record is
reduced to such an extent as to be essentially a rejection of his world; he
is withdrawing from the world [7] and is not making use of his abilities
[8]. Once, taken off guard, he permits himself freer response, and here his
perception becomes quite inaccurate [9]. The serious constriction in the

* Bracketed numbers refer to Notes on Interpretation, which for this chapter will
be found on pages 138–154.

thinking [10] as a whole, with the subsurface confusions [11] and over-all disregard of outside stimuli [12], is foreboding; unless redirected, it can settle into fixed reaction pattern of ego inadequacy and immature emotional reaction trends [13].

A serious deficiency is also present in this child's emotional life [14]. Harry permits himself little affective contact with others [15]. When he does express his feelings [16] they are primitively strong, explosive, impulsive [17]. He has not as yet learned to modulate his feelings by ego direction; he is either indifferent [18] or explosive. These two extremes in his emotional make-up, which are both disturbing, produce inner tensions which he cannot cope with [19].

While he would like to respond to others in greater measure [20], he is unable to do so [21], and this inability to respond is sensed by him as a threat. In fact, at one point [22] when confronted with the emotion-toned stimuli, he senses the threat of disintegration: "My mind! I'm getting all mixed up. I notice the colors and nothing else." We see here some evidence of latent, healthier trends [23], but these are not now available to him. It is to be noted that because of the lack of any modulated control over his strong feelings, tantrums and outbursts are to be expected [24].

This threat of unpredictable behavior is the greater because of the constricted fantasy life [25]. Harry permits himself little day-dreaming by which he could absorb some of his strong feelings inwardly [26] and thus reduce his tensions [27]. The reason for this freezing [28] of fantasy potential becomes only too clear when we see how much pain there is in all of his mental content [29]. What little fantasy he now permits himself is evoked by "father" imagery, which is a lead to the source of the anxiety [30].

Unbearable pain is the core of the anxiety, and while it is a chronic condition [31], it becomes especially intense at father and masculine imagery, the focus around which the maladjustment is hardening. The most important idea of his life—the parental image—is an extremely fearful one [32]. It is a shadow. The ambivalence he feels creeps in when he limits the class "bad giants" only to those that are black. Then he robs the image of all substance (ghosts). This is manifest in all of his human percepts: he makes them all ghosts, sometimes from Mars, keeping them distant, unreal [33]. In this way he solves his unbearable life experience. The maternal figure is also experienced as oppressive and threatening, but less so [34].

A mood of deep unhappiness is etched [35]. Harry is very sensitive to the grays and blacks of the test figures [36], projecting in this fashion his heavy, dysphoric mood. And while this mood, as passivity, is some countermeasure [37] against the expression of his strong feelings [38], it all only adds to the inner tensions [39], with the total effect being an inactive withdrawal from his unsatisfactory world [40, 41].

The present pattern of an essential freezing of the intellectual life [42], the flight from emotional contact with others [43], the indifference to environmental stimuli [44], the inner tensions springing from strong feelings urges, on the one hand, and dysphoric, oppressive emotions, on the other [45]—all result in a painful withdrawal from the world [46] which is now deeply a part of the character [47]. The evidence is, however, that it is still a reaction [48] to an unbearable situation [49] and that it can be redirected [50].

Psychotherapeutic exploration is imperative [51] from these test findings, with a view toward relieving tension and unhappiness [52]. The psychometric findings give clear evidence of assets [53]; in fact, Harry's full capacities are not even known [54]. The release of these, with concomitant ego-satisfying goals [55], can set going a benign, healthy course and growth [56]. But unless his situation improves, there is great danger that his present maladaptive trends will become more hardened [57] and that his general condition will worsen [58, 59].

## Notes on Interpretation

[1] This paragraph condenses the over-all findings. This child was referred by a pediatrician who wanted to know how serious the child's personality disorder was, whether to advise the family to consult a psychiatrist, and if so, how urgent the need. Under the press of his own practice, the psychiatrist may not have had time to read a full report immediately on receiving it and to digest its technical meanings. The psychologist, in such an instance, serves best in presenting at the outset a brief statement that tells the essence of the condition and makes clear the implications as to the next step. However, this practice of an initial concentrated summary is also a good one to follow in all reports to a consulting therapist.

[2] This very bright boy produces a total of only 13 responses. The mean for normal 6–9 year olds is 21.93 (SD 9.20). Bright children are much more productive than the average. This child can achieve the more difficult additive W's (R 2, R 4), but he misses the easier ones (in figures I, VI). He could then, so far as his intelligence is concerned, give more associations than he does. His is a much reduced performance at present, narrowed in range. His mental capacity is fettered.

[3] Harry is much preoccupied with the same topics, especially ghosts and shadows. We see here a personalized stereotypy. Yet, the scope of his interests, narrowly channelized though they now are, can be broader as is

obvious from some of the content (see below). Some of his ideas manifest the originality, even if only a gleam, to be expected from his intelligence.

[4] This shutting-out is an inference from (a) the data already noted, i.e., the fact that his achievement in the test is not consistent with his ability, and from (b) the evidence of a resentful attitude (concerning which, more below). We conclude that in his constriction he is reacting against the world, defending against "outrageous fortune." It is a maladjustive defense.

[5] His intelligence quotient is 132. It was obtained in a Stanford-Binet examination immediately following the Rorschach test.

[6] For examples of such formal thought pathology, see the Rorschach test protocol of the Orthogenic School boy (pp. 155–159). In that record, there is a circumstantial thought process in which a detail is a "chimney" because the rest of the figure "looks like soot." Also, the idea "someone shooting dust out of this" is suggested from the percept "a dusting gun," and " shooting fires" leads to the inference "a rocket going fast in the air" for the entire test figure. In the same record, there is a sample of confabulation in that "skeleton" and "blood sections on it" become in the Inquiry "a fox skeleton with some blood." For a discussion of such responses, see *Notes on Interpretation*, notes 4–7 on p. 173. Concerning perseverations, see Mrs. E., note 39, p. 112. The question can be raised whether Harry's "ghosts" and "shadows" are perseverations, but the certainty and strong feeling with which he so associates each time warrants our judging these as new percepts educed afresh from the particular stimulus figure before this boy at the time. Another kind of thought disorder consists of queer ideas, qualitatively so judged. The Orthogenic School boy's first test protocol (pp. 155f.) contains numerous examples of such idiosyncratic thinking.

[7] Rejecting the world is, of course, only a technique for withdrawing from it, a tactic in defense strategy. See note 4; also notes 42–47.

[8] Evidence independent of that in the Rorschach test are the psychometric findings (note 5). Internal evidence within the test that Harry's abilities are high includes the fact that his Z score of 14.5 is well above the mean of 7.15 (SD 7.40) at ages 6–9. Then, too, this total Z score of 14.5 is high for a response total of 13. Patients whose normal productivity is at this level have very low Z scores, not far from zero. They are either not capable of grasping meaningful relationships or they achieve only the simplest kind since they do not have the requisite drive. This boy's organizing ability is reflected in the kind which he does achieve: the additive W's (see note 2). They are what Rorschach has termed built-up W's, reported by him for his *intelligente*. In my own experience, subjects who produce the additive W are almost always of above average to superior

intelligence. Further, in his theme content Harry shows flashes of the original and the differentiated, and so discloses a potential that is straining at the prison-like constriction. Among these gleams of originality are the "Indian" in figure VII and the "log fire" in figure IX. The "Mars" association in figures IV and V may not be out of the ordinary in our space travel age, especially since the topic is by now an established reality in the "comics," a medium which has no doubt been part of this child's experience; thus, it cannot be labeled a differentiating and original idea. On the other hand, the "Indian design" for figure X is such. Art percepts of various kinds are not unusual here, although they are usually the work of more sprightly minds. A specific "Indian design" is rare and differentiating. We see in these scattered samples the ore to be mined out of a mentality represented by an intelligence quotient of 132.

[9] See the associations to figures II and III. Technically his perception here is accurate and the responses are scored F+. But the deviations stick out: in R 3, in "half a hat ... half a face ... half clothes;" and in R 6 in the "shadow ... and a hole in both." There has been a breach in the ego's critical controls.

[10] Referring to the low quantity of associational activity in general, rather than to the thinking specifically.

[11] See the rapid interchange of percepts and their fusion in the Inquiry for R 2. He does this again in R 3 and in R 10. The process is similar in R 7, although the varying ideas are bound together by one unifying motif. In fact, throughout the several flighty perceptions, the basic forms remain accurate: a core of firm ego can be detected underneath this boy's agitation.

[12] As indicated in the lamba index of 0.86. This is a very low finding (see p. 75). It would indicate that Harry is inadequately focusing on external or environmental events, so much is he in the grip of his own emotions. Measuring Harry's lambda index by the formula all-F/R, it comes to 46.2; findings for normal 6–9 year olds are 78.40 as the mean (SD 12.25). He is functioning inadequately in respect to this trait.

[13] Is this schizophrenia? But it is best to avoid using this ominous word in a report, especially in the early portion of a report. When the test findings build up to an unequivocal schizophrenia I do call it that after having detailed the data, but the wisest rule is to let the data speak. The term "schizophrenia" is too fraught with a sense of finality, too identified with a diagnostic land of no return. The therapist, for his part, may well find salvageable assets in his patient, or his own view of the person may highlight benign trends which the Rorschach test description has missed or minimized.

[14] We turn now to the externalized feeling reactions, those stirred up by the lively toned stimuli and understood as being of pleasurable affective

quality, i.e., the color-determined associations. The term "emotional" in the report actually covers too much semantic space, since it refers also to the painful feelings. The words "affective contact" in the following sentence are usually understood, however, as indicating a reaching outward of feelings, with attendant pleasurable experience. I may seem to be laboring a point excessively here. Yet, communication is the first task of a report and clarity is the first need in communication. At the same time, the practical demands on the reporting psychologist's time, as on that of the therapist reading the report, necessitate economy in the formulated message. Happy the writer with a talent for writing so as to meet the needs both of economy and of clarity.

[15] Harry uses the color determinant only twice. Even more significant is the extremely low affective ratio: 0.18. The mean is 0.53 (SD 0.23) for the 6–9 year age. He is almost entirely incapable of any pleasurable experience. The full rejection of one of the color cards of the test (VIII) supports this reasoning. However, there are also contrary indications, as will be seen in the notes immediately following.

[16] In R 12 and 13, the boy's two color-determined responses. Here is a sign that Harry can achieve some feeling contact with his environment, as any association scored as color-determined, whether in whole or in part, indicates.

[17] Harry's color associations are scored without any F component. Once his emotions are set free, they are altogether free, without ego restraint. The feeling contact with the environment (note 16) is achieved, but it is an egocentric contact, one in which the environment's feelings are being disregarded; hence, the contact is primitive, explosive, impulsive.

[18] "Incapable" would have been a more accurate word here than "indifferent." This boy has the urge to relate emotionally (see note 20). In fact, the trait exerts much pressure within him. He repeatedly reaches for the colors but fails to weave them into any percepts. Tantalus-like, he has the thirst for emotional relationship and the related gratification, but as he moves towards the waters which could satisfy him, they always recede. (See notes 19 and 21.)

[19] Harry betrays these tensions in every test card that contains color. In figure II his immediate reaction is one of annoyance or resentment explicitly directed at the color. Concerning his defensive flight from the affect here aroused, see note 22. He delays long before verbalizing a scorable association, a typical color-shock pattern which is, in turn, evidence of the anxiety which is here mounting. In the first of the all-color cards, VIII, the child's inhibition is complete: he rejects without scorable association. He is explicit in verbalizing the color shock (see note 22). The disturbance was sufficiently severe to emerge in motor behavior, since the

examiner makes a special note here of the child's agitation. Similar feelings
break out in figure IX as irritability. His one scorable response here, "fire,"
is an anxiety motif. A feeling of resignation: "That's all I get for this one,"
is then verbalized; it is of a kind found in patients with depressive mood
tones. Then he discloses his unsettlement in an open counterattack: "Stop
that business."

In figure X Harry relates his difficulty at associating more specifically to
the colors as such. Significantly, he lays open to view here a symptomatic
thought: the brother and Harry's sense that he is inferior. His initial response time is here the slowest for the eight test figures to which he associated with scorable responses. A tendency to reject this figure shows up:
"Too hard," and only more encouragement by the examiner elicited a response, which turns out to be an original and one of his few healthy ones.
Color shock is in evidence in each of three color figures: over and above his
chronic anxiety condition, the child is acutely vulnerable to feelings stirred
up by exciting stimuli. Such vulnerability due to color shock, I take to
reflect the anxiety which the excitement arouses. My further reasoning is
that we are seeing in these anxiety disturbances exemplification of Fenichel's theory that the patient feels threatened by his own impulses.

[20] The colors interest the child enough so that he attends to them in
all the figures (except III). In one instance, he manifests apparent pleasurable affect at his success in associating to a color figure in spite of the difficulty which it presents to him: figure IX, "Another hard one; now, I get
it," and an association follows. The "Indian design" in figure X is a socially
healthy theme and promises at least a latent ability in this boy for satisfying interrelationships with his fellows. It will be noted finally that the
test card which he prefers is X, and the reason is "the colors," i.e., a tinge
of cheerful mood. Thus, evidence for that affective reaching commented on
in note 18.

[21] See note 15 concerning the low affective ratio. Viewed in the light
of the color shock and of the anxiety which produces shock, we are justified
in reasoning here concerning the deadly effects of his emotions in denying
to Harry the use of his high intelligence.

[22] In figure VIII. It would be difficult to formulate the lethal work of
color shock in undoing intellectual efficiency more clearly than this bright
child so spontaneously does. Truly, "out of the mouths of babes..."

[23] These have been indicated in note 20.

[24] The response determined entirely by color, without influence of
form, is generically the test's representative of unrestrained affectivity. We
could so interpret such an association out of the context of any whole
Rorschach test protocol, but it is axiomatic that no response is viewed by
itself. The potential for tantrums and outbursts to which the report refers

is indicated in his two undiluted color associations, but only in the context of his entire reaction pattern. As we have seen, this pattern is one in which the feelings are holding strong sway over the ego, with moments of actual outbreaks.

[25] Only one response scored M (in R 8). The question arises whether there is not also an M in R 2. Harry's language in R 2 appears to be not much different from that in R 7. However, it differs in the degree to which the child is emphasizing the characteristic "bad" in R 2 as compared to R 7. In the former it is mentioned once and as if parenthetically; in the latter it is emphasized again and again. Rorschach's explicit rule is to score M for human-form action. From some of his examples of scored M, however, we can infer that humans characterized by attitudes connoting action are so scored. In Harry's R 2, I would have to assume too much from his phrase "bad ghosts" if I were to score M. That is, I would be assuming what needs to be proved. In R 7, the three times repetition of "bad" and the four times repetition of the percept "giant," known to be phobic, puts the association within Rorschach's rule for proven M. The mean for M in the average 6–9 year old is 0.87. Harry, with his intelligence quotient of 132, is no average child. Then, too, there is just enough vestigial evidence in his Rorschach test record of a differentiated mentality, a mentality from which to expect imagination.

[26] Fantasy living serves as an internal shock absorber. It is to the personality what steel springs are to the automobile. The M or fantasy person habitually turns his feelings inward; he is the introvert; hence, the feelings do not have to break out (see ref. 57, pp. 85f.). Harry is now lacking in fantasy life, and as he experiences rough going in life, he will react not smoothly but with a jolt.

[27] "Reducing tensions" is not to say that the patient is relieved of his strong feelings. These feelings persist, since the M experience consists of just that. It differs from the feeling indicated in the color-determined association only in the direction that it takes, inward rather than outward. The tension it reduces is that generated when the ego has to maintain the effort to keep the feelings from expressing themselves dangerously, an anxiety-laden situation against which the ego defends. With the feelings absorbed in inner living the patient is safe from the kind of externalizing that will bring trouble. In human society, M is an adaptive psychologic structure in the Darwinian sense.

[28] The low quantity of M is itself the result of a defensive maneuver in my interpretation, and hence the terms "freezing of fantasy" and "permits himself." My conclusion has been that Harry cannot face the horrid monsters which inhabit his unconscious and so he locks them deep in the subterranean passages of his mind. Two other possibilities, other than

defense motives, need to be considered in explaining this child's low quantity of M: (a) the sheer devastation of his mental life has also shattered his ability to imagine; and (b) he may simply be constitutionally incapable of M. Which of the three is the fact cannot be known in this child's present disorganized state. Only in the circumstance that his course changes to a healthy one and that he may then be studied again by psychologic test methods could these questions be definitely answered.

[29] The "ghosts," the "shadows," the "giants," the bodily deformations, in men and in animals, speak for themselves.

[30] In structure, the M in figure IV is sound, being accurate (+), ascribed to a whole human, and perceived in a whole blot figure frequently seen as M-determined. One may generalize that any M which is scored W M+ H in figure IV (as also in figures I, II, III, V, and VII) is of sound structure. Judged only on this basis Harry is capable of healthy imagination. But the structure in his R 7 includes also the Y determinant, and this is sufficiently prominent in Harry's association to warrant setting it before the M in the scoring formula, i.e., it is the primary determinant. The fearful emotion thus alters the structure into an unhealthy one. From this fusion of Y with the M, the accent on the Y, and the painful affect that so saturates the fantasy experience, I infer that it is intensely lived. However, it cannot be classified among those M which, by the Levy scale, are energetically lived. The rating by that scale would be 1–2. As I have noted elsewhere,[11] the high intensity of the emotion in the M is in some responses indicated by techniques other than the rating on the Levy scale. These are, one, the theme itself in the association or its elaboration, or both; for example, "a flat fish, a flounder; malevolent looking profile, an angry individual." The patient continued, in the Inquiry: "Looks like he's blowing a gale out of his mouth." The scoring is D M− A. On the basis of the amount of overt bodily activity, I would have had to estimate the degree of movement by the Levy energy scale as low, 1 or 2. My rating, dictated by the terms "malevolent," "angry," and "blowing a gale" actually was 6. Secondly, there are the fusions of M with other emotional determinants: frequently M.C; occasionally M.Y, as in Harry's response; more rarely, M.V. To be consistent in my use of the scale my rating of Harry's M remains low, owing to the lack of overt activity, i.e., 1–2. At the same time, I am judging the feelings which he is here investing as high. The rule may be stated that all M's with a high activity rating by Levy's scale indicate that strong feelings are being lived in the fantasy, but a low rating does not in itself point to the absence of strong feelings.

[31] It is chronic since it is not restricted to one, two, or even three points in the test that particularly stir up anxiety while the response pattern in the rest of the record remains relatively integrated and normal. Such are the

protocols usually produced by most patients in anxiety states, including severe ones. In Harry the entire associational production is shot through with the signs of an abiding fear state. But see note 32.

[32] The anxiety in figure IV is all-absorbing, excludes any vestige of thought content not related to the giant that is bad, declares an inexorable conviction that "all giants are bad." His single response here is out of unconscious layers (M) and so is not of the world of reality, and the emotion that fuses into it is a painful one (Y). Concerning the intensity of the experience represented by this blend, M.Y, see note 30. We infer that Harry at times lives the awe, the "not me" experience described by Sullivan.[67] Harry can suffer panicky dreams. Consistent with this fearful state of mind is the mood reflected in his language. There is utter discouragement and finality in the resigned phrase: "My only answer," and similarly in the "nothin' " formula, although this may also be defensive (see note 37). Then, too, there is the child's explicit identification of "black" with "bad." Here is evidence that this color denotes the emotion which is usually associated with it in our culture, evidence the more impressive because issuing out of the mouth of this unsophisticated child (compare note 22).

For an example in fictional literature of the relationship between a color and mood the reader is referred to Chapter 42 of Melville's *Moby Dick*. The mood that Melville there conjures up is the eerie feeling and impending doom inherent in the book's all-dominating figure, the great white whale. The color symbol here is white, and Melville's phrases and allusions include "ghastly whiteness," "abhorrent mildness," "white-shrouded bear or shark," "White Steed of the Prairies" (of American Indian tradition), the "White Squaw" of the Southern Seas, the "marble pallor" (of the dead), the "hue of the shroud," "the snowy mantle around phantoms, all ghosts arising in milk white fog," and so throughout the pages of this chapter Melville piles one aspect of nature upon another, invoking now perception through the ear, now through the eye. "The muffled rollings of a milky sea . . . the bleak rustlings of the festooned frosts of mountains . . . the desolate shiftings of the windrowed snows of prairies," and he closes his chapter, "and of all these things the albino whale was the symbol."

For Harry the dominating fact of figure IV is that "it's black, only black ones are bad," and he concludes "color is black." Such is the one thought and the emotions agitating it which are stirred up in our young patient by this very masculine figure. Whether it is rightly or wrongly called a "father" figure,[27] the fact is that the anxiety which it liberates, whether as structural reaction or in theme, is frequently validated as related to the father: he is a stimulus awakening ideas in which the relationship with him is a dynamic factor. The great amount of affect which this test figure generates in Harry is grounds for the hypothesis, to be tested in the clinical exploration of the boy, that his relationship with his father has now reached a critical pass. Evidence at another point supports this reasoning, i.e., in what happens to Harry at figure VI with its phallic imagery; there is a total blotting out of his mental processes. He complains about the difficulty set up by this test card and about his inability to think; he gives motor expression to his pained state of mind (the sigh); he manifests resentful rejection at the end of his free-association effort and, with mounting intensity, in the Inquiry. Finally the full collapse comes: he cries bitterly. He has been unable to produce any scorable association to this test figure, and we cannot be sure whether this is neurotic inhibition or more pathologic blocking (in Bleuler's sense; ref. 20, pp. 32–36). Why this severe mental crippling by figure VI? Is it produced by the blot's phallic contours? Or by a more impersonal mounting pressure of anxiety in the patient? The heavy anxiety in figure IV lends weight to the first of these two possibilities, i.e., that ideas related to the male are very threatening to him. But the question, so far as the Rorschach test goes, must remain an open one.

The argument for specificity in figures IV and VI (their masculine significance) has support in the child's differential reaction to the other figures of like quality, those that release anxiety from superego sources, the all-black ones. In figure V he gives vent immediately to one of his few expressions not weighted down with gloom: "That's easy." For the first time in the test he experiences relief, although the general tone remains consistent with the heaviness of his test record throughout. The resignation formula ("That's all") gives a depressive flavor, which is reflected also in the protestation of inability ("I don't know"). He vigorously repels the examiner ("Leave me alone."). Structurally, one response has to be scored as determined by the indicator of anxiety and passivity (Y). Also, there is intellectual dysfunction ("a butterfly ghost"), i.e., regression, which is a sign that the ego has slipped. Yet, neither in the extent to which it is mobilized nor in its intensity does Harry's oppressive state approach that which he suffers at figure IV. In figure VII the unhappy reaction is similarly mild, although he complains of difficulty here too. One of his hitherto preoccupying themes flits across his mind ("shadow"), he tends to reject ("nothing"), is unique in seeing the human profiles here as "unfriendly," and is confabulating, i.e., the ego is slipping again, in seeing the profiles both as an "Indian" and as "girls." Yet, in this figure, and in this one alone among the ten, the boy can express what seems like satisfying affect, "Now, I get it." As in figure V, the quantity and intensity of painful affect are much reduced as compared with that in the other figures, especially in IV and VI. Were the anxiety in figure VI impersonal and the result of mounting tension, it should mount even higher in the following figure, VII. But

the contrary is what we find. So, Harry is reacting differentially. In figure
I the mood is also a heavy laden one, about at the level of figure IV. Initial
shock is here one of the operating factors. For another, following Bohm's
theory,[21] we are seeing in the disturbances at both figures I and IV a pattern
characteristic of boys reacting with hostile affect against the father. All
in all, chronic and severe as Harry's anxiety is, he is more vulnerable to
some than to other stimuli; some of the ideas stirred up in him upset him
more than others. In the long run this is a salutary finding. It uncovers an
ego sensitive about certain issues. Certain treatment implications follow.
Where there is ego there is hope.

[33] For the possibility that in these percepts Harry is using defense
tactics, see note 28.

[34] Concerning the difference in quality and in intensity of reaction to
figure VII as compared with figure IV, I comment fully above in note 32.
The additional observation is made in order to call attention to Harry's
more benign mental state in figures VII and V in that in both of these figures he sees the P form. To be sure, he contaminates and he confabulates
in V but he is capable of accurate percepts here, and in figure VII there is
even a dash of originality ("Indians").

[35] See notes 29, 31, and more especially 32.

[36] Referring not alone to test figures IV, V, VI, VII, and also I, but to
all the shading nuances throughout the test and the influence of the dark
tones on the child's associational themes. He even sees shadow effects in
the all-color figures IX, X. In the structural summary this shows up in the
high accent quantitatively on Y: five Y-determined associations out of a
total R of thirteen, and of these five, two are without modulation by form
(R 4) and in one the shading element is dominant over the form (R 8).

[37] The depressive mood together with the behaviors which it breeds,
passivity and resignation, are such countermeasures. This is to say that
passivity and resignation are not the absence of behavior; they are positive
activity. To not do some one thing, such as attack, is to do something else,
e.g., stand still, play possum, or run. Any of these expedients saves the individual from engaging in an action which could be destructive to him. A
depressive reaction is thus a defensive one, ego-motivated. This thinking is
consistent with the psychoanalytic theory of depression which sees these
conditions as the work of the superego, i.e., a specific form of ego.

[38] Harry provides evidence at several points of swirling feelings on the
verge of outbreak. See his vigorously resentful, attacking expressions in
figures V, VI, and IX. He projects the aspect "unfriendly" onto the "girls"
of figure VII, the more unique since when girls are seen here they are almost
always perceived in a light and playful aspect. Concerning the strong out-

going feelings indicated in the two color-determined associations (R 10, 11), see note 17. The content in one of these is that destructive phenomenon, fire.

[39] Referring in the first instance to the anxiety which so saturates this test record. Then, see again note 37. It is clear that painful affect is implicit in the mood, the passivity and the resignation, and is a defensive measure of the ego. Thirdly, the feeling pressures (described in note 38) have not vaporized and so are still seeking an outlet. The patient is thus experiencing this competition between two kinds of feelings, of differing affective qualities, which can only make for emotional turbulence.

[40] This is to say that Harry's entire reaction pattern is to a world that has been imposing only frustrations and their related pain on him. It is the total adjustment at which he has arrived, the net result of disastrous events in his environment and the confusion which they have brought about in a boy at the green-stick age of under six. One may theorize that it is defense of a very pathologic kind, but in the absence of such maladjustment, the alternative might well be catatonic immobility.

[41] The original report did not describe the defenses. In a child so young and so disturbed as Harry is, they are of especial importance in offering a clue to the ego potential. They may help to answer the question whether we need to think of schizophrenia in view of the fact that he is so storm-tossed emotionally and so channelized in his thought content. To the extent that we can detect defenses in the picture, to that extent ego has been operative and the outlook is perhaps less ominous. But the question will not only be are there defenses, but also what are they like? how pathogenic? how adaptive?

Harry's outstanding defensive maneuver is one of resistance to and rejection of his world. He may take this attitude to the entire situation presented to him (the entire test card), as in the "I don't know" on being presented with figure I; or to some aspect of the situation (the colors), as in figure II; a general negation, as in figure IV, "nothin' "; a direct attack (on the examiner), as in figure V; or general negation, as in figure VI. To what extent this child's reaction is rejection, to what extent it is a flight from or evasion of stimuli, is a moot question. The complaints about the difficulties which he experiences at figures VIII, IX, and X point to a positive rejection; his color namings at several points without color-determined associations are examples of avoidances, what Rorschach identified as "color shy."

A most arresting question is that opened up by Harry's adhesion to the themes "shadow" and "ghost." As phobic themes they must be binding some deeper, more unbearable anxiety. As "shadows" they also testify to the lack of substance in these phobic images, however, and so Harry is here engaging in denials of his fears. The "nothing" expressions in figures IV and VII may similarly be negating the anxious affects which he experiences. The very fast time for first response in figures IV and V looks like over-reaction. We may also be seeing here a nice example of undoing: the patient rids himself of the affects which the stimulus arouses in him by quickly disposing of the stimulus by jumping into the task which it presents without delay.

Reflecting a regard for precision is his qualifying of his descriptions in R 2, 3, and 6, while in figure VII this need results in the narrowing down of his vision, vitiating what was first a more liberated response (the feather, which is an Adx, after seeing the entire "Indian"). Stemming from the same source is the apologetic, "Once in a while it burns that way" (IX). The complete shutting-off of associational activity in figures VI and VIII raises the question of whether massive inhibition is needed by Harry to protect him from the anxieties generated by these two figures. If so, it would be over-reaction of hysteric proportions; for the theory as to the blackouts under such conditions the reader is referred to Fenichel.[32] Concerning passivity and resignation as defensive measures see note 37, again extreme measures although not to the point of total blacking-out.

Harry, thus, defends against the unhappy realities of his world by withdrawing from it, rejecting and sometimes attacking it, denying some of the painful affects which he suffers, and binding his anxieties in phobic thinking. The phobic thinking is the most severe of his symptoms. He does not go to the more pathologic extreme of paranoid projection. He does not twist his realities. His ego takes losses, heavy ones, in terms of much reduced, impoverished living, but he does not regress, although he is under a push toward doing so (see notes 2–12).

[42] Concerning the evidence that he has abilities, see notes 5 and 8. Concerning their reduction to the point of freezing, see notes 2–4, inclusive.

[43] This retreat before the emotion-toned stimuli has been described in notes 15, 18, and 21.

[44] Referring to the low lambda index; and see note 12. It should be clear that the term "indifference" does not here mean indifference to reality such as is indicated by inaccurate perception or distorted percepts. The indifference indicated in the lambda index is the not noticing of relevant facts in one's environment. Those that are noticed may be seen quite accurately.

[45] See notes 19 and 39.

[46] As shown in exposition of the defenses, note 41, and see especially the concluding remarks in this note.

[47] This is an inference from the indications in the test record generally as to how extensive this child's unhappiness is, how saturated he is

with pathogenic affect and pathologic thought content. Refer also to notes 28, 29, 31, 36, and the related text.

[48] It is a reaction rather than a condition of arrested growth or a regression, i.e., the pattern is of a neurotic not schizophrenic structure. We deduce this from the color shock, especially in figures II and VIII, and from the shading shock, especially in figures IV and VI. Even though this boy's pathologic state of mind is chronic, within this general pattern he does react differentially to varied stimuli. See also note 32.

[49] To what extent it is the pernicious external situation that is calling forth Harry's reaction, to what extent it is his own excitement, is something to be established from his social history and from study of his personality. The essential contribution in the test finding is that as a *reaction*, it is ego sensitivity to worldly values, and when the ego is sensitive the patient can be redirected. Treatment is in order.

[50] The *Interpretation* for Harry, including the comments on treatment, are reproduced in this book exactly as sent to the referring pediatrician. Certain additional observations can be made, however, concerning Harry's total adjustment picture by using the list of 170 behavior items in my "trait universe" (see comments p. 210 on the application of this instrument to clinical evaluation). Those items in what was formulated as a research tool I find now a constant influence on interpretation. In the observations that follow I am exemplifying the use of the trait universe for the Rorschach test by translating the behaviors of the one into the other directly. These are:

He is uncommunicative, makes little effort at verbal rapport; this is seen principally in the low productivity and also in his refusing outright, on examiner's urging, to attempt further associations.

Unique attitudes and beliefs are aspects of the boy's adaptation; this is inferred from the channelization of the thought content into the individualized ideas of the ghosts, shadows, and related themes.

He construes "reality" in terms of his own needs. This is also judged from the content with which he clothes his otherwise accurate percepts. This behavior item is manifested in a totally different way in some patients: they totally misshape the "realities" at which they are looking and see them in a fashion determined by their inner needs; that is, they misconstrue reality. Their Rorschach test percepts are largely F— and, depending on how serious the misconstruction, are signs of schizophrenic perception. It is one of the critical findings in Harry that unique though his ideas are, they are formally accurate. He is not schizophrenic.

He is socially withdrawn, i.e., withdrawn from, or inadequate with respect to, social participation. This observation must be made of this child in view of his resistance to his environment as general defense strategy (see notes 40 and 41) and his absorption in his special thought content. The caution is in order, however, that his withdrawal is not the affectless asociality of the schizophrenic or the equally affectless antisociality of the psychopathic personality. On the contrary, Harry's withdrawal is consequent on his need to be in contact, a need which has been defeated. See again concerning his affectivity and notes 19–22, inclusive; also note 32.

Persistent, unresolvable conflicts are in evidence. This states, in fact, the core of Harry's present maladjustment. It is clear from (a) the heavily oppressive mood that saturates the response pattern; (b) the findings of neurotic shock and anxiety shock, which are evidence of conflict (see note 48); and (c) the intense anxiety activated by father imagery (see note 32).

All these items stem, it will be noted, from one common underlying source trait: self-absorption. This is one of Harry's characteristics in his present adjustment. Another set of items in the trait universe applicable to Harry and describing his social adjustment derive from another source trait: self-deprivation. These items follow:

Excessive repression (to a pathologic degree) of gratifying images. The absence of gratifying imagery is only too pathetically clear in Harry's test record.

Inability to initiate activity. We infer this from the serious inadequacy of his ego at this time, which is, in turn, indicated in his intellectual reaction pattern (see note 42).

He permits himself little pleasure or enjoyment. This is found in the test especially in his inability to respond to the lively toned stimuli, i.e., the color cards.

His thinking is impoverished, as indicated in the almost monotopical restriction of the thought content, a personalized stereotypy (see p. 213).

There is withdrawal from social contact, but not into autistic fantasy. This is an important differential: the presence or absence of fantasy living. In its absence, as in Harry's case, the feelings cannot be absorbed inwardly and so they find outward expression, which is so manifest in his test protocol.

Potentialities for pleasure and learning are hindered. The hindrances to pleasurable experience are apparent in his response pattern to the color figures, in the tensions and interferences that develop at these stimuli (see again notes 19–22, inclusive). The hindrances to learning are set up by his impaired intellectual response pattern (see notes 2, 3, 8, and 10). An additional observation is in order here concerning his approach type (Ap): excessive accent on the whole (W), with partial or total disregard of everything else (D, Dd); in psychological terms, inefficient holistic perception and failure to discriminate the meaningful details and minutiae of one's environment. Persons so reacting are not able to adapt to varied conditions —they do not change, they do not learn.

Interests are narrowed (relative to ability). The discrepancy is very sharp between Harry's probable ability (notes 5 and 8) and the extreme narrowing of his thought content.

Two other source traits account for the remaining overt behaviors that characterize the social adaptation pattern. One of these source traits we call "restitutional." It includes the items: "delusional thoughts–systematized, hallucinatory." Does this Rorschach test with its preoccupation with ghosts and shadows indicate delusions and hallucinations on Harry's part? I could not in the light of the underlying form accuracy arrive at such a conclusion. The point at which I had most to suspect it was in figure V in which "a butterfly ghost" is essential contamination and archaic thought content. I did have to ask here how much does this child slip into the unreal, primitive world of earliest childhood? How much does he so retreat as a defense against unhappy realities? The response pattern as a whole did not warrant my so concluding. The other source trait consists of constructive life objectives. The items relevant to Harry are:

Drive and energies are mastered by intellectual control. This is indicated principally in the accuracy of his percepts but also in the constricted reaction pattern, i.e., the control is excessive, pathogenically.

In the realm of aspiring and achieving, in figure IX Harry is at first stopped by the difficulty—"Another hard one"—but he immediately reacts with apparent pleasurable affect to his ability to solve the difficulty, "Now, I get it." This is a trace only but, especially in the light of Harry's generally despairing attitude, it is a spark that a therapist certainly will want to know about.

Two items, closely related, are that he is capable of real pleasure and enjoyment. There is emotional warmth and the ability to sympathize with others. The response pattern to figure X offers this clue. For one thing, there is his moderately original association, "an Indian design." What mental living survives the holocaust of the color shock is of original potential and of socially satisfying cast. Secondly, as Harry informs us following the test administration, he prefers figure X "because of the colors," and so gives evidence of appropriate reaction to these pleasure-toned stimuli. Compare also note 19. These are still not much more than sparks but they are in this important sphere of the emotions and they give promise that the therapeutic effort can fan them into a healthy reaching out to the environment.

[51] This is strong language. It is dictated in the first instance by the child's obvious suffering. But the examining psychologist cannot permit

his sympathy for the patient to carry him away. He owes an obligation not only to the patient but also to the therapist. Into what sort of a treatment problem is he steering his referring colleague? In evaluating Harry's treatability the questions which his psychological test findings, Rorschach and psychometric, open up are really a summary of the major treatment problems (Chapters 11 and 16). Should any treatment effort be invested in Harry? Does he have personality resources which he can bring into play? And does he have the ego reserve such that he will exert himself in activating his resources? Assuming he can be treated, at what level shall it be? A surface, supportive psychotherapy? A deep, psychoanalytic treatment? Environmental only?

[52] That is, the immediate objective is the sheerly humane one of healing, of softening and binding up a psychological wound.

[53] Helping to answer thus the question raised in note 51 concerning personality resources; see also note 42. For evidence as to ego assets, see notes 41, 48, 49.

[54] High as the psychometric rating (I.Q. 132) is, the question is in order whether in this child's distraught state it is a representative finding. Concerning evidence within the Rorschach test finding of more abilities than Harry is now using, see note 8. The EA score of 4.0 is also a promising note, for a productivity of only 13.

[55] The planning of such goals, of course, becomes routine once the therapist has the information as to (a) the patient's assets as well as his liabilities; (b) the resources in the immediate family; and (c) the resources in their environment, i.e., the community in which the patient and his family live. When, as with Harry, the transactions among the family members are of the essence of the child's illness, they must obviously be subjected to the treatment impact. In a broken family, as the present one is, father and mother cannot be a treatment unit. The problem becomes a mental health opportunity for the psychiatric social worker.

[56] The word "can" here may be begging the question. It assumes what needs to be proved. In any event the course will be watched and therapy directed and redirected as indicated by the course.

[57] The character is already extensively involved in this illness; the pathology has made deep inroads into the child, as must be apparent from the exposition, especially in the notes, so far. Without the intervention of treatment the present maladjustment is bound to become more and more deeply entrenched, and any future treatment effort is bound to be less successful in effecting change.

[58] What would this worsened condition be? As we have seen above, the ominous word schizophrenia can be held off. The danger that faces Harry as this Rorschach test now sees him is of fixing into a neurotic character, a

reaction pattern in which, in Fenichel's language, "the personality does not appear to be uniform or disturbed only by one or the other interrupting event, but openly so torn or deformed and often so involved in the illness that one cannot say at what point the 'personality' ends and the 'symptom' begins" (ref. 32, p. 18).

[59] As for the transference possibilities, the Rorschach test describes a patient with all the ingredients: conflict, suffering, emotional fluidity; readiness for hostilty, so much so that he discharged some of it toward the examiner; and an agitating anxiety focused on the father image. What more can the therapist require?

## Clinical Note

This boy, under six years of age, was referred by his pediatrician who had become concerned over the child's being easily upset, saucy, argumentative, and sometimes inclined to strike out. He was extremely jealous of a brother fifteen months younger. The patient was described as "emotional, sensitive, does not thrive on competition."

The parents were separated. The father had inflicted severe physical punishment on the patient. At the time of this report, the boys seldom saw their father, and they became noticeably wound up when he visited.

The home is described as "a woman's world." The children have no close contacts with other adults. But the mother reports she is now calmer and better able to cope with Harry so that "he won't grow up a peculiar character."

# CHAPTER 10

# Clyde's schizophrenia in three Rorschach test patterns

## A. First Rorschach test. Clyde at age nine years, seven months.

### Response Record

#### Figure I (8″)

|  |  |
|---|---|
|  | 'This is a real house ... I like to come to people's houses. |
| 1. D YF+ War | 'This looks like one of ... like the Korean War. I think it is the shape of smoke, coming from a bomb (smoke from war). |
| 2. D F+ Hd,An | 'I ... maybe kind of like the bottom of a skeleton of a person, from Korea. Just an old Korean person. |
|  | 'Smoke from a big campfire or a house on fire. |
|  | 'Some black ink spilled.' ('Blackness'.) |
| 3. W Y Ink | 'Someone had tracked some ink all over. Just track it around like that. |
| 4. D F− Na | 'It looks like soot (W, except D 4) in a chimney' (D 4). ('Soot in it.') |
|  | 'There is not much else.' |

#### Figure II (10″)

|  |  |
|---|---|
| 5. D F− A | 'Oh ... it looks like an animal.' ('Part of a bear ... the spine.' Both D 6). |
| 6. D C.Y Bl,Fi | '... being slaughtered or killed in war.' ('The blood.') |
|  | 'The red part being fire, and the black being smoke. |
|  | 'It looks like red and black ink being spilled. |
| 7. D VF+ Ls,As 3.0 | 'It looks like a kind of a sunset (red sun) against black smoke from a fire or something.' ('I thought of some- |
| 8. D C.Y Fi | thing [D 3]: a funny sunset with an eclipse ... the black part ... with the moon eclipsing over the sun.') |
| 9. W CF+ Fi | 'A bomb, blowing with fire (D 6, D 3, D 2). |
|  | 'It might be a bunch of firecrackers blowing off at once.' ('Red, shooting fire') '... ten tons of T.N.T. bombs ex- ploding.' |

* Only the third of Clyde's Rorschach test records is analyzed in detail with the explanatory notes. Considerations of economy dictated omitting the analyses for the first two records, since it would have meant duplicating much description for the same person. But the course over time which the three records trace out is of highest interest, and I am therefore including the full protocols, scorings, and interpretations for all of Clyde's tests.

*Figure III* (10″)

10. D C.Y Fi     'Well ... that looks kind of like a ... (12″) fire (D 3) giving kind of smoke' (remainder of figure acts out). (Always seems abstracted.)

11. D C Bl     'Blood left around.' ('Some persons that got hurt by a car collision.') 'Some black ink.' ('Blood over black dirt, silly bomb.' And he repeats. 'See this scar? I stumbled over something.')

12. D F − Ar     'Black soot and fire flying up the chimney.' (Chimney: D 6 with D 11.)

13. D F − An     'Some blood around, something like intestines (D 9) or something.' ('They look like that.')

14. D Y Na     'Let's see ... smoke around some black dirt and tiny bits of fire.
'It must look like black stuff around blood ...

15. D F − An     'A piece of skeleton with some ...
16. D C Bl     '... blood sections on it' (red D's). ('A fox skeleton
    4.0     and some blood.')

*Figure IV* (1″)

17. W Y War     'Oh! Gosh! A big bomb that exploded the whole state of Korea.' ('The smoke ... whew!')

18. W F+ AP     'A piece of bear skin' (W). ('The back of it, the way it
    2.0     looks. It looks quite sloppy sometimes.')
'Some smoke over a small portion of the city' (W).
'A bomb exploded out in the alley.'

19. W F − An,Sc     'A big, gigantic skeleton ... a piece of dinosaur skele-
    2.0     ton' (W).

20. W Y Na, War     'Some kind of dust and black dirt and silt, going over an army camp.
'Smoke ... from ... gosh ... a campfire. Someone puts the fire out and makes all that smoke. Soot in the fireplace.
'It might be a piece of a bear skeleton.
'Silt that has been washed up from a flood ... gone over the flood wall.
'Smoke passing over a little bit of the city.'

*Figure V* (5″)

21. W F+ A     'A penguin flapping all over' (W).
    1.0

22. W FY − War     'A bomb, exploding in all directions. It bombs out like
    1.0     that and does like this.' ('Because of the Korean War, it works out well ... the smoke is black.') 'Smoke going from a big bomb or ten million firecrackers.'

23. W FY – Na     'A rock that's been splattered with black, been fired.'
      1.0        ('Someone threw ink on a rock [laughs] to be silly . . .
                    looking for trouble.')

24. W Y Na      'Dirt spread around on a floor' (black). 'Real black coal
                    dust kicked up by wild horses . . . kicked up on dry
                    sand.' ('The horses are under the dust. This is [D 3] the

25. D F – Ad     horse's tail. I forget things.')

*Figure VI* (1″)

26. W Y War     'Boo-oo-oom! Boom! It looks like the Korean War.'
                    ('From bombs making so much smoke, it just blacks
                    out all over.')

27. W F – A      'It looks like the shape of an octopus.' ('It looks like it').
      2.5        'It looks like a person named Billy, blowing off fire-
                    crackers in that kind of a shape.' ('The smoke.')

28. W Y Ink      'It looks like some ink being smashed down to the door.'
                    (W. 'Yes [laughs and walks over to the door], like
                    some silly person splashed ink.')

*Figure VII*

29. W YF – Ink    'Wow! It looks like ink shaken all over in a funny-
      2.5        looking shape.' (Black.)

30. W F – Mess   '. . . It looks like someone just really made a mess' (the
                    shape of it, and the mess square) 'all over the bed.

31. Dds F Hh     'Someone had diarrhea and had a bowel movement on
      4.0        a bed' [laughs].
                    'Someone exploded a bomb in this room. That's what
                    it looks like . . .' ('It would blow everything up.' Laughs).
                    'It looks like someone put dirt down on the floor.'
                    (Black.)

32. DW YF – Im,Na   'Like an explosion from a light bulb, breaking out a
                    whole shadow of dust.' (D 6. 'The explosion forcing the
                    dust.')
                    'It looks like someone shooting dust out of this, like a
                    dusting gun.' (D 11 and W.)
                    'People had blotted ink on the paper.

33. W F – Ls      'It looks like the ocean coming up (W). The way it
      2.5        washes up.

34. W Y Na      'It looks like sand . . . dark, silty sand (black) washed
                    up from the ocean . . . sewer water.
                    'A big ten thousand ton had skidded on wet sand and
                    shot some dust and smoke.' ('The darkness of it.')

*Figure VIII* (5″)

35. DdW CF + Rc   'Gosh! A rocket going fast in the air.' ('The center
                    shooting fires, blasts out fire.')

36. W CF− Hh
    4.5
'The shape of a carpet.' ('Some carpets have this picture.')

37. D F+ A
'Two animals (foxes . . .?) climbing up the sides, climbing on a rocket (gripping on it) that's blasting into the

38. D F+ An P
ground. A bomb. A sky rocket! A sky rocket on the 4th of July, making colors, skeletons and all that.' ('They go in that shape. A coon skeleton.')
'Like some big mines, time bombs, have blown high in the air, and thrown from a window.' ('Looks like it. They make fire.')

39. W C.Y Fi,Hh
'A big fire, making all colors of smoke.
'A light bulb of all different colors.
'A big rocket, shooting into a tunnel.' ('No picture of it.')

*Figure IX* (5″)

40. DW CF+ Hh
'Wowee! That looks like another type of light bulb in all kinds of colors.' (D 6 is bottom; D 5 is filament wires; and all is the bulb.)
'Insides of radio tubes lit up' (C).

41. D F+ Im
'Something like a big war gun, shooting in all directions (D 7) and clouding over.' ('The smoke the bullets leave.' D 1.)
'A big thunder and lightning storm, thundering overhead . . .

42. W CF− Na
    5.5
'. . . and rains of different colors and a sunset appearing through the clouds.' ('The sun [D 6] and reflecting on here [D 3]. The clouds [D 1], the form of it.')

43. D C Fi
'A big bonfire of a big army camp . . . or robbers trying to start a house on fire.' ('The fire [D 6], an army camp, and something like in a house.')

*Figure X* (7″)

44. W CF+ Rc
    5.5
'Whoo gosh! It looks like looking through a kaleidoscope.' ('All different colors . . . shapes of all different kinds.')
(D 1 is octopus, octagonal.)
(Long pause.)
'It looks like several colors of ink being spilled all over.' ('Yellow, orange, blue, and purple.')

45. D F− A, Sc
'Some animal.' ('A dinosaur being slaughtered a lot.' (D 11, D 9, and adjacent D's, 'meat.')

46. D C Art
'A painting.' (Indiscriminate D's; color.)

47. Ws C Oj
'A certain type of radio tube, all lit, in different bright colors.' (W; white is the tube; and the colors.)
'It looks like a light bulb, shattering, of all different colors being shadowed all over.'

48. DW C Rc          'A balloon bursting.' (D 12, and all the colors).
49. D F+ Rc          'Some fireworks.' (D 11. 'Firecracker. Bursting. Boom!')
                                  'Nothing I can think of.'

Total Time: 28 minutes, 25 seconds

Likes best: X. "The colors."
Likes least: IX. "Different. Not as much colors."

### Response Summary

R: 49

| | | | | | | | |
|---|---|---|---|---|---|---|---|
| W | 22 (s,1) | C | 6 | Hd | 1 | F+ | 39% |
| DW | 3 | C.Y | 4 | A | 6 | A | 14% |
| DdW | 1 | YF | 3 (2−) | Ar | 1 | P | 2 |
| D | 22 | CF | 6 (2−) | Ad | 1 | S | 4% |
| Dds | 1 | Y | 8 | An | 4 | Af r 0.44 | |
| — | | FY | 2− | Art | 1 | L | 0.62 |
| | 49 | VF | 1 | Bl | 3 | T/first R (9 cards) 5.8 | |
| | | F+ | 7 | Fi | 5 | T/R 34.6 | |
| Z f | 14 | F− | 11 | Hh | 3 | Fln T/first R (8 cards) 3.12 | |
| Z sum 41 | | F | 1 | Im | 2 | Fln R 1.78 | |
| Ap. W!! DW (D) | | — | | Ink | 3 | | |
| | | | 49 | Ls | 2 | | |
| Seq. Irregular | | | | Mess | 1 | | |
| | | EB | 0/21.0 | Na | 7 | | |
| | | EA | 21.0 | Oj | 1 | | |
| | | | | Rc | 4 | | |
| | | | | War | 4 | | |
| | | | | — | | | |
| | | | | 49 | | | |

### Interpretation

*Summary of findings:* Extensive pathologic involvement of the personality, with retarded growth, especially serious in the ego sphere and therefore manifest also in the sphere of the emotions. A fixation in a schizophrenic pattern is the only conclusion to be drawn from this Rorschach test record. The ego's inadequacy is particularly severe in the thinking processes, which lack the coherence and the critical evaluation expected for this patient's age. Ideas are unique to the degree of "private world" production. The perception disorder includes distortion of, as well as indifference to, the objective world. The attention wanders and is not adaptively distributed to environmental stimuli. Emotional reactions disclose the primitive drive as largely unmodulated by ego considerations. At the same time, a deep-seated passivity has set in and is crippling the personality. It is of a painful, anxious coloring, a derivative from an older anxiety. At present, however, essentially no free anxiety is indicated in the test findings, and the patient appears bland in this respect. The boy engages in no fantasy and so does not absorb his feelings inwardly. Passivity is thus his principal defense against primitive affectivity, and against an aggressiveness which is projected in the content—an aggressiveness which is itself a defense against a devastating insecurity, apparently displaced on to his household.

The ego's insufficiency is apparent in the accidental and tangential thinking processes; in the elaborations that are irrelevant, whether to the stimulus or to his own percept; in the perseverations, especially of personalized thought content. These so dominate as to exclude attending to normal interests. Reasoning is at times alogical and usually lacks any set pattern. Samples of the queer ideation:

"Looks like sand ... dark, silty sand, washed up from the ocean ... sewer water."

"The shape of a carpet. Some carpets have this picture."

"Two animals climbing on a rocket that's blasting into the ground."

"A sky rocket on the 4th of July, making colors, skeletons, and all that. They go in that shape. A coon skeleton."

"A big rocket shooting into a tunnel."

The perception, as well as its erratic and distorted quality, includes a vividness in which there is an hallucinatory potential. There is a question of a Klang association. Much inappropriate laughter; immature exclamations.

The primitive pressure of the emotions is manifest not only structurally and in the consistent domination by one level of affect, but also by the content which is saturated with violence ideas and projects preoccupation with destructiveness. Fire, smoke, a bomb blowing up, ten tons of T.N.T., blood left after a car collision, an army camp or house started on fire by robbers, a bulb with filament wires, the inside of a radio tube, meat. Very rarely are a "carpet" and "a painting" healthy themes.

*The essential absence of free anxiety* is striking. The patient may well be binding it in all the violence thinking, doing so habitually, and so insulating himself from this painful emotion. There are signs of vulnerability to the phallic and to the maternal figures, especially to the latter. No doubt, his attitude toward his mother is a source of threat. He also engages in counterphobic and phobic thinking at the father stimulus. There has been chronic anxiety but it is not now an active dynamic at the conscious level. However, it has left its residue in the passivity which is deeply imprinted on the character. There is material here for an apprehensive mood, one that can be very painful. Should the ego retrace its course and begin to grow, distressing, dysphoric mood moments must be expected.

This passivity has been serving as the main defensive strategy, especially since fantasy living is not available to the patient. He does use other defenses: an isolating narrowing of the attention; reaction formations; and intellectualization much beyond the ego's present growth. But the core of the pattern is: aggression defending against the insecurity and passivity defending against the aggression.

*The total functioning.* The superior potential of this boy is apparent in his vocabulary and in his many original ideas of superior caliber. Structurally, he is capable of conceptual achievement at a very high level, in fact, at an excessively high level which reflects a symptomatic need for self-display. While difficult problem-solving is well handled, it is not consistent with the conceptual drive. The ego's insufficiency in using its resources is seen in the disorganized intellectual life and in the narrowing of the interests. The boy is seriously below normal in focusing on objective stimuli, so responsive is he to his emotions. When attending to reality he is inaccurate, critically below normal. He disregards social canons to the point of being asocial intellectually. An inelastic intellectual pattern will make change and learning difficult.

*The content.* The all-absorbing insecurity and violence have already been noted. The "house on fire" appears early and recurs. It is a frequent motif in very anxious or panicky children. The "Korean War" theme is the focus of many related associations. The interest in destruction also emerges in "slaughtered, killed, animals," "skeletons," "person from Korea," "intestines." Recurrent themes are "a big war gun shooting in all directions," "clouding over," and "bullets." A very regressive content is: "looks like someone made a mess all over the bed (laughs), it's black; someone had diarrhea and had a bowel movement on the bed." The "light bulb," "radio tube" interest requires investigating for its projection value. Of especial interest is: "a sunset" and "the moon eclipsing the sun." Also: "real black coal dust, sand, kicked up by wild horses, and the horses are under the dust." Of possible broader interest are: "looking through kaleidoscope" and "a dinosaur."

*Treatment outlook:* Reconstruction is likely to be a very slow, discouraging process. The boy does have assets in the intellectual sphere, the potential for superior mental activity, and the affective resources can be converted into drive. But the essential lack of ego in the sense of central motivation and of standards must make for pessimism in predicting the ultimate personality structure. A benign environment will help, but love will not be enough. The critical therapeutic problem will be that of planting the seed of an ego.

### B. Second Rorschach test. Clyde at ten years, eleven months.

#### Response Record

*Figure I* (6″)

1. W F+ Ink
1.0

'Some have good looks.' (Patient has candy in hand.) 'Looks like ink ... splatters and so on'. ('On a piece of paper.')

2. W F— Ashes     'A mixture of ashes, magnified sort of.' ('Like one ash magnified 1000 times; they are very crummy shaped.')

3. W Y Na.     'Soot in the fireplace, something like that.

4. W FY+ Art     'A design on a rug, maybe.' (Form, shading.)
      1.0

5. Ws F— A     'Might look like some animal skin.' (W. 'The shape of
      3.5     it. White is where the coloring is on it . . .')

### Figure II (6″)

'Hey, that's got . . .

6. W C.Y Fi     'Looks like a fire burning up from the ashes.' (D 2 and D 1; color, form. 'Doesn't have much form, but it's the color.')

7. D Y Cl     'Looks something like a . . . something like a . . . storm,

8. Dd CF Na     a wind storm with red lightning flashes.' (Dd of D;
      3.0     color of the clouds.)

9. W Y Ar, Fi     'Sort of looks like a chimney on fire . . . like the insides' (patient appears distracted). 'I have to think.' (W. Shows the insides of the chimney; the color of black soot and ashes.)

10. D Y War     'Maybe a bomb exploding.' (Patient does constant sniffing). 'I can't think of anything.' ('It doesn't quite show the bomb, but the smoke . . .')
      'The fire in a fireplace.' ('All the oranges and reds.')

### Figure III (35″)

(Patient appears distracted.)

11. D CF— Rc     'Sort of looks like the fireworks shooting up in the air.' (D 2. 'The orange and stuff like that.')
      'I think it looks like a small fire.' (In the orange.)

12. D Y Ashes     'Could be partly ashes, I think.' (D 9. 'Mostly color.')
      'A picture of a modern design on a rug.' ('Most all of it . . .')

13. W FC+ Art     (Patient looks around.) 'Could look like a bomb.' ('The
      5.5     way the smoke shapes up.')
      'Could look like a painting.' ('Of fireworks and orange things.')

### Figure IV (1″)

14. W F— Ashes     'Ooh! That looks like ashes spread around.' ('Sort of the
      2.0     shape to it.')

15. D F— War     'Looks like a bomb going up in the air.' ('Most all of it.')
      'I think it looks like smoke from bonfire.' ('Yeah, it does . . . bonfire going up.')

16. W FY+ Cl     'I think it could look like a rain cloud.' (Very oddly
      2.0     shaped; one half of form and one half of color.)

17. W Y Na                 'Could be a cloud of dust.
                           'Not that I know of.'

                           *Figure V* (5″)

18. W F+ A P               'That looks like something like a moth.' (W; wings.)
        1.0
19. D F− A                 'Might look like another animal . . . the skin spread out
                           sort of.' ('Most of it.')
20. W YF+ Na               'I think it might look like a tidal wave bringing up
        1.0                dust or something.' ('Going up like that.' Patient traces;
                           patient does much yawning.)
21. W FY− Na               'I think it might look like a big cloud of dust left over
        1.0                from ashes or something.' ('The ashes being thrown
                           around.' One-half form and one-half color.)
                           'I think we could go on to the next one.'

                           *Figure VI* (15″)

22. W F+ A                 'Looks like (patient appears amused) kind of a turtle
        2.5                or something.' ('Could have been a turtle; right around
                           here . . . about all of it . . . mostly the shape.')
23. W Y Ashes              'Looks like ashes thrown around.' ('The color of ashes.')
                           (Patient laughs, amused.)
24. W YF− War              'I think it might look like a trace of a smoke of a time-
        2.5                bomb.' ('Ooooh . . . around here . . . a cloud of smoke
                           and left that trace.')
                           'I think we could go on.
                           'It could look like an ash storm.' ('Ashes going up like
                           that with a terrible bang [D 6] . . . going out like that.')
                           'Not that I know of.'

                           *Figure VII* (10″)

                           (Patient appears amused.)
25. W YF+ Na               'Looks like something moldy.' ('Mold in a pumpkin.
        2.5                Mold sometimes forms like that; the color mainly.')
26. D YF+ Ink              'Might look like some ink marked around the wall
                           sort of.' (D 3; shading and form.)
                           'I think . . . I don't have any other idea.
27. W F+ Cl                'Could be a very odd shaped rain cloud.' (W. 'Rain
        2.5                clouds are not usually shaped like that, very seldom.')

                           *Figure VIII* (15″)

                           'Hey, that's' . . . ('It was surprising, unusual colors to
                           it.')
28. D F+ AP                'Might give an idea of two animals . . . (D 1) climbing
29. Dd F− Bt               . . . up a tree, sort of.' (Dd 27, with Dd 30.)
        3.0

30. D C Fi        'It might look like a bonfire here.' (D 2. 'A brush fire
     3.0         lit by accident.')
                  'Might . . . it might just look like a tree catching on
                  fire.' ('At the bottom, some trees do that thing going
                  up.')

31. D CF— Cl      'Sort of an odd shaped rain cloud in a very bad storm
                  or something.' (D 4. 'The color of the cloud . . . I don't
                  know exactly . . . blue and stuff.')
                  'I don't think so.'

*Figure IX* (5″)

32. D FC— War     'That looks like, really like a timebomb.' ('Altogether,
                  it sure does . . . fiery smoke goes up in the air.' D 9,
                  with D 3; form, color.)
                  (Patient appears distracted.)

33. D CF— Bt      'A tree caught on fire.' (D 5 'is the stem . . . the red
                  colors and stuff.')

34. D CF— Na      'Maybe lightning.' (D 7. 'The colors and flashes.')

35. D F+ Cl        'Flashing and rain clouds.' (D 1. 'The shape.')

36. D C Na         'The sun shining on a cloud sort of.' (D 3. 'The orange
                  of the sun going down.')

37. D C Fi         'I think it looks like some part of smoke left over from
                  a fire.' (D 6. 'Smoke looks like that color.' D 6 with
                  Dd of D 1.)
                  'I have no other idea.'

*Figure X* (1″)

38. D FC+ A       'Hey, that looks like the bottom of the sea a little bit.'
                  ('I didn't.' D 1, D 4. 'Odd sea animals.' Form, color.)

39. D F— Fi        'It looks like the inside of a blast furnace to me.' ('A
                  fire injector.' D 5 and D 4. 'The way it looks and the
                  way the fire would shoot out.')

40. D C Fi         'Some of these yellow parts look like sort of a fire.'
                  ('Sort of.' Color.)
                  'I think it looks like two sea animals.' (D 1. 'I don't
                  know exactly.')

41. D Y Fi         'Some of it looks a little like smoke.' (D 9. 'Sort of
                  black like smoke.')
                  'I think it looks a little like dust.' ('Dust looks like it.'
                  Dd of D 9.)
                  'I think we could go on to the next one. This is the
                  last one!
                  'The beginning of a wild bonfire.' ('Fire parts are burn-
                  ing.')
                  'Part of a . . . like a blast furnace down here' (D 5).

42. D F+ A          'Might look like two reindeer jumping.' (D 7. 'They
     4.0             sort of do look like it . . . jumping away from the fire.')
                    'I think we've gone through all of it.'

Total Time: 20 minutes, 45 seconds.

Liked best: 'Probably the last one . . . I don't want to take too much time; I don't
feel like it; the colors and (D 5).'

Liked least: 'I'll have to go through; maybe figure IV; it doesn't have much coloring on it.'

### Response Summary

R: 42

| | | | | | | | | |
|---|---|---|---|---|---|---|---|---|
| W | 19 (s,1) | C | 4 | A | 7 | F+ | 50% |
| D | 21 | C.Y | 1 | Ar | 1 | A | 17% |
| Dd | 2 | CF | 5 (4−) | Art | 2 | P | 2 |
| | 42 | FC | 3 (1−) | Ashes | 4 | S | 2.5% |
| | | Y | 8 | Bt | 2 | Af r 0.55 |
| Z f | 17 | YF | 4 (1−) | Cl | 5 | L | 0.50 |
| Z sum 41.0 | | FY | 3 (1−) | Fi | 6 | |
| Ap. W!! (D) | | F+ | 7 | Ink | 2 | T/first R 9.9″ |
| Seq. Ir. (cnf) | | F− | 7 | Na | 8 | T/r 29.64″ |
| | | | — | Rc | 1 | Fln T/first R 11.2 |
| | | | 42 | War | 4 | Fln R 0.89 |
| | | | | | — | |
| | | | | | 42 | |

EB  0/14.0
EA  14.0

## Interpretation

*Summary.* This boy's lag in ego growth is persisting seriously. It is at
present manifested in a type of self-effacing that is very destructive to the
functioning of the personality. He is essentially de-egotizing himself. The
gap is a wide one between his intellectual living and reality. Defenses
developed by the ego are essentially lacking, although he does use a pathogenic preoccupation with world destruction as a defense. There is an all-
absorbing, intensely felt, dysphoric mood, with probable overt passivity.
At the same time, strongly mobilized, exciting feelings, chiefly primitive
and of diffuse discharge quality, are present. The anxiety remains unbound
in spite of much phobic thinking. The boy uses no fantasy, leaving him
just that much more exposed to his strong feelings since he does not introvert them. Fortunately, opposition urges are absent, which supports the
passivity findings. In all, he is a child showing much self-deprivation
as well as absorption in special, pathologic thinking. Concerning treatment
implications, the resources continue meager in all spheres. A benign environment will necessarily be the first requirement.

*The defenses.* Avoidance of what must be a terribly experienced anxiety is reflected in this boy's emphasis on violence and world destruction themes. An undoubted depersonalizing is here projected. There is much displacement of emotion by means of phobic thinking. The passivity indicated structurally is also intense enough to be essentially depersonalizing emotionally. A hold on reality is lacking, and there is rather little hold on the self. Thus, there are few or no defenses of adaptive quality.

Saturation by a painful mood is in evidence throughout. The patient does not even escape it at the pleasure-toned stimuli. The content uncovers a fear-laden and probably agitated state of mind. So extensive and deep-set is the agitation as to argue for a central anxiety and insecurity which set in very early in life and developed into one of the autistic pictures described by Kanner.[41]

The anxiety, to some extent, has a focus in father imagery. Yet, it is general as well. It is a free anxiety which the phobic thinking fails to bind. In brief, this is an ego very vulnerable to painful ideas.

The ego is vulnerable, too, to exciting emotions. Reactions are predominantly uncontrolled, although there is still some modulation by the ego—partly at the child's immature level but partly as mastery by the ego. The quantity of ego mastery is small but it is indicative of some growth. In all, however, the emotional structure confirms the ego findings: immature and with a trend to unrestrained discharge. The content is principally fire and destructiveness, but there is also an occasional trend to the healthier, raising a question of a restitutive trend.

Total absence of fantasy may be another sign of the ego's growth lag. An occasional trend to it uncovers empathy with destructive forces at least and a potential for introverting the intense experience: for example, "an ash storm, ashes going up like that with a terrible bang." However, the present structure is entirely extratensive. Only the fearful mood leading to the passivity serves as a counterforce against the excitement pressures.

The absence of structural findings indicating opposition is consistent with the finding of passivity. The essential question here is whether this pattern became set in earliest infancy. The unknown factor (in the science of personality generally) is, of course, to what extent a trait is constitutional.

The ego's insufficiency is reflected in the fact that the boy's perception in frequently indefinite; his attention wanders and he appears suggestible. There are many inaccuracies in his perception, which permits inadequate central criticism to be postulated. The thinking is highly unique in its content, with emphasis on special themes. There is some perseveration. Excessive over-all, global reactions result from inadequate analytic thinking. Language includes inappropriate verbalizing, immature expressions, and even echolalia. However, there is occasional superior language and clear diction. A self-devaluating attitude and overtly compliant behavior are indicated.

*Total adjustment.* Released intellectual energy is at about expectancy, or, if anything, somewhat above the patient's age norm. It is maldistributed in over-attention to the larger stimulus, which occurs uncritically and unanalytically. Four test indices that relate to the objective world converge in telling one story: the patient is below norm in over-all grip on accuracy, in attention to external stimuli, and in recognition of the more common stimuli and of the conventional. The occasional better diction does point to fluctuation, however, as do the sporadic content themes of wider interest.

*The content.* The concentration is on storms and violence: lightning, fire, and ashes. For example: "looks like a fire burning up from the ashes, like a storm, a windstorm with red lightning flashes, looks like a chimney on fire . . . color of black soot and ashes." "Could look like a rain cloud." "I think it might look like a tidal wave bringing up dust." "Lightning flashes and rain clouds . . . the sun shining on a cloud sort of." "A couple of reindeer jumping away from a fire." Of healthier potential is "sunshine" and some art themes, although one of these is "a painting of fireworks."

As compared with the first Rorschach test, there is a slight improvement in the ego's functioning intellectually, although in a negative sense. The second test does not show all the serious dysfunction of the first test. More significant is Clyde's remaining essentially stationary in his ability to recognize familiar stimuli, due to his greater absorption at present in the special theme of world destructiveness. The speculation is in order of whether the anxiety projected in this destructive thinking uncovers a dawning of ego. Clyde's failure to change in conformity or to achieve fantasy means, of course, that he is standing still. The important, and possibly critical, change is in the sphere of the lively emotions: a significant reduction in total reactions at a purely infantile level even though these continue in high quantity. Also, he has for the first time achieved some mastery over his feelings. The content does not contain quite so many pathologic themes as formerly. In all, then, some slight movement forward in the emotions, essential stand-still in the ego.

*Present treatment outlook.* Assets are essentially lacking in the ego and are limited to the sporadic, more mature language forms and slightly original thought content. The insufficiently analytic approach will make learning and change a slow matter. The inner world is characterized by no fantasy and by the domination of strong feelings. The instances of mastery over these are too few to be viewed as a therapeutic resource. The one asset may be his very painful mood and the related fears. It follows that a benign and watchful environmental therapy must still be the approach.

## C. Third Rorschach test. Clyde at fourteen years, five months

### Response Record

(Behavior note: Odd, tight posture. Keeps saying "Yeah." Brings cards very close to eyes. Smiles. Seems preoccupied.)

### Figure I (45″)

1. Ds F+ Adx

'Looks so like the wings of a bird.' (D 2; form only.) (Hesitates.)

2. Dd FV+ Ls

'This here ... looks like two hills off in the distance.' (Dd 22; form and distance.)

'I think I'm through.' (Seems to be saying things to himself.)

'I notice these spaces here' (Dds 29). 'Looks like holes going through the bird's wings.' (Patient is very absorbed, hesitant. Yawns.) 'Part of feathers are missing.'

### Figure II (80″)

(Attention is distracted.)

3. D FY− A
    3.0

∧ > ∧ > 'Looks like two wild animals when I look at it like this.' (Stutters, distracted, picks at card edges.) (D 1; their shape; dog fur. Form and shading.)

4. D C Fi

∨ 'The red part looks like little bits of fire.' (D 3; color only.)

5. D F+ A
    5.5

∧ 'Looks like two sea lions coming together up here.' ('Facing each other ... touch each other ...' D 2; form only.)

> 'Looks like the hind legs of these two animals (of R 3) are touching together' (D 4).

6. Dd F+ Adx

'Two little bits of fur hanging down here.' (Dd 27; form only.)

7. Dds M − Ad

'One last thing ... they have their mouths open.' ('It's out of proportion.' Dds at 22. 'A loud screech.')

### Figure III (10″)

8. D M+ H P
    4.0

'This one looks like two people meeting together.' (D 1. 'Holding mops ... sort of like women ... their shape and their breasts look like natives, that effect. Their hands will meet but not the rest; in a mood to dance; a game.')

9. Dd F− Cl

'These look like clouds ... these lines here.' ('Some look like that ...' Dd of 8; form only.)

10. D M.Po− Ab

'This is keeping them apart ... this red part.' (D 3. 'Yeah, that's the way it looks, right between them.' Patient stutters. Form only.)

11. D CF+ Oj.Rc      'Two decorations hanging down from the ceiling.' (D 2; color and form.)
'Also holding two mops right here' (D 4).

12. Dd F Oj      'This little line looks like a stick going between the two.' ('Mops gave the effect of it.' Dd in D 7; form only.)
'Two things coming out from their knees.' (Dd 26; part of their costume; form only.)
'I think we've covered it all.'

### Figure IV (75″)

13. W F+ A      'Mm.' ∨ (Tips card back and forth, distracted.)
      2.0      'Looks like a bird with a funny tail.' (∨ 'Lower part is tail; rest is bird.' W; form only.) (Very distracted.) 'These are attaching his wings.' (Dd in 1. Stammers.) (Is amused, self-absorbed, laughs.) '. . . A real funny one . . . I'll tell you in a minute.'

14. Dd M − Hd      'These two look like the lips of a wild native . . .' ('Their shape, African, a man . . . stretched out . . . acting like an ape; Dd 26) or something.' (Is almost convulsed with laughter, which is almost silent, however.)

15. Dd F Ad      'It looks as if the bird has spines on his wings.' (Dd on D 2; and laughter continues; looks at back.)

16. D F+ Adx      ∧ 'These look like elephants' trunks if you look at it like this.' (Covers half. D 4; form only.)
(Amusement continues; yawns.)

17. Dds F Ls      'Two little gulch-like things . . . like a gully you might say.' (Dds of Dd 21. 'Dug out.' Form.)

18. D F − Ad      ∧ 'A camel hump . . . like the hump on a camel's back.' (D 3; form only.) > (Laughs.)

19. Dd F − Adx      'This looks like the head of a pig.' (Dd of 2; form only.)

### Figure V (95″)

20. Ws F+ A      (Amused. < Covers half.) ∧ > 'This looks like a bird
      1.0      with its mouth open.' (W; form only; concentrates on D 3.)
∨ 'And this part, his tail' (D 2).

21. D F − Adx      ∨ 'Their feathers are hanging out of his wings.' (D 1 and Dd 22; form only.)

22. Dd VF Ls      < 'This looks like a mountain.' (Dd of D 6. 'Very far.' Form.)
(Waves card; distracted.)

23. D F − Ad      ∨ 'These look like sharp spines on his wings.' (D 11; form only.) 'That whole line of sharp spines on that other card that reminded me of a bird' (amused).

24. Dd F − Adx      ∨ 'Little claws sticking out' (of the bird; Dd 26; form only. 'Very odd angling.')

*Figure VI* (15″)

25. D FY+ AP        'Sort of looks like a bear skin.' (D 1; form and color a little.)

26. Dd F+ Ad       'These look like cat whiskers.' (Yawns and drops and waves card. Dd 26; form only.) 'This is part of the bear's tail (Dd 28). Yeah, a little bit of fur.' (Quite self-absorbed.)

27. D F+ Art        'Some kind of Indian design.' (D 3; form only. Speech is badly blocked.)
(Picks nose.) 'These were his legs.' (D 9 and Dd 25 of the bear.)
(Very odd tipping and angling.)

28. D VF.Y+ Ls     'Also something like a road going through a desert.' (Very far D 10 and D 4; distance, the shadings and the form.) 'That's it.'

*Figure VII* (45″)

29. Ws F− Ls        'Looks like a piece of land spreading out into the ocean.'
         4.0        (W; the black is the ocean; Ds 7 is land; denies vista.)

30. W Y.F+ Na.Ar   (Waves card.) 'Two stone shelves (D 5 and Dd of D 1;
         4.0        the color and form) over a valley' (Ds 7). (Very, very slow and absorbed.) 'Looks like two pieces of stone (Dd 21; leaning over; the color) are hanging onto a wall.' (Excessive blocking throughout). 'Looks like two stonewalls balanced on one.' (Each D 2 on D 4; good balance; form and some distance.)

31. D F+ Ar         (Starts laughing.) 'And two other walls are facing right here.' (Each half of D 6. 'Stuck together; the flatness.' Form.) (Twirls, waves card vigorously.)
'That's it.'

*Figure VIII* (70″)

32. W F+ A P       (Distracted.) 'Looks like two animals climbing (W) up
33. D FV+ Ls       a mountain.' (D's 4, 5 and 2; form and distance.)
         4.5        (Twirls; giggles.) 'Looks like the top of the mountain is barely balanced on the bottom, and as if it will fall over any minute.' (In two parts; balanced at Dd 29.) (Laughs hard.)

34. Ds F+ An P     'Part of the skeleton of an ape' (Ds 3).
35. Dd FV+ Ar     'On top of the mountain two spires sticking up and touching.' (Dd 24; form and distance).
'It's not the card I'm laughing at . . . it's about the skeleton you wrote down. I said the word ape and in school I write it down an awful lot.' (Laughter is more audible.)

|  | ∨ 'Animals look as if hanging by their tail.' (Twirls card.) |
|---|---|
| 36. Dd F+ Na<br>3.0 | ∨ ∧ 'And the animal's legs look as if they are caught in the rock.' (Laughs; Dd 25. 'The way the color goes into this; will try to break loose.' Distracted by books on shelf; gets up and reads "Rorschach's test" and is amused.) |
| 37. Dds Y Ls | 'Top of the mountain is carved out by running water.' (Dds between D 4 and D 5 as between the mountains). |

### Figure IX (45″)

| 38. D F+ Hh | 'Oh, golly! This part sort of looks like a bowl.' ('The way it is balanced.' D 12; form only.) |
|---|---|
| 39. D CF.V+ Ar | 'Looks like an arch here.' ('Of colored stone.' Dd 25; color, form, distance.) |
| 40. Ds F+ Oj<br>5.0 | (Playful.) 'A hole in bottom of the bowl, balancing it on a pin.' (D 5 is pin; form.) (For Dds selected, see R 43.) |
| 41. D M+ H P<br>4.5 | 'Two people holding up a stick ... these are sticks.' (D 3 and D 7. 'About to fight. Men ... just starting ... warlike, middle-aged.') |
| 42. Dd F− Oj | 'Pins sticking down' (Dd 21 ; form) 'into a rock.' ('The color of rock and shape.' D 6; color and form.) |
| 43. D CF+ Na | 'Two carved-out holes' (Dds 29) (twirls card) 'in the bowl or rock, and similar here' (Dds below D 12). |

### Figure X (15″)

| 44. W CF+ Rc<br>5.5 | 'Looks like the Fourth of July.' (W. 'All the fireworks. The colors and how it sticks out.' Color and form.) |
|---|---|
| 45. D C Fi | 'Two bits of fire (D 2; color only) jumping together ... |
| 46. D F+ A P | '... like dogs.' (D 2. 'Two fire dogs.' Form only. 'The color of it; first pieces of fire, then it looked like dogs.' |
| 47. D F+ A | < ∨ 'Two strange animals (D 6) are meeting together.' |
| 48. Dd F− Ad<br>4.0 | 'And only one head.' ('Only one head for both.' The mouth at Dd 34.) ∨ 'And can't get apart, because they have only one head.' Form; laughs.) |
| 49. W F+ Art<br>5.5 | ∨ 'Whole picture is balanced on this stick.' ('Yes, just about all are attached to this one [first W, then D 14] right here.' |
| 50. D FC+ Oj | (Scratches on card, twirls, laughs.) 'Some odd decoration hanging down ... |
| 51. D F− A<br>4.0 | ... from these two animals.' ('A string hanging, but it doesn't show.' (The shape and color; D 10 as both decorations and animals.) |
| 52. D F+ A | ∨ These look like two dogs jumping down.' (To bottom of picture; D 13; form.) |

| 53. D F − Hh | < ∨ 'Two spoons attached together.' (D 3; form.) |
| 54. D FC+ Oj | ∨ 'Two sticks stuck on to one.' (D 14. 'Form just |
| 4.0 | about, and some color . . . brown.' Form and color.) |
| 55. D M − A | ∧ 'Two frogs trying to jump . . .' (D 7. 'They want |
| | to get in on the act.' Form only.) |
| 56. D C Fi | '. . . at the fire.' (D 9; color only. 'The display of fire |
| 4.0 | works. They will burn.') |
| 57. D F+ A | (Laughs.) 'Two whales in the picture . . . it just tickles |
| | me . . . like killer whales because of their sharp spines.' |
| | (D 12; form and position of mouth.) |

Total Time: 66 minutes, 16 seconds.

Liked best: fig. X because of the colors.

Liked least: hard to decide; fig. V is just one thing, not much color or detail in it; only the light and dark.

### Response Summary

R: 57

| | | | | | | | | |
|---|---|---|---|---|---|---|---|---|
| W | 7 (s,2) | M | 5 (3−) | H | 2 | F+ | 63% | |
| D | 33 (s,3) | M.Po− | 1 | Hd | 1 | A | 42% | |
| Dd | 17 (s,3) | C | 3 | A | 12 | P | 6 | |
| | 57 | CF | 3 | Ad | 12 (x,6) | S | 14% | |
| Z f | 17 | CF.V | 1 | An | 1 | Af r | 0.84 | |
| Z sum | 67.5 | FC | 2 | Ab | 1 | L | 1.37 | |
| Ap.(W) (D) Dd!! | | Y | 1 | Ar | 3 | T/first R | | 49.5″ |
| Seq. Ir. (cnf) | | V | 1 | Art | 2 | T/R | | 69.7″ |
| | | FY | 2 (1−) | Cl | 1 | Fln T/first R | 42.2″ | |
| | | V.FY | 1 | Fi | 3 | Fln R | | 2.22 |
| | | VF | 1 | Hh | 2 | | | |
| | | FV | 3 | Ls | 7 | | | |
| | | F+ | 19 | Oj | 6 | | | |
| | | F− | 11 | Na | 3 | | | |
| | | F | 3 | Rc | 1 | | | |
| | | | 57 | | 57 | | | |
| | | EB | 6/9.5 | | | | | |
| | | EA | 15.5 | | | | | |

### Interpretation

Viewed in the perspective of the ominous reaction pattern in his first Rorschach test (at age 9 7/12 years), and the even more regressed picture at the time of the second test sixteen months later, this boy (at his present age of 14 5/12 years) is developing more realistic perception, is making an effort at controlling himself, less readily responds to primitive feelings; and can for the first time convert his feelings into some imaginative living. In a word, he has progressed. Where the ego was formerly nonexistent, it is now a directing factor. However, he is far from having grown to the level of an integrated personality. The signs of the ego's impairment are numerous and prominent.

In the intellectual sphere the impairment shows up in perceptual inaccuracies, which are sometimes severe [1]* and reflect indifference to reality [2]. Attention is frequently in flight [3]; the thinking is marked by unique ideas [4], and it recurrently shows the drag due to perseverations [5]; confusions are noted [6]; and at times the boy retreats to contaminatory [7] processes. Shifts in the quality of the productions are sharp [8]. Apparent thought blocking is of serious proportions [9]. Numerous motor symptoms: giggling, inappropriate and uncontrolled laughter; immature play, e.g., whirling of the test cards [10]; an apathetic attitude [11]. Yet, neither in quality nor in quantity does the intellectual impairment have the severity found in the first two tests. The boy has moved up from his condition [12] of fixation and archaic mental life to the less malignant one of inadequate disciplining [13] and a less primitive immaturity [14]. He is still in a condition of ego lag [15].

In the emotional sphere, explosive reactions are notably fewer than at either of the two previous times [16]. They still appear but play a much smaller role relative to the entire expression of the feelings [17]. Ego modulation of the affects is now the rule [18], and while an easy irritability is the dominant nuance [19], a more measured self-control and reaching for healthier contacts also appear [20]. Most striking, even dramatic, is the great reduction in the total push of feelings for outward expression, a reduction not only absolute but relative to the now higher total productivity [21]. He has grown away from the former condition of uncontrollable excitement. Content in this sphere now only rarely centers around the destructive and anxiety-provoking, and it does include healthy social interests [22].

This containment of the feelings is further highlighted by the boy's present ability to introvert them into imaginative living [23], something new in his mental life. In itself this activity would be evidence of maturation since it emerges generally with unfolding intelligence [24]. But it can be a two-edged talent, enabling autistic living, and, in fact, it is so used by the present patient, with dominantly immature regressive structure [25] exposing essentially dream material. Such, for example, is the anxiety-laden, of panic quality [26]: "Two frogs trying to jump into the fire, into the display of fireworks ... they want to get into the act ... they will burn." This painful affect characterizes all his inner living [27]; thus, it is not wish-fulfilling but phobic [28]. This affect is reflected, too, in evidence that he avoids or fears his fantasies [29]. The aggression theme appearing

* Bracketed numbers refer to Notes on Interpretation, which for this chapter will be found on pages 175–195.

in them [30] indicates what trends in himself he fears. Oral phobic ideas [31] also appear. In quality, it is usually a low energy [32] fantasy activity, reflecting the weak trait it is in this boy and that it is not an effective personality asset [33, 34].

The painful affect at present centers especially in feelings of inferiority. These are numerous [35], strongly experienced [36], and the pain in them is aggravated by dysphoric mood trends [37]. Significant for judging this boy's course is the fact that this trend is now appearing for the first time in his three tests, and, painful as it is, paradoxically it is also the sign of a favorable trend; he feels himself inferior as he measures himself against a perspective of world values [38]. The themes that he emphasizes are those of the distant objective [39], the difficult task [40], and also that of inner inadequacy [41]. A strongly experienced anxiety [42] offers the lead that he is sensing the need for participating in the world's struggles [43]. An occasional other association points to a possible compensatory striving trend [44]. The passivity (of the former findings), although still present, is now much in retreat [45] and no longer dominates the total picture.

Another critical shift is in the stimulus that now provokes his most acute anxiety shock: maternal imagery [46]. Disruption of the mental life is here most severe [47]; and the content accents the insecurity (balance; R 29) motif and that of protection (walls; R 29, 30), nicely exemplifying the theory of mother-child relationship as so dynamic in personality disorder.

A marked outcropping of the resistiveness trait [48] for the first time [49] is consistent with the decline of the passivity [50] and in itself must be looked on as growth. The unstable emotional trends [51] and the aggression themes [52] do, however, raise the issue of maladaptive externalizing of the feelings [53].

The defenses in the main take the path of self-constriction, avoidances, denials, undoings [54], some phobic thinking [55], some symbolisms [56]. The release of fantasy [57] is another tactic. A trend toward the adaptive is the ability in phases to hold well on to reality and, rather less well, to master himself [58].

In the total present adjustment mental energy is well released [59] and the boy can achieve intellectually at above average to superior level [60]. A number of superior original associations emerge [61]. But content in the main is channelized by his still immature ideas [62]. It is in over-all critical regard for reality that he manifests his most significant growth; he now about reaches the minimum of the normal range [63]. Clyde's ego growth potential is disclosed at a more surface level in his recognition of the conventional within normal limits [64]. The numerous incidents of pathologic thinking and perceiving cannot be overlooked, however [65]; and with these as the most serious dynamic at present are the inferiority feelings and his pathogenic view of the self [66]. In all, thus, he has made definite progress as compared with the findings in the first two tests, and the outlook is more benign [67]. But Clyde's is still an impaired personality [68], one that is moving into a more adaptive reaction pattern but will probably always need sanctuary from the world's stresses [69].

The dynamics [70] in the content very much accent the insecurity (balance) motif [71]; and as reactions to it, aggression ideas, usually screened [72]. Oral themes recur, both phobic and aggressive [73]. The anxiety appears in repeated fire [74] associations. A very frequent "together" motif [75], unique to this boy, requires exploring as pain-over-separation thinking. Of probable significance as traces of healthier, striving ideas are R 32, 33, and the quite original R 35 may stem from the same urge; also, the dream fantasy of the frog who wants to get into the act (R 55). Among the better originals is R 39 [76].

*Treatment implications.* Assets have emerged: the ego's growth [77]; self-consciousness reflected in the inferiority feelings [78]; the move away from passivity and toward self-will; the opposition [79]; the emergence of imaginative activity [80]; the regard for the conventional [81]; the occasional broader interest [82]. Yet, the impairment still pockmarks this personality picture sadly. Nor is there enough evidence of a healthy central urge toward an adult goal [83]. The affective fluidity is such that he will respond to his surroundings [84]. A situational and directive treatment is indicated for the critical years ahead [85]. Stresses will need to be minimal since these patients remain vulnerable. Directed into ego-satisfying training and vocation, this boy can settle into a relatively stabilized adjustment [86].

## Notes on Interpretation

[1] In R 9 the "clouds" seen in a very small Dd. The clouds percept is unknown for figure III and would be a serious departure from accuracy for any of its details. The intellectual dysfunction here is more severe because of the very tiny detail to which the patient is attending. This convergence of data from two sources testifies to the patient's not being under central direction.

Similarly, R 18, the "camel hump" to D 3 of figure IV; and R 19, the "pig's head," to a Dd of D 2 in figure IV. These percepts are just not evoked here. They are not only statistically F— but are even more inaccurate than the F— associations that are sometimes produced at these portions.

R 24, the "claws" to Dd 26 of figure V—an animal part very seldom, if ever, assigned to this "bat" figure. Nor do I recall that this rare Dd is ever picked in itemizing the details of the "bat." Rorschach's fourth rule for F+, i.e., critical preception, is here being violated.

In R 29 we have a double reversal of figure and ground, the usual land is sea and sea is land. Here is a twisting of the usual realities, whatever the dynamics behind it may be: Nietzsche's *Umwertung aller Werte*.

R 42 is unknown as a response to Dd 21 of figure IX. As a probable perseveration (from R 40) the likelihood is stronger that the percept will be a vague one (see note 5 concerning perseverations). Rorschach's first criterion for F+, the ability to concentrate, is being violated here.

[2] Indifference to reality as contrasted to distortion. In the former, no personal need, so far as can be surmised from the Rorschach test indications, has any part in misshaping the percept. In distortions, a personal dynamic is predicated and is a lead to be explored. The difference here is that between the impersonal and the personal F−. The former are more common in patients with brain pathology and in the mentally deficient. It is in such patients that clinical logic would lead us to expect the inability to concentrate and to criticize one's percepts (see note 1). For the responses in note 1, I judge only the F− in R 29 to be probably personal, the ones in R 9 and R 42 possibly so. The F− in the others are probably impersonal.

[3] This is inferred from (a) the impersonal F−, since an unsteady attention is implicit in the inability to concentrate, and (b) the greatly excessive number of small details. The Ap expectancy for 57 associations is: W, 11 D, 41 Dd, 5. Clyde is thus having his attention requisitioned by the less essential elements of his presented world at the expense of attention to the larger situation and to the obvious. While such a finding could be that overweening absorption in the minute characterizing the obsessive neurotic, the picture as a whole warrants our seeing this finding rather as fragmented attention. The same reasoning holds for (c) the extraordinarily small and very rare Dd's which grasp Clyde's attention. From the pattern as a whole we judge these to be a flight of attention, possibly the passive but nonetheless keen attention which Bleuler found in some schizophrenics.[19] (d) The examiner's observations throughout the test, as the record shows, report the patient chronically distracted or absorbed in himself and so not attending to the stimulus.

The Ap with its disregard of the obvious fact (D) and of the broader concept (W) indicates, of course, a maladaptive attention to life's problems.

[4] The "mops" of R 8 are off the beaten path without having the originality found in the responses of the healthy, superior person; see also the undirected elaboration around this association in the Inquiry. Other examples are the "walls ... stuck together" of R 31; and the "pin sticking into a rock," of R 42–43. While not the totally "foreign idiom" (C. McF. Campbell) of some schizophrenics, these ideas are still peculiar and in a measure perplexing.

[5] R 6 as a perseveration from R 3. In R 12 the "mops" is a persevera-

tion from this percept in R 8. The "spines" of R 23 in figure V the boy himself tells us is a perseveration from this association, R 15, in figure IV. In figure VI, "a bear's tail" and other parts of the animal are perseverations, after intervening responses, from the "bear skin" of R 25. The "pin" of R 42 is a perseveration from R 40. The relationship between perseveration and F— has been brought out in note 1.

[6] In R 8 the nonrelated ideas, "mops," "breasts," as a part of the same association (Inquiry). There is a question of confusion in R 14 in which the man's and ape's "lip" is equated. In R 47–48 we have the archaic "two animals with only one head and mouth." In R 50–51 Clyde puts the "decorations" on the animals. In this figure, X, the first association, "fireworks," continues to dominate, with the resulting confused and archaic thinking of R 45–46, "fire dogs," and in R 55–56 in which the "frogs" will "get in on the act" by jumping into the fire. Structural evidence for disorderly thinking is found in the Sequence: very confused in figure IV; irregular in figure III; approaching confusion in figure X.

[7] Where does confusion end and contamination begin? The dividing line is not always a sharp one. The "spines" on the "birds' wings," R 15, is a contamination, as is also the "spines" on the bat, R 23; and we find this again: the "spines" on the "whales" of R 57. Under this heading we need to consider also R 45–46 and R 50–51 (note 6).

[8] The shifts are observable both in quality and in quantity of the productions. Concerning quality: in figure III following the most frequent and what may be considered the most normal association in R 8, Clyde produces that R 9 which is inferior intellectually on two counts (note 1); and this impaired intellectualization is continued in R 10 with its accidental thinking process (the position determinant, Po). In figure IV the patient starts with a realistic percept, shifts immediately to a regressive fantasy, and concludes this figure with two severe departures from accuracy. In figure V inaccurate perception is clearly the rule; and figure VII stands out for the distortion of the realities in it (R 29; and see notes 1 and 2). Between these two figures, in VI, all perception is of plus quality: a height of accuracy between two valleys of errors.

The quantitative fluctuations are found both in the initial response times and in the productivity in the respective test figures. Thus, in initial response time a slowing from figure I to figure II of 35 seconds; a speeding up between figures II and III to the extent of 70 seconds; and between figures III and IV a slowing again in the amount of 65 seconds; then figure V to figure VI the time speeds up by 80 seconds. The mean fluctuation in his initial response time is 42.2 seconds. The mean for children in the 14–17 year age is 14.10, SD 12.90.[68]

Fluctuation in productivity: the small productivity in figure I stands

out in contrast to that in all the others, as does the high quantity in figure
X; and the range set by these two figures, two to fourteen, is very wide.
Also, the increase by three responses in figure VIII over figure VII is a
sharp one as compared with those in figures III, IV, V, VI, VII, and IX
over each preceding test figure. The mean fluctuation in productivity for
the 14–17 year old group is 1.67, SD 0.60. For Clyde in this Rorscrach test
it is 2.22.

[9] Thought-blocking is not to be mistaken for inhibition; nor inhibition
for thought-blocking. In inhibition, conflict and anxiety are at work, as the
entire structural pattern shows; and the personal dynamics are the effective cause of the on-going conflict. In blocking, it is as though for the time
being there is no thought content in the patient, as if the flow has been
stopped by turning off a valve. See Bleuler's elucidation of thought poverty.[19] In the present patient the very slow initial response times in figures
II, IV, V, and VIII show differentials too violent as compared to those in
the other figures; and they are not explicable as due to shock phenomena.
That is, they are not the work of a current reaction nor does the reaction
pattern as a whole indicate a current conflictual condition. My inference is,
therefore, that what we are seeing here is thought-blocking; the examiner's
observation to the same effect made while taking the test will be found in
the record (figures I, VI).

[10] Clyde manifested these throughout the administration of the test,
as the examiner observed, and as a reading of the record will show.

[11] The apathy is apparent in the yawnings, e.g., in figures I, VI. One
wonders also about the patient's state of mind during the several long
delays and the periods of absorption which the examiner reports at several
points. See also at R 26 the manner of his handling the test card.

[12] The condition at the time of his first Rorschach test, four years
and eleven months prior to the present one, and also at the second test,
one year and six months prior to the present one. See the reports, pp. 165f.
and 170f.

[13] In the present test the confused Sequence (figures III, IV, and the
trend in X), the flight of the attention to the out-of-the-way and the
trivial, the impersonal departures from accuracy, the sometimes severe inaccuracies, the shifts in quality, the anomalies of motility, all described
in the above notes, are the measure of Clyde's present intellectual and ego
impairment. Also, disturbances in speech forms occasionally appear, e.g.,
R 13. The outpouring in figure X is an undirected spontaneity of a kind
which I have observed principally in schizophrenics and in some severely
disturbed neurotics. It is an associational push in which the central (ego)
directives are notably lacking. The Sequence disorder is the principal
present residue of the boy's former more disintegrated condition. The more

seriously archaic mental life in Clyde's earlier growth phases will be discerned from a study of the first two Rorschach test records. The differences between those two stages and the one manifest in the present test is a gauge of his change. Inadequate though he now is, he has clearly grown as compared with what the earlier tests mirrored.

[14] In fact, the findings enable us to state the changes in positive terms: as moves towards maturation. A nucleus of F+ or controlled perception now characterizes this boy. His present F+ per cent for the record as a whole is 63, compared with 39 and 50 for the first and the second tests, respectively. Actually, he is now accurate in his perception within the lower critical limit of findings in neurosis. Inspection of the scoring summaries for the three test records also show a significantly higher count at present in P (greater conformity); where formerly he was deviant in this respect, he now scores within normal range. He now perceives whole human forms, something of which he was formerly incapable, supporting the evidence in the P findings as now having other persons in mind and to that extent as relating with them. The present Ap, even with its imbalance with respect to Dd, is still very much healthier than the badly one-sided accent on the holistic approach of the first two tests. A significant improvement appearing in the second test as compared with the first and maintained in the present one is found in Clyde's giving up the DW and the DdW approaches, i.e., he no longer jumps to conclusions from facile, alogical reasoning. The increase in productivity may or may not be a sign of better health, since it may, on the one hand, reflect liberation of mental energy and so of drive but, on the other hand, as undirected spontaneity it would reflect the ego's inadequate hold on the mental processes. It should be added that the actual increase in R at present over those obtained in the first two tests is not a significant one. The other change is in respect to per cent of animal forms. This is a significant one. In being higher, it shows that Clyde is now capable of seeing a larger percentage of the more common forms and that as compared with the small percentages of animal forms in his former tests he is now less individualized. This finding reflects the same move as the one in the P finding. But in his percentage of animal forms Clyde has shifted too far, to the level of stereotypy. Having overcompensated, the ego is taking a loss.

[15] Judged, that is, from the findings in the third Rorschach test viewed by itself alone. The intellectual dysfunction described in the text and in the notes so far indicates the present operations of the ego. Insofar as these fall short of expectancy for a boy of Clyde's age, they show his ego as lagging in growth.

[16] As shown in the number of undiluted color (C) responses: in the first Rorschach test, 10; in the second, 5; in the third, 3.

[17] Referring here to the sums of the color values in the three tests: 21.0, 14.0, 9.5, in the first, second, and third tests respectively.

[18] We judge this from the CF and FC associations, i.e., those in which the form, or ego, element moderates the C, or affective, element. As the summary of the scorings show, Clyde reacted with no FC in his first test while the number of his CF associations came to 6 in a total of 16 color-determined associations. In the second test, the number of CF together with FC comes to 8 in a total of 13 color-determined responses. In the present test, CF and FC together account for 6 out of the total of 9 color-determined responses. It is clear then that F, or ego, now plays a much more effective role in affect-toned associations. Here is a real move forward.

[19] The number of CF is greater than either that of undiluted C or of FC. That is, Clyde shows more inadequately mastered affectivity than he does either unrestrained impulsivity or understanding emotional contact with others (see the note following). Qualitative observations confirmed this indication of only partially restrained activity. See, for example, R 44, R 45–46, and R 50–51, and the Inquiry concerning them, with their indications of a high-strung tempo and push of feelings.

[20] The emotional contacts indicated in the FC responses, those in which the regard for the environment, F, masters the affect and draws more of it toward the environment. While the actual quantity of FC in the third Rorschach is no larger than in the second test, it will be clear from the figures in notes 17 and 18 that the two at present play a larger role in the total affectivity, i.e., Clyde now shows relatively more self-mastery. He shows this also in the themes which channelize his feelings (see also note 22).

[21] This reduction stands out whether we turn our attention to the individual number of color-determined associations in each test or to the sum of the color values. By the former criterion the findings are 16 color determinants in a total of 49 responses in the first test; 13 color in a total productivity of 42 in the second test; 9 color in a productivity of 57 in the third test. Using the second criterion, the findings are: a sum of 21.0 in 49 responses; 14.0 in 42 responses; 9.5 in 57 responses, in the first, second, and third tests respectively.

[22] These are reflected in the content of the color-determined associations. The socially more appropriate themes now dominate, since five of the associations in this sphere now have this quality, while only three are anxiety-determined and the other is indefinite. More socially related interests appear, to be sure, in the color-determined associations in the first and second tests, e.g., carpet, paintings, radio tube, balloon, fireworks, sun shining, sea bottom. But in both these earlier tests these topics are in

the minority, as Clyde's strong feelings center predominantly on blood, fire, lightning, and other violence themes. In the present test, fire anxiety appears in R 4, 45, and 56. The other themes are, decorations, in R 11 and 50; nature objects in R 39 and 43; and fireworks in R 44. In the "sticks" the personal emotional significance is unclear. Again, we can say that as seen in the content of the color-toned associations Clyde is showing a change in the direction of growth; he is more in contact with his environment in the way he invests his feelings.

[23] The six M are evidence of Clyde's ability to live his feelings in his inner, imaginative world. However, he does not contain all his feelings, and the report really overstates the case on this point. The EB of 6/9.5 is extratensive and indicates that an overflow of feelings into the environment must be expected. But compare the present EB of 6/9.5 to that in the second test of 0/14, and to the one in the first test of 0/21.0! At both the first two times, not only was the patient much more freely releasing his affects (note 17) and so nearly all of it was explosive (note 16) but, in addition, he could not cushion it at all by inner living. As indicated in these EB's this patient's move has been away from an infantile explosiveness, from egocentric childishness, into a state of mind such that he has (a) both grown out of the immature emotionality and also (b) built a stabilizing resource into his personality.

[24] A correlation between M and intelligence was observed by Rorschach (ref. 57, pp. 94ff.) and is assumed by a number of writers because M, or fantasy, is the work of imagination and imagination is likely to go with high intelligence. To assume a consistent such correlation can, however, be deceptive. For one thing, imagination is available to persons of moderate intelligence, being found both as Rorschach's M and indicated in achievements in the world at large. Secondly, some very intelligent persons use no or very little M. They are the extratensives. This raises the question of whether M is a constitutional trait which a person is either capable of or is not. This, in turn, opens up the question concerning the theory of M, or fantasy living, and there have now been numerous contributions on this point. Much of it is opinion of armchair quality. Some of it is hypothetical and deductive, but with the hypotheses not proven. The systematic inductive study of M is still to be done. However, barring evidence to the contrary in a given individual's Rorschach test, the generalization that there is a positive relationship between M and intelligence can be depended upon.

[25] Of his six M, four (R 7, 10, 14, and 55) are M−. The reality in them is a distorted one (the F in the M is F−) and this is dream M. Of these four, two (R 7 and 14) are seen in Dd, a kind of M to which young children are prone. These are also found in the Rorschachs of more regressed neurotics,

and they may or may not appear in a schizophrenic's record. In R 7, furthermore, Clyde compounds the pathology by reversing the figure and ground and then converting a white space into an activity in his imagination. The pathology is also apparent in R 10 in which free association mingles inner living with an accidental thinking process (Po). In a word, Clyde's fantasy living is at present of sick structure.

[26] R 51. The dream quality in this R 55 as well as its fearful affect. I am assuming these from our general knowledge of psychopathology and of content whose source is anxiety. Neither the dream structure nor the affective value to this boy can be proven from the Rorschach test record directly. These are assumed, and clinical sessions with this patient will either verify or refute them, although the Rorschach is opening up a lead based on data obtained by it (the M) and on the previously established general significance of such data. In ascribing a dangerous thought to animals, especially animals having an unpleasant connotation, a thought involving being consumed by fire, Clyde is uncovering his double anxiety of (a) his complete destruction through (b) a very painful mode. The association recalls the feeling of primitive awe described by Sullivan, something from which the individual dissociates himself and so spares himself experiencing the sharp anxiety and anguish. It is the "not me" experience of Sullivan.[67] As in dreams, we can participate in experiences usually carrying emotions and yet we do so without suffering these feelings. So this patient can be bland here while living this awful experience. He does it in the guise of a frog, screening it from himself exactly as a dream would.

[27] "Nearly all" would have been more correct, since in R 8 there is a pleasurable connotation in the "dance" theme, while the "mops" topic is, so far as we know, a neutral one to this boy. Affective quality in all the others must be judged as carrying a disagreeable flavor: the "screech" in R 7; "keeping apart" in R 10 (see note 75); the latent phobic motif in the "wild native" of R 14. Concerning his laughter as defensive warding off of troubling emotion, see concerning the defenses (notes 54 and f.); hostility and the related tension occur in R 41; and primitive awe in R 55 screens a probable panicky state.

[28] The term "phobic" is here used in its general sense of fear-laden, not in its technical sense of anxiety-binding phobic thought. The distinction between wish-fulfillment and fearful thinking is one of affective quality only: the one is pleasurable, the other painful. Both express a wish, either that something will happen or that something will not happen. We recall our troubles with our high school Latin, with its *timeo ut non,* and its *timeo ne.* This ancient grammar more correctly expressed the blending of wish with the negative attitude to it, our wish that it does not happen.

[29] In R 5 the "sea lions coming together" raises the question of a latent

M screening a coming together of humans. The "keeping apart" theme of R 10 supports this surmise, the more so because of the delaying action: Clyde produced it only as an afterthought. "Togetherness" is, of course, critically important to all of us—the oxygen to us as social organisms as Freud some place puts it. Even more critically important is the togetherness of the young child with his mother as psychiatric and sociologic research has been showing now for many years. The lead from these Rorschach test data is that we are seeing in Clyde's concern with this theme, and his walling himself off from it, a need which is at the nucleus of his illness. It is so dynamic to him that he cannot even face it as fantasy living.

R 14 is a borderline M and could as properly have been scored F—. The patient's defensive laughter at this association (see note 27) is a sign that he wants to deny the emotion here awakened, which would be evidence that he fears this fantasy. Other signs that he avoids fantasy are the failure to introduce any M in figure VII which frequently elicits such responses even in persons incapable of as many as six M (Clyde's total), the delay in producing it in R 41, and his fourth association in figure IX. When these two details are seen in action in figure IX, they are usually so seen as the first or second response to this figure.

[30] The aggression trends are apparent more in the M responses that Clyde verbalizes than in those which he suppresses. But even in these liberated fantasies, his aggression is more latent than open since the manifest content is more recognizably that which the analysts call the other side of the aggression medal, namely, phobic. But in R 7 and also in R 14 the significance may be either phobic or aggressive. The aggression is explicit in R 41, and I assume it in R 55, accenting as it does that destroying agent, fire, and its activity, burning.

[31] Referring here to content other than M-determined. See concerning the dynamics in the content generally, in note 70f.

[32] The energy ratings by the Levy scale would be:

$$
\begin{array}{ll}
\text{R } 7 & 3 \\
\text{R } 8 & 3 \\
\text{R } 10 & 1 \\
\text{R } 14 & 3 \\
\text{R } 41 & 3 \\
\text{R } 55 & 6 \\
\end{array}
$$

[33] Another indication of this weakness is the total absence of any extensor M, i.e., of any indication of a self-assertive pose in Clyde's unconscious.[58] Such direction of the activity in the M responses in this record that can be judged with confidence is centripetal (R 8, 41, 55), uncovering a clinging or dependent attitude in this boy's unconscious. In R

10 the activity is static. Even in the "fight" association of R 41 the characters are "about to fight...just starting," i.e., in Clyde's mind they are poised but not yet really engaged in the contest. This fantasy has the quality of arrested motion. Still, some traces of stronger character trends are in evidence. For one, even in his three centripetal M's, he does not develop the explicitly bowed stance, and to this extent he is neutralizing the dependency need. Then, too, the aggression trends (note 30) have in them the seed of assertiveness. In R 7 and 14, while no direction of the motion in Rorschach's sense of a stretching or a bowing activity can be identified, the directions of the "screech" and of the "lips...stretched out" are of a reaching-out variety. All these are only traces, but to the therapist searching for treatment resources in Clyde, they will be the seed of an independence-seeking, hence material for ego building, the more promising in being at the deeper layer of the personality as M data are.

[34] Additional indications in Clyde's fantasy productions (not included in the original report) are that, with the possible exception of R 8, all his fantasying is autistic, i.e., a solving of his problems by way of daydreaming that is only self-serving and is not imagination of socially constructive potential. The very regressive quality in much of it (note 25) confirms this indication of autism. Still, his content in this sphere is not a monotopical one. A variation in themes will be apparent on reading the six M-determined associations. In only two is there something approaching repetition of topic: R 7 and 14. In the others, even though he is so dominated by the unpleasurable and by the phobic aggressive, he does vary his specific imagery. It should be noted, too, that two of his M associations are entirely sound structurally (R 8 and R 41). Finally, one of his two most regressed fantasy responses (see note 26) contains in it also a theme denoting social participation (to get into the act); I refer to this again in the text (p. 175).

[35] A total of seven vista-determined associations is high by any standard. The mean for 14–17 year olds is: 1.92.[68] For 155 normal children it was 1.12; for 60 schizophrenic children, 1.00; for 50 neurotic children, 1.10.[15]

[36] In R 22 and R 28 the vista is more effective than the form percept in determining the association. The blend in R 39 with a color determinant discloses a mixed emotion and one in which the experience of each heightens that in the other and tells of the pungency with which both emotional experiences can be tasted.

[37] In R 28 and 30. The shading determinant (Y), a product of an anxiety-toned passivity, blends with the unpalatable feeling in the inferiority (V) attitude itself. The "desert" motif in R 28 with its connotation of aloneness adds a depressive mood-loading and so aggravates the unhappy mental state.

[38] This reasoning is, of course, not on the basis of Rorschach but on clinical principles. One feels himself as better or as worse only by comparison with a standard outside himself. The trend is a favorable one since to measure oneself by values outside oneself is to be conscious of such values and hence to appraise oneself by a social norm. This takes ego, always a hopeful sign.

[39] The "far away" motif is accented in R 22 and 28; while distance is a factor in R 2, 35, and 39.

[40] As mirrored in the mountains and hills of R 2, 22; and more vividly in the complex development of this theme in R 30.

[41] The architecture associations in R 35 and 39; and see Rorschach.[58]

[42] Referring to the effect resulting from the blending of the Y with the V factors, the two emotions deepening each other; see also note 37.

[43] Since he now judges himself by reference to the world's estimates of him. Again, an inference from clinical, not Rorschach, test principles, as set forth in note 38.

[44] See in note 76 concerning the climbing and the striving themes in R 32 and 36.

[45] In each of his two first Rorschach tests, Clyde utilized the shading determinant respectively in 17 and 16 associations! In his first test the form element was lacking in all but five of these Y-determined associations (Y, 8; C.Y, 4); i.e., emotion was all-dominant and ego mastery (F) proportionately lacking. In his second test, ego modulation (F) fails in nine of these responses (Y, 8; C.Y, 1); it is a force in 7 (YF, 4; FY, 3). In his present test, Clyde achieves a notable shift to only 5 associations in which Y participates at all. Passive withdrawal and undertone of sadness together with the pull to depression have critically diminished at the time of his third test. The painful mood now plays a markedly smaller role in the entire reaction pattern.

[46] Figure VII.

[47] The full reversal of figure and ground, the severe departure from accuracy and the essential distortion which this is of reality (R 29); the preoccupation with his symptomatic thoughts (especially as seen in R 30 and 31, but probably also in R 29); and the consequent failure to perceive the human profiles, one of the most common forms in the test—all add up to evidence of the disturbance which he suffers at this "mother" figure.

The question has been raised about the accuracy of designating this figure by the term "mother."[27] Implicit in such a designation is the assumption that this stimulus always evokes the thought "mother" and the accompanying emotions. There is no such one-to-one relationship between any idea and any of the Rorschach test stimuli. Still, figure VII does, in my own experience and that of others, very frequently activate the image of this parent, especially when the thoughts about her carry conflictual emotions. The content in Clyde's association to figure VII are evidence that it has excited such thoughts and feelings in him. The social history notes provide the external evidence for this test reasoning.

[48] A white space count of eight, for a percentage of 14, in the total productivity is very high by Rorschach's criterion that more than one space percept is deviant. My own means are 1.14 for normal children; 2.38 for schizophrenic and 2.06 for neurotic children.[15] My mean percentages are 4.9 in 14–17 year olds, 5.87 in adults.[11]

[49] As can be observed from inspection of his first two Rorschach test records, Clyde attended to much less space detail in each.

[50] The drastic reduction in shading (Y) determined associations, as set forth in note 45.

[51] Unstable (CF) and also impulsive (unmodulated C) emotional trends are the reactions that are easiest for Clyde when he is exposed to an exciting situation (see note 19). Regard for form—ego restraint—plays a lesser role in what he will do when his feelings are stirred up.

[52] These are spelled out in notes 72 and 73.

[53] Seen in the cluster of (a) high white space count, or oppositional trend; together with (b) the C, CF associations, or labile affectivity; together with (c) the aggression content or ideas that mobilize the affectivity and the opposition trends. It loads the dice against the patient to predict that the result will be maladaptive, and one may hypothesize as well that the feelings and the stubbornness will be converted into a socially useful effort. In some persons, this will no doubt be so and this judgment can be made from other content in a test record as well as from its structure. Clinical experience, however, makes one cautious and warrants setting up storm warnings with the word "maladaptive."

[54] The very slow time for first response in so many of the test figures raises the question of thought-blocking. Even more emphatic in pointing to blocking is the exceedingly slow mean time for all his responses: 69.7 seconds. I do not have systematic statistics for mean time per response, but from empirical observations it is known that not even extremely retarded, depressed patients take more than about 60 seconds per response on the average. Examiner's impression that Clyde was blocking in his speech or much self-absorbed will be noted throughout the record. Another quantitative effect is the very limited productivity in figure I, where perhaps the interference with the mental processes may be related to initial shock.

The avoidance of the fantasy responses described in note 29 has a constricting effect since it cuts down on the boy's imaginative living. In R 5 when he attributes the "coming together" to animals he is utilizing a specific technique for avoiding the painful idea which this same motif would hold if seen in humans. But it is constriction, paying as it does the price of giving up an imaginative experience. In his laughter at several points Clyde strikes a familiar pose: he is undoing some idea.

A structural restriction on his breadth of vision is reflected in his x associations: R 1, 6, 16, 19, 21, and 24, and perseverative x trends will be noted also in figure VI. This boy's intellectual energy and potential are high enough so that such limitation on his vision would not be expected (see notes 59 and 60). Rorschach observed this response (ref. 57, pp. 42 and 43) and ascribed it to defective intelligence (his scoring sign for it was a Do, i.e., oligophrenic detail). As Loosli-Usteri[48] later showed, it is really an indicator of anxiety. It is an avoidance expedient, since by narrowing in the range of vision, one shuts out the undesired. More correctly stated, one shuts out much that is both undesired and desired. The latter is the ballast that goes overboard in the tempest, the price of stabilizing the emotion-tossed vessel. See in this connection comments by Bleuler on the price of neurosis (ref. 20, pp. 495–67). The unusually heavy laughter at R 14 has the earmarks of a denial of the phobic loading in the association. The mechanism in R 41 is an undoing of the aggression: "they are just starting," and by making the combatants "middle-aged" Clyde is also taking the bite out of the fight.

[55] Animals of menacing connotation, or parts of animals used in aggression, especially their mouths, and frightening expressions in men or animals are leads to be explored for their phobic significance in any patient, especially in children. In Clyde, these are: R 3, 5, 7, 14, 20, question of in 23, 24, and 57.

[56] Interpretation of symbolism is always hypothetical. It has to be validated by the patient himself in the course of therapy. What the test does do is to alert the therapist to topics which, as possible symbolisms, may be screening ideas of dynamic significance, together with their emotional loading. In the present Rorschach test record they are: R 30–31, 35, 36, 39, and probably also 28. This is not to say that some of the other associations are not symbolisms. By an extended definition of symbolism, all fantasies would be such because the manifest content in them screens a latent meaning not in the patient's awareness.

[57] Fantasy activity, whether it is of healthy or pathologic quality, is one of the ego's defensive recourses. It gives vent to pent-up feelings and so relieves the individual of the tension which he endures in holding them in. By containing the feelings within, as day-dream living, fantasy protects the individual from being the menace which he would be if he discharged his feelings on the environment. By the transforming art of the unconscious, he hides from himself the unsavory meanings of his wishes,

is thus saved from seeing himself as he is, and so can live at peace with himself. This is that psychologic economy of which Freud writes and which is the equivalent of living the serene life.

For the first time in the three stages at which the Rorschach test has sectioned out his personality structure, Clyde is now liberating fantasy responses. His total of six is an above average, even a high, quantity. Means are: in normal children aged 14–17, 3.04; in schizophrenic children, 2.34. The quality of this inner living is, to be sure, in large part regressive and Clyde is using it mainly for obtaining his satisfactions autistically (see notes 25, 34). But it is still evidence that the ego has had sufficient reserve force to activate this imaginative ability; also, that Clyde possessed the imagination but that it had remained a buried resource until the time of this third Rorschach test. Important reflections are to be derived here concerning the treatment effect on him of his residence in the school, with corollary reasoning as to the outlook of further treatment effort.

[58] The hold on reality which Clyde demonstrates in his perceptual accuracy, undeviating in figures VI and VIII; also in figure I, where it is less convincing because the smaller number of associations provide less opportunity for error; and also in figure IX but less consistently since form accuracy breaks down in R 42. Yet, in view of the emotional strains on him in this figure, his ability to remain as accurate as he does is further evidence of the ego's ability to meet a challenge.

The occasional hold on the self is inferred from the occasional adhesion to D while disregarding W and Dd. Clyde does this in only two test cards, VI and IX (the single Dd in each of these is within normal expectancy). He apparently does it also in figure X, where, however, the eleven D are artifacts rather than adaptive attention to the D which he perceives, since these are simply the product of his excessively high productivity to figure X, i.e., all the D are incidental to an unchecked spontaneity. As such they do not represent a hold on the self. However, F+ perception demands not only a hold on reality but also a grip on the self. It thus supports the indication in his attention to D.

[59] As judged from the total productivity, together with the W count and the Z score. Total R of 57 is not only far above the mean of 41.35 for Clyde's age group, the 14–17 year olds,[68] but also exactly at the mean of a very superior adult sample.[6] Then, too, his total W score is now in a much healthier proportion to the entire productivity than it was in the first two tests, in both of which the W's overbalanced the D's and the Dd's (compare the response summaries for the three tests). At the same time, his present W's include five (R 29–30, 32–33, 44 and 49) that require a vigorous intellectual effort, the kind that Rorschach reports as stemming from the

drive to grasp relationships—*Indikator der dispositionellen Energie des Assoziationsbetriebs*—and also product of the wish for complex achievement—*komplizierteren Leistung.*

[60] While the W, as just described in note 59, is index to this achievement, still the W is a special variety of a more general ability to organize the stimuli of one's world meaningfully, indicated in the test in the Z score. The findings for Clyde in his present test: 66.0; mean for the 14–17 year olds, 28.90. In part, again, the score is happenstance, resulting from the outburst of response to figure X which alone contributed 27.0 to the total Z score.

[61] The associations are: R 11, 30, 35, 37, 38, 49, 57. Some of these are, to be sure, tinted by the symptomatic needs of our patient, but all are original in terms of frequency and they are in varying degrees "superior" and disclose in Clyde a differentiated breadth beyond the pedestrian range of the normal average. Of significance, too, is the appearance of "a human" content for the first time in this Rorschach test record. Concerning this content, see note 83.

[62] "Immature" since they are the residuals of his older, still unresolved needs and thus are leads at present to his symptomatic thinking. This content is explicitly reported in note 70 and ff.

[63] His F+ per cent of 63 is actually above the cricital minimum. For practical clinical purposes this critical cutting-off point is 60 per cent.

[64] The P count is six. It was two in each of his first two tests. The means for ages 6–9, and 10–13, Clyde's age groups in his first two tests, are respectively 3.19 and 5.23. Mean for age 14–17 is 6.75. Thus, from the state of mind of a child unable or unwilling to know his world's conventions, Clyde has developed to about where we would expect him to be at his present age.

[65] See the text, p. 173; and the exposition in notes 1–15.

[66] See p. 174; and notes 35–46.

[67] This is more fully spelled out under "treatment implications," p. 175, and the notes relating thereto, i.e., 78–87.

[68] Clyde's ego is inadequate for the tasks put upon it. See again notes 1–15. In addition, concerning his total adjustment, we should observe that unique ideas, percepts, and hence attitudes are still a part of his way of life; from time to time he construes reality more as his needs dictate rather than as it is; and on occasion he is indifferent to reality. Motility is subject to peculiar manifestations and he engages in more than the usual amount of wasted effort. Between his inefficient use of his intellectual abilities, his undervaluation of himself, and his still persisting submissiveness—much as he has improved in this respect (see note 45) —the prediction is in order that his achievement will not, as his personality

is now constituted, measure up to the promise in his ability. He is incapable of realizing the daydreams in which he does indulge himself. His judgments are often unwise. His handling of the various problems of his daily life is not adaptive (see note 3). Still, he can veer much better with changes of conditions than he could at the times of his first two Rorschach tests (compare his present Ap with those of the first two). He does try more to master his high drive by means of intellectual control and he succeeds in so doing. His responses to environmental stimuli as compared with the amount of response to stimuli from within (emotional reactions of any affective quality and fantasy living) were formerly seriously low: lambda index in his first test was 0.62; in his second test, 0.50. In the present test it is 1.37. The normal range (as an empirical rule; I do not have the necessary statistics) is 1.50–2.50. That is, he was formerly very much the plaything of his strong feelings but now approaches a normal equilibrium. Mindful of social canons intellectually, as we have seen him to be, he corroborates this indication by showing some understanding of the emotions of others (note 20); he can make some friendships. Also, his feelings frequently center around needs of appropriate quality and so he is capable of some normally pleasurable experiences. In all, then, he is now socially adaptive both by conscious effort and, to a degree, emotionally.

[69] As to the diagnostic picture emerging from this Rorschach test:

The question of color shock is raised by the initial response time to figure II, but it is not tenable (a) in view of the very long initial response times in the other figures and the probable thought blocking (note 9), which would explain the retardation in figure II. (b) The intellectual upset is not worse in figure II than in some of the other test figures; the F+ per cent is higher in it than it is in III, IV, VII; the Seq. is better in figure II than it is in figures III, IV, V, VI, and X. Pathologic thinking processes are worse in figures III, IV, VII, and X. So the pathology that does appear in figure II (two very rare Dd selections, one of which is a Dds; an F− in his first association; P is lacking; the M−; and the unrestrained affectivity indicated in the C determinants) cannot be laid to color shock. (c) In the color-toned figures proper, the initial response time is very slow in figure VIII, but the F+ per cent is here the best for the ten test figures; the Seq. is normal; and there are two P responses. It is thus among the freest from thought pathology. Clyde's deviations in figure VIII are his one too many Dd's, especially since one of them is a very rare one and a Dds. In figure IX, his thought content becomes notably unique and he commits one serious perceptual inaccuracy (R 42). But F+ per cent holds up here too; and the initial response time, while slow, is faster than those in four other of the test cards and equals it in two

others. P appears, belatedly. Seq. is fairly orderly. Thus, deviant ideas
and a brief break with reality, but not general disruption commensurate
with these deviations. The evidence here does not warrant our reasoning
to an emotional impact productive of typical color shock. Rather, we see
here the chronic dysfunction more consistent with findings in schizophrenia. The boy has improved but he is still impaired.

In terms of our six schizophrenia reaction patterns, Clyde is moving
up from more malignant conditions, principally SR-1 and with even the
more pathologic cast of S-1, toward the more stabilized sanctuary patterns delineated in SR-2. That is (ref. 15; p. 132), in the intellectual sphere
he shows trends toward control alternating with still-frequent disruptions. His defenses are primarily of the constriction variety, with a trace
of the adjustive. In the latter respect, however, not all that glitters is gold.
His fantasy activity is the reason for so describing him, but to be adjustive, fantasy needs to be creative, and in view of the drag still on the
ego, we cannot look to too much promise yet from Clyde. Nor is the quality of the fantasy associations themselves such as to warrant looking for
creativity. It is more regressive than healthy, autistic, and of small caliber (cf. notes 23ff.). But inner living does now serve to stabilize the boy
and is thus a step toward more adjustive defense. Meanwhile, Clyde's
emotional state continues very labile, at the same time that he manages
some control over his release. The sanctuary in this pattern generally
consists of the patient's ability to retire into some fantasy living, to
heighten the respect for reality, and to tighten up the defenses. However,
such patients remain vulnerable and cannot stray too far into the world's
corroding air.

[70] Referring now to the personal dynamics. The exposition so far
has focused on nonpersonal psychologic processes, the structural dynamics, what may be looked on as the psychologic machine. But two vehicles
with motors exactly alike can be headed in quite different directions. What
these psychologic directions are, the personal foci of the conflict and of
the pain, the ideas latent in the fantasying, these are gleaned from study
of the content. Much of this has already been elucidated in the discussion of dynamics, e.g., the themes in the color-determined associations
(note 22); the fantasy-determined (notes 26–30); and the vista-determined (notes 39–41).

[71] Most acutely expressed in R 32–33, and this motif is also stressed
in R 30 and is probably present in R 31. It appears again in R 38 and the
theme perseverates in R 40. Then, once again, in R 49.

[72] Screened as fantasy associations (see note 30).

[73] Described in the main in note 55. Additional observation: R 46
"dogs" again, and they are equated to that awe-inspiring, destructive

force: "fire." In R 48, another "mouth." In R 52, "dogs," without specific identification of the mouth but in light of the amount of oral content in the record this animal percept is suspect. The three associations here noted, as well as most of those referred to in note 55, are nonfantasy. They are thus, hypothetically, percepts at less disguised, i.e., at more conscious, levels. It would follow that the patient's phobic attitudes and the aggressions implicit in them are in large measure known to him. This again is only a lead for further exploration. If verified, the important clinical finding is that thought content from Clyde's much more immature years are persisting into his present growth phase. It is a finding which affects both the diagnostic and the prognostic thinking concerning a patient.

[74] In R 4, 45, and 56; see also note 22.

[75] Even one "together" need would be an individualized and personally significant association. In the present record we find it five times: R 5, 10, 47, 53, 54. Most arresting is this motif in R 10 in which it is expressed as a prevention of two (humans) coming together; it is the more impressive insofar as the association is structured in fantasy. An unconscious process is going on and the personal source of the thinking is therefore deep.

[76] See note 61; as there indicated, some of this content has in it the flavor of personal emotional loading. Other associations of probable especial significance, not reported in the original interpretation and not yet discussed in these notes, are:

R 9. "Clouds." See note 1 concerning the intellectual dysfunction connected with this percept. In view of the general dysphoric connotation of "clouds" the question here raised is that the inaccuracy is a personal $F-$, on the supposition that a painful mood tone is breaking down the form accuracy.

R 12. "Sticks ... mops." Both are unique. No clue as to significance to the patient.

R 17. "Gulch-like ... gully." Individualized. Its meaning to the patient ...?

R 27. As "art" category some differentiation of interest is here indicated. But the specific topic, "Indian design," is fairly frequent in figure VI and it is not original to Clyde.

R 29. Much speculation can be aired concerning the possible symbolism of this "lands ... in the ocean" association. But only the patient has the answer as to the meaning of this or of any other symbolic content. To interpret it here as disclosing a personally dynamic meaning to Clyde is to beg the question: we make an assumption that has to be proven and proceed to reason from it as though proven.

R 32, together with R 36. The "climbing" (aspiration?) theme, the pre-

carious position of the animal, "barely balanced ... as if it would fall
any minute," the unhappy predicament of the animal, "legs caught in
the rocks ... will try to break loose." The obvious themes here are insecurity and frustration, and this may actually be expressing Clyde's
percept of himself as he recalls himself over the years and as he feels
himself to be in relation to his environment. Since the description would
also be so much a human vicissitude, a Rorschach critic may properly
ask why not score M? Why adhere inflexibly to Rorschach's rule about
M? The answer is that to do so would again be begging the question; it
would be to assume what has to be proven. The sense of being in a predicament, in danger, frustrated, may well be what Clyde is here communicating. But the seduction of interpreting first and then scoring in
accordance with the interpretation, while it may at times give the right
answer, gives it for the wrong reason. The effect of such a practice would
be to rot the test's foundations. The question is in order, however, whether
the activity of the animal is not actually anthropomorphic. If so, there
is no problem. We score M and the fantasy becomes a true dream production, with all the importance that a dream carries clinically. My resistance to such scoring is on the ground that the "climbing animal" is
here too frequent, and too frequently an F+.

R 37, "the running water," and R 40 and R 42, the "pins," leave us
again without a clue as to their significance to the patient. The "bowl"
is rather frequently seen in figure IX and does not therefore mirror originality of mind. But, similar to R 27, there is a differentiated interest, and
this speaks of some capacity for breadth in Clyde.

[77] As indicated in notes 12–14 inclusive. One may demur that the
intellectual inadequacies described in note 13 are scarcely an asset.
Granted. But the pattern is an indication of growth when compared with
the more primitive adjustments delineated in Clyde's first two tests. As
the report puts it, his present condition, even though disturbed, is a step
forward. Furthermore, the new ego–affect balance is growth, relatively:
much more regard for reality (F+ per cent), many fewer feelings on the
loose (the color-determined associations) at the present time (see especially notes 18 and 20). The possibility that Clyde's fantasy associations
reflect growth, with the reservations on this point, are stated in note 23.
For a summary of the ego's assets and deficits, see note 68.

[78] See especially note 38 for the reasoning as to why this trait, painful as it is, can be the point of departure for a treatment effort. The
qualification is that the amount of this painful feeling, or of anxiety
generally, must not exceed the patient's stress tolerance point. Anxiety
can be a big help, if it does not disrupt. In Clyde, both the frequency and
intensity of these reactions are high enough to indicate that the feeling

is more pathologic than healthy. Treatment tactics will, therefore, need to be directed toward relieving his discomfort and helping the boy to understand his emotions better. Knowing the extent to which they are symptomatic, as well as the extent to which such feelings are "normal," will enable him the better to master his anxieties.

[79] As described in note 49. In reacting with some opposition, which is to say self-will, Clyde is growing. But from note 48 we know that he is overdoing the opposition, just as he excessively reacts with feelings of inferiority (note 38).

[80] The questionable asset which fantasying can be is indicated in the report; also in note 25. Structurally the emergence of M, fantasy living, is an asset. The question with relation to imaginative fantasy always is: how is the individual using it? In view of the largely autistic service to which Clyde is now putting this ability, the answer in his case as to the outlook must be a cautious one and await further evidence.

[81] For a more general exposition of the thought content now in Clyde's mind, see note 82. But refer also to note 64 concerning his greater regard at present for social canons.

[82] These more original themes are listed in note 61. The ability to spread out one's interests rather than channelize them is of course an encouraging sign. Clyde is emerging out of the channels set by his symptomatic preoccupations. A specific and even more encouraging finding in this connection is the H count. Low as it is, two H, one Hd, it is still progress as compared with no human percept or even part human percept in the second Rorschach test, no whole human but two part humans in the first. A dawning recognition of his fellow man is now part of our patient's mental content, always welcome news to a therapist. A downward course is observed in his inability to see any human details at all in the second test although they do enter into his first. A regression while a patient is under treatment is not an unusual finding. We may speculate that about the time of his second test, Clyde was avoiding humans in his thinking, since therapy made him aware of his painful interrelations. By the time of the third test he was gaining the strength whereby to face these thoughts. The regression was temporary.

[83] Not yet a formulated one, but the makings are there. Clyde's improvement in integration, his relatively improved attention to his environment, his intellectual drive as seen in his present W and Z scores (see notes 59 and 60), together with the spread in his interests, would be evidence that he can invest his energies toward objectives that carry social value.

[84] As shown in the exposition concerning pleasure-toned affect, and see especially notes 18 and 20–22. Clyde's responses to his environment

are still likely to be more frequently egocentric than allocentric (unmixed color and color-form responses are more numerous than form-color) but there will be responses, i.e., he will engage in that contact with others without which no progress can be made in therapy. It is axiomatic with some therapists that a bad interpersonal relationship is better than no relationship.

[85] Situational because of the fact that he can be in affective contact with others, directive as reflected in the potential for striving toward a goal (see in note 76 concerning R 32 and 36). The critical implication with regard to treatment is that deep therapy is contraindicated. The boy is as yet too vulnerable; thought content out of his regressive system (note 25) still too readily communicates with ideas in his conscious mental life.

[86] Clyde's present Experience Balance, 6/9.5, and the EA of 15.5 contribute in important measure to this favorable outlook, guarded as one must be about prognosis in a person with this kind of personality and history. Clyde's EB is such that he can absorb the shocks from the affects inwardly. His emotional state is one of readiness to let his feelings go, explosively at times. But he can also continue just on the verge of letting go; he can feel strongly and direct himself and his feelings toward socially useful effort. Can we look for a transference relationship? *A priori* the answer would be no. The reaction pattern is not that of a neurotic conflict. It is that of a personality still in ego lag, a schizophrenic reaction pattern. He has improved, but he is still in arrears in respect to the ego's growth. The outlook that he will transfer resentments in him to a therapist, that he will live through the emotional experiences that bred his resentments, and set out on a fully adult ego course is now small. He has reacted to his frustrating sources not with conflict but with withdrawal and retreat. The transference outlook can for now only be regarded as poor.

## Clinical Note

Clyde was nine years and four months old when he entered the Orthogenic School. He had been referred by a child guidance clinic (in another State) after having been in treatment in that clinic for nearly three years. The symptoms when he came to the school were as follows: intense preoccupation with electric fans, motors and electrical appliances, and an interest in things rather than people. Hyperactivity, with self-destructive and aggressive behavior. He talks in opposites, e.g., cold is intense heat. Ritualistic and compulsive behavior patterns, e.g., he does not eat away from the table. He thinks of his insides as being electrically driven. Clyde does not talk to children; he refers to them as "small persons."

This boy is the eldest of two children. He has a sister six years younger. She is an attractive, bright child with whom Clyde is rivalrous and aggressive. The father is an executive in a machine industry. He is quick-tempered, irritable, and has been quite punitive with this boy. There is little understanding on the father's part of Clyde's serious personality disturbance and there has been a poor relationship between the two since Clyde was an infant. Although this child was planned for and wanted, the mother rejected him from birth on. His early training was rigid and lacked warmth. The mother feels quite overwhelmed by this boy and is detached and vague in her feelings about him. He refers to his mother and father as "parents" and addresses them indirectly as "him" and "her."

The boy has a severe laceration on the right wrist caused by his thrusting his hand through a glass door. This resulted in numbness of the thumb and first and second fingers. The accident occurred about six months prior to admission to the school.

In the school Clyde has been acting out his mechanical and electrical preoccupations. He carries a small tube and motor with him constantly. He frequently makes noises like electrical devices and machines. He uses adults as tools fitting in with his fantastic and elaborate constructions. He is very explosive in temper and hits, kicks, bites and scratches himself, as well as inanimate objects and adults. He is extremely self-destructive, stating that he wants to break his own bones as well as to explode the school and kill the counselors. He imitates the symptoms of the other children. He does not engage in any structured activity in the school, but it is known that he does read. He has cognizance of the school's protective function and is constantly testing this out.

# III.
## The Test and Treatment

# CHAPTER 11

# Treatment and change

The purpose of treatment is to help bring about learning. All learning is change. To be treatable a person must be able to change. Starting with these premises the corollary is obvious that insofar as the Rorschach test is an effective instrument in evaluating a person's ability to change, it is useful in judging his treatability. The logic of the test's findings in indicating willingness for or resistance to change, and therefore readiness for psychologic therapy, forms the substance of this chapter and those that follow.

Concerning learning as change, my point of view is the clinical one. The general principle that to have learned is to have been modified is an old one. In the language of that astute psychologist, Sherlock Holmes, it is elementary. Old as it is, problems in learning are obviously among the newest ones in our science. Else why would the present generation of students in our field be finding themselves exposed to the controversial schools, their theories and supporting experiments on learning that are all so prominent a phase of contemporary psychology?

I am not here rushing into the arena of controversy among the learning theorists of the universities and the laboratories. Yet, the learning which I have in mind and the changes which it effects includes the kinds which have been studied under conditions of careful control: at the physiologic level, in conditioning experiments, in habit-forming, in investigations on memory. All are on one unbroken continuum with the learnings induced by the therapies directed at the complexities of mental disturbances and disorders. Pavlov's dogs, Watson's babies, and all the generations of school children, college students, their professors and other adults, those from Ebbinghaus to Hull, Tolman and Köhler, all who have been subjects in uncounted researches on learning, all have changed. However each theorist may have seen his results, the observation was in order that the experimental animal or human was, to a degree, changed after the learning. The dog salivated at the sound, formerly meaningless to him, of the tuning fork; the baby became alarmed at the furry touch of the rabbit. Each of these stimuli had previously left these subjects unmoved. Then they learned.

The principle extends to the field of the personality in its purposive, adaptive, developmental course. Benedek,[16] among others, has shown that the baby, a mass of uncoordinated discharges at birth, has by the fourth month learned to know the source of its satisfactions (mother) and to control himself; he has learned to wait. The undirected discharges are changing into something that is becoming a human being. Another writer, Bartley,[2] reports some experiments on the pupillary reflex and interprets the observed changes in this reflex as psychosomatic learning; the individual is adjusting to the changed conditions represented by the stimuli. He is thus, after the learning which each adjustment is, to that extent a changed person.

Of much more complex personality significance, although still occurring in the infantile months of life, is the case of one baby who utilized her alimentary experiences as appropriate response in her pleasurable interpersonal relations. Grinker,[35] (citing Engel and Reichmman) uses this case to exemplify his theorizing about identification. It also demonstrates learning entirely by means of one of the somatic systems, learning which transforms a personality and in a sphere essential to this little human being in terms of the grown person she will eventually be.

Then there is the commonplace that each of us is born so much alike with regard to certain general needs but we grow up so differently with regard to what satisfies them. Murphy[53] makes the point. Every baby is hungry, but the hundred thousand or so born over the world in any one day will grow up differing in what they will love to eat: bread (rye? or white?), ice cream, peanuts, raw eggs, rice, whale blubber. Murphy's bill of fare does not include oysters, snails, fried grasshoppers. Yet, people love them. They have changed in these differential directions from the undifferentiated hungering babies which they were at their starts. They have learned.

Take these same hundred thousand or so persons and the presumption is a safe one that by the time of his adult years, each will be speaking some language. Yet, if one could look at them all on the day of their birth, could he have any hint that at the age of twenty-five one would be speaking in the rounded, controlled accent of England's upper classes, another in the Cockney's squeaky inflection, in a Bronx twang, or in our southern Negro's soft drawl? Or that he will be speaking not English but Swedish, or French, a German dialect, or a Russian or Chinese? Bantu or Masai? So far as his undifferentiated condition at babyhood was concerned, it might have been any of these. Each learned and changed with the conditions in which he lived, with the environment that was constantly impinging on what he was at birth. All this is elementary too. Yet, there is a fateful finality in these environmental effects. Operating through the agency of our parents, these are arrestingly, sometimes comically, obvious in those outer personae which we present to our social familiars. Liss[47] vividly summarizes: ... "gestures, grimaces, voice, postures and many types of physical emulations which are uncanny in their mirrorlike quality in the infant. Many of the subsequent mannerisms of the child recall the parent."

Liss here puts his finger on that learning which is of the essence clinically. For at the source of the mirrored behaviors in the child are his psychologic traits. The reasoning is in order, in fact, that the child has absorbed from the parent the latter's anxieties and full-blown neuroses, manifest as these were in the parent's gestures, voice and other mannerisms; and now in the child. Here we see one kind of learning that malforms the personality. The other, even more significant clinically, resides in the fact that the environment is always so critically important in what the child learns. In psychoanalytic terms, learning is overdetermined by superego forces. To the extent that it is so the ego is unfree. The individual is overloaded with restrictions, impeded by expectations of punishment or of disaster and dares not exercise his abilities. He seldom tests out his wings, clings to the well-built nest or ventures only an ever-so-safe distance from it. It is not an *ego* learning, using the term "ego" in Federn's sense of wide-open boundaries. When these boundaries extend to the horizon and beyond, we see the ego at its freest, as in the most creative men and women.

But the ego in most persons, far from extending its boundaries, shrivels them. We may paraphrase, with an apology to Gray for the mutilation of the meter:

> "Full many a gem of purest ray serene
> The dark unfathomed caves of the unconscious bear."

The gems remain locked away. The person has learned only too well to inhibit, to channelize, to immure, to stay immature and to cling to his immature artifices. Thus incapacitated and neurotic he presents himself for therapy. Can he *un*learn his self-defeating and character-deforming ways? The problem is not that of undoing the past. It is one of learning anew.

Concerning treatment as learning, I can only refer to the vast literature that has been written in our generation on the subject of psychotherapy. Whatever the orientations of the several therapies, at their cores the central principle is the same. The patient is obtaining insight, understanding. He is seeing realities which had formerly escaped him. He is seeing himself in a perspective hitherto obscured in relations to others, to his conflicts, his emotions, and his potential for drive and achievement. The patient-therapist relationship is always a learning relationship. It takes, to be sure, the deeper psychotherapies to attain these understandings. At the more directive treatment levels, the capacity for learning is less. The change in these persons does not reach deeply into their personalities. Restricting the term psychotherapy to the meaning inherent to the two roots of the words, it is therapy of the psyche. In the psyche, deep changes are effected. It is here that the person learns. He does so by calling "upon the 'distance receptors,' a relatively enormous superstructure possessing million-sided connections with multitudinous other nervous arcs and representing untold potentialities for redistribution of, so-to-say, stored stimuli by *associative* recall" (Sherrington, ref. 64; p. 351). He uses, in a word, that marvelous piece of human equipment, his higher brain centers. By the *redistribution* he is something different, he has changed.

And now a third premise on which this chapter rests, one which is a clinical axiom. It is: a person's ability to change varies with his defenses. More accurately, it is the converse of his defensive state: the more rigid the defenses, the less changeable the person, the less treatable. The principal emphasis in the pages that follow is, therefore, on those test data and patterns that correspond to the psychologic defenses. Too, I indulge myself in some speculations concerning that all-important phase of the treatment experience, the transference relationship. These speculations follow from the reasoning concerning the affects, ego, defenses, and personal dynamics behind anxieties. With the intention of preparing the ground for some of the complexities of these psychologic interactions, I proceed first with some general exposition concerning clinical changeability. This demonstrates something of the way in which the test affords evidence of intellectual adaptivity and emotional fluidity. As my next point, I describe the clinical pictures in the order of their known treatability. This exposition follows.

# CHAPTER 12

# Who can change?

Let us consider, first, two concepts which Rorschach derived out of his test and which we can firmly set on statistical bases. They are his *Erfassung*, or Approach, and his *Sukzession*, or Sequence. Both are derived from W, D, Dd. Normal distribution statistics readily distinguish between D and Dd, and my colleagues and I have so established these categories.[12] The term W is itself a definition. Any finding, such as Approach (Ap) based on a patient's selection of W, D, Dd, can therefore be viewed with confidence as constituted out of quantitative data. The norm, or frame of reference, for what is a healthy distribution of W, D, Dd, adjusted for total productivity, is also found by frequency statistics.[2] A meeting of the minds among researchers regarding the population that can appropriately serve as such a norm is all that is first necessary.

Concerning the indications in Ap for changeability and hence for treatability the answer is given again empirically. What kind of persons yield the Rorschach test patterns with the several kinds of Ap? I am using as my normative population a sample of presumably healthy adults in the average intelligence ranges for whom a W, D, Dd distribution has been established: it is 6, 23, 3 for their mean R of 32.65. Possibly this represents the optimum for getting on in the world, in the average intelligence ranges.

Inspecting now the Ap patterns in the light of personality patterns whose changeability is known, here is what we find. The persons who excessively, in instances exclusively, accent the major detail (Ap: (W) D! Dd; or W D! (Dd)) have great difficulty in changing. They are either very limited, by reason of intelligence, in the ability to attend to anything other than the obvious—this is the person who proverbially cannot see beyond the end of his nose—or they must concentrate on and cling to what is most plain and tangible. They dare not stray. They are, therefore, unable to see the woods for the trees. They cannot change because they will not.

When in his test pattern the subject overaccents the whole (Ap: W! (D) Dd; or W! D (Dd)), he is again handicapped, being now unable to see the trees for the woods. He cannot break up his mental field into its meaningful components. Some persons live with this habitual pattern and are often being carried away by larger enthusiasms. In others, their mental sluggishness prevents their detecting the salient features within a situation. These two kinds of persons can be differentiated from each other through their different kinds of whole percepts. In either event the ideas which should shape up in a therapeutic effort fail to do so. They are all persons who cannot learn, who are not likely to change.

Then there are those whose selective observations excessively accent the minute. Some do so because their regard is splintered. They are over-distractable. They are too unstable to focus their attention adaptively on the major, tangible fact or to abstract out any larger significances. Others with this defective (Ap: (W) D Dd!; or W (D) Dd!) approach are under an irresistible compulsion for reasons of anxiety to concentrate on all minutiae, and in doing so they disregard matters of larger import. Percepts which could effect learning are fended off. Since the press of the underlying psychologic forces which dictate this defense is self-perpetuating, these persons too dare not change.

The sophisticate in the Rorschach test and in psychopathology will recognize in these two approaches, both of which accent the less obvious (Dd), the two different conditions that produce this same finding. One is schizophrenia, which splinters the attention, and the other is obsessive neurosis, which compels the attention. The same overt behavior is thus the work of differing underlying personality organizations. The effect on the treatment potential has been in the one instance to dissipate, in the other to congeal it. It is thus critically essential to know the entire person-ality reaction pattern in order to understand what the manifest symptom tells concerning the personality source from which it arises. This principle holds for any of the approach types. Each must be judged within the frame of reference of the patient's whole reaction pattern. Only from this sphere of reference can we know its significance in judging treatability. This qualification should be axiomatic. Yet, it is one of those axioms which an examiner loses his sight of as he concentrates on some one finding as sig-nificant. The value of a Rorschach test datum is as a psychologic depth actuality. Its meaning as symptom is a function of the whole person who so behaves.

As a generic indicator, then, Ap tells how perceptive the person is as he attends to the data of varying significance in his field. Does he adequately attend to the major ones? To what degree is he sensitive to the minor ones? Can he grasp the more general significance of events? As presented situa-tions vary in importance, can he shift his focus with these changing events? In terms of promise of response to therapy, it is a representative sample of how adaptive he can be, whether he has the necessary intellectual "give" such that he can open up new perspectives on himself and follow them.

Sequence gives evidence, at one extreme, of the fixity of S's intellectual procedures and, at the other, of its unregulated disorderliness. When the patient unvaryingly follows a W, D, Dd sequence for the ten test cards, he is too set logically in his ways, cannot relax adequately for purposes of thinking out alternate ways of working out his problems. It is a trait which makes him impermeable to the perceptions which the treatment process would open up. Learning is forestalled. For the persons at the other extreme, the thinking carries little or no predictability. It is arbitrary in its lack of orderliness. Hence, these persons cannot lay a grip on the ideas which are the new perceptions of a treatment effort. The patient continues disorganized. He is not changing. Between the two extremes, intermediate forms are found.

The optimum sequence, that affording best promise for response in therapy, actually departs within certain recognizable limits from what may at first thought appear to be the best. The empiric facts are that the healthy, those with more "give" in their mental structure, show variations in the order in which they attend to W, D, Dd, in the respective test cards. They are relaxed in their orderliness. These are the persons who can change, i.e., they can learn. An unvarying adherence to a norm in the Rorschach test—and one may so reason for any of the tests of clinical psychology—is not found in normals. The cliché is by now well known: the strictly "normal" is not normal.

The observations concerning Approach and Sequence refer to two variables that are primarily the work of the intellect. They are thus among the test's indications as to the condition of the ego in its role of consciously attending to the environment and controlling the subject's intellectual method within orderly ranges. Insofar as these two variables reflect the ego's facility in modifying the individual's course, they tell us something about the subject, about his plasticity, a character trait critically important in treatability.

The ego's share in carrying on the therapeutic process is, however, a much more extensive, active one. The outcome of any treatment depends in fact on the ego's basic stamina, its toughness. It needs to be tough in order to manage those biologically more primitive forces in the personality, the feelings. In the Rorschach test findings, it is the Experience Actual that communicates information concerning the sphere of the feelings. This (the EA as reported in Chapter 2) is the patient's total emotional reactivity. It is thus information concerning the very center, the core, of the personality. In some persons, under certain conditions of human life, these are the forces least subject to the ego's criticism or mastery. They contain the sources also of what is most exciting, most creative, on the human scene. In one's total life course, EA may be the road either to Waterloo or to Olympus. In the resources which the EA uncovers, the patient and his therapist have their great opportunity: they can direct the patient's mental assets into activity that will bring healthy results or they can release the potential dynamite which EA is, with the well-known effects to the personality of dynamite.

A rationale for a relation between EA and treatability is readily available from an inspection in one perspective of (a) certain patients with low EA in their Rorschach tests and (b) the known psychologic treatability of these persons. The diagnostic pictures under consideration are: mental deficiency, extensive loss of function due to brain pathology, depressions. In their Rorschach tests, all these individuals are very constricted in EA, with very few color-determined associations and essentially no human-form movement responses. The feebleminded are as a group emotionally sluggish and unresponsive. No doubt this is due to the lack of ideas and of acquired interests because of their inadequate brain equipment. Ideas and interests are the triggers that mobilize our feelings and activate us into their display. Defective brain equipment must theoretically be the fact behind lack of imagination (M).

Concerning the deficits consequent on brain pathology, the rationale is parallel to what it is in the feebleminded, both with respect to lethargic emotional response and dearth of imagination. These persons have no inner life such as is indicated in EA. They are not amenable to psychologic therapy, not in any penetrating sense.

In the depressed, the EA is also characteristically very restricted. Depending on how deep the depression, the M,C findings may be 0,0. This is, in fact, so frequent in depressions that when, within such a reaction pattern, the patient does produce some M or C determined associations, we are alerted to active neurotic features in the clinical picture. The cortical tissues of the depressed are, however, intact. This is abundantly clear from the behavior of these patients following recovery. In their illnesses, therefore, their emotional responsivity is submerged. The term "depressed" is a statement of what is happening to these persons only psychologically. It is as though the mental stream is actually being pressed down—de-pressed—and prevented from normal flow and functioning activity. The illness achieves functionally what amentia and dementia are doing by reason of tissue inadequacy. The inability of the depressed to respond to psychotherapy per se is well known. Fortunately for them the community of therapists does not throw up its hands when faced by this illness. Care of the patient in an appropriate, tension-free situation, whether home or hospital, is the usual first step. An ingress into his troubled state is eventually made, with support at first of dependency needs, and gradual emotional warming up is attempted so that an active therapeutic effort can be made. The EA is expanding. It is expanding too when the remissions are spontaneous, which is frequent in this illness.

Here, then, we have three groups of patients that are not responsive to psychologic therapy. All are without inner life in the Rorschach test language: no C, no M, or very little of these. They are possessed of very limited, if any, EA. EA is a statement concerning a person's emotional mobility. It requires emotional mobility to live the personality changes that are the essence of the therapeutic process. These two sets of data, the one Rorschach, the one clinical, confirm each other.

Turning now to persons who are known clinically to be treatable, Fenichel[32] lists the several groups in the following order with reference to their accessibility to psychoanalytic therapy: hysteria; compulsive neuroses, and these vary according to whether the conflict is active or the condition has hardened; neurotic depressions; character neuroses; perversions and impulse neuroses. After these he makes note of the psychoses, with special reference to the manic depressions and to the schizophrenias.

In the Rorschach test, the inner living of these patients is characteristically as follows. Hysteria: EA, medium, with an extratensive EB (C total greater than M). Compulsive neuroses: EA broad, and EB ambitendent (C about equal to M). Neurotic depression: EA, medium to restricted; with the EB more likely to be introversive (M greater than C total). Character neuroses: EA, medium; EB may be extratensive or introversive. Perversions and impulse neuroses: EA varies, usually with the patient's intelligence resources; it can be broad, medium, restricted; EB is most likely to be extratensive.

It will be kept in mind that Fenichel is here discussing *psychoanalytic* therapy. I have been applying his principles to three levels of psychotherapy: directive without insight; with insight but without ego reconstruction; and deeply penetrating, with effort at full ego reconstruction. In so doing, I am consistent with the broad tenor of Fenichel's thinking. The *accessibility* of the patient is the thing. That is, is the patient open to, can he be opened up, to ideas that will alter his way of seeing things? Can the treatment experience change him, and to what degree, from what he is in his illness?

Reasoning now from the Rorschach test's EA and EB findings in the persons at these three levels of treatability, we observe that some inner living is present in all. They are all to some degree emotionally fluid. They react in varying amounts with an outward show of feelings (C), and they introvert feelings (M). But this is as far as the EA and the EB alone can take us. No EA or EB is specific for any reaction pattern. We cannot, therefore, use the findings as to total emotional responsivity (EA), or as to introversive-extratensive balance (EB) for placing a patient on a given point on Fenichel's continuum of treatability. What an inner experience balance (EB) which is clearly extratensive does tell us is that, given a Rorschach test record that patterns out into a clear-cut neurosis, with evidences of keen ego-affect conflict, and with certain specific foci of the conflict, and indications also for restrictions of the mental field, then the extratensive EB points to a probable hysteric reaction form. This EB is information to the effect that the symptoms are not likely to be contained by introversion, that there will be some form of outward expression. From the nuances of the color-determined associations themselves, i.e., from color responses which are not at all modulated by regard for form (C) or those in which the color determinant dominates over that in the form percept (CF)—and these are the nuances which usually characterize the color responses of these patients—from these data the story is filled out: an hysteric overreaction. The information which the EA provides concerns the total breadth of the emotional life, or the limitations on it. How much feeling is ready to be mobilized in the patient? The essential fact is that the hysteric, far from being inert, as is the feebleminded, the brain damaged, the deeply depressed, responds. He even overresponds. He seeks contact of the kind which is most essential to a person in communication with another, emotional contact.

In the compulsive neurotics, the inner mobility as sheer expansiveness (EA) is greater than in the hysterics. Yet, it is notorious that these patients are less easily treatable as a clinical group generally. Some of these patients are so recalcitrant to the treatment process as to present the therapist with his own most stressful professional labor, one in which the rewards are scanty and the frustrations persistent. They are in a more hardened state rather than in the flux of conflict (Fenichel). The roots of their neuroses reach to earliest infancy. They are sincere in their urgent wish for therapy, since their anxieties are intense ones and are taking heavy toll as their obsessive thinking and compulsive acting play havoc with their day-to-day routines and normal pleasures. From the extensive EA in so many of these persons, we should expect individuals with rich personality resources. Many are. Yet, they are also—to repeat and accent—among the most resistant to the therapeutic process. Their opulent emotional life— whether more introversive, more extratensive (rarely) or ambitendent (most frequently)—is just not a help to treatment.

Obviously, then, factors other than EA are of the essence of the whole therapeutic experience. They are: the defenses, the patient's need for them and his ego's ability to maintain the personality's integration if he discards any of them. Implicit in these considerations is that of the nature and degree of pathology in the patient. His EA may be no asset. Rather, its features—the structure of the M, the nuances of the C, the content in both —may more sharply delineate the illness. These observations hold also for those other clinical groups of less treatable potential in Fenichel's appraisals: the neurotically depressed, with their orality; the character neurotics in whom the ego is so embedded in the neurosis that it will not reach across to the therapist in an effort at changing. Then there are those persons with perversions who just enjoy their primitive love patterns too much. These feed too gratifyingly on the pleasure principle to be interested in change. All these groups, among the more recalcitrant to learning, are yet in their Rorschach tests possessed of EA, of inner resources in varying amounts. On the other hand, persons who, by reason of character structure, are not treatable are also lacking in the ingredients of EA in their Rorschach tests.

The general principle is: a finding of EA in the Rorschach test is essential for psychologic treatability. Patients without it are not likely to be directly treatable. But the possession of EA, however extensive, is not alone assurance that the patient will be responsive to psychotherapeutic effort.

Returning now to the two kinds of compulsive neurotics and the Rorschach test findings in them, in those that are more treatable, the anxiety is free rather than bound. Whether manifest as shading shock or as color shock, the effect is more obvious, acute, and disrupting. The patient fails to master anxiety through the effort at hold on the self, i.e., through accent on D, on F+, on P, on animal forms, at the same time that he extrudes the affectivity determinants (see p. 211). Nor does the compulsive neurotic who is less treatable have recourse to these relatively adaptive defenses. However, he does master himself. His expedients as communicated in the test are: much overattention to Dd; excessive productivity, with little synthesizing of his percepts; excessively fast time for first response; and, even though animal forms are many, percentage-wise, the number of P may be small; the content may include two or even more anatomy themes. All this is binding the anxiety. This defense is pathologic. It binds the anxiety in tactics and in ideas that on the surface are safe, but it also so tightly hobbles the mental life as essentially to cripple the patient. He has security but at the price of that freedom which is intellectual adventure and all its zest. Total associational productivity is usually greater in the less treatable, as is the total Dd. The emotional charge is more limited, the EA less extended, in the less treatable. They give up their potential for richness of experience under stringent command from within.

A curious and general finding in obsessive compulsive neurotics is the ambiequality of the EB, in both the treatable and not treatable. Whether the test yields up many or few M, many or few color-determined associations, the number of M tend to equal the weighted total of the C responses. In fact, given a neurotic Rorschach test pattern, the ambiequal EB, the balance or nearly so of M,C is usually the cue to the reaction type being obsessive compulsive. F+ per cent is within the same compromise range of neurosis (65–75% in both groups). An important differential in the two is in their thematic content: oral themes characterize the less treatable, both as oral-gratifying and oral-phobic. The themes are in some responses patently oral; in some they are screened. Examples are the breast; sucking, whether by humans or by animals; food associations; less frequently, drink, although containers of drink are frequent as an evasion of this need.

These associations may emerge with M determinants, and, as language of the unconscious, their essential meaning is not manifest to the patient. But these themes appear also at more conscious levels. The oral threatening percepts are usually of phobic animals (wolf, alligator or crocodile, tiger, lion, eagle, hawk). In some patients it is a topic specific for him with which he binds the anxiety, and the test uncovers it in his adhering to it (repeats the association at more than one point). Phobic themes are observed both in those neurotics with more active conflicts, i.e., those with free anxieties and therefore more treatable, as well as in the more indurated conditions which are less amenable to therapy.

When produced with M, these associations may point to a very vulnerable person psychologically, and so to one more treatable, since they are communicating active dream work, pregnant with heavily painful affect. The patient shows himself in this communication sensitive to that within which he also finds alien to himself. Liability to panic reaction resides in these Rorschach test M's. As something about himself which he wishes were otherwise, such fantasying is a wish to change. It is one that can come to expression all too dramatically, as in homosexual panics or in a hostile aversion impulse which may reach the extreme of homocidal or suicidal urge. These storm-laden M may, therefore, be the paradoxical promise of readiness for that psychologic catharsis which will leave the patient stronger. But it is also a measure of the Damocles' sword that is hanging over the patient, the danger of psychotic disintegration. The test's message is thus both a warning and a preventive opportunity to the therapist: can he so direct the catharsis as to forestall any tragic discharge and start the patient on his remission?

The two kinds of obsessive compulsive neuroses, with their differing readiness for therapy, illustrate my second major guiding principle in judging the treatment implication in a Rorschach test pattern. This principle is: the patient's readiness to respond beneficially depends on (a) the fluidity of the conflict and (b) the fixity of the defenses. Two variables are thus involved. It will also be seen by the sophisticated clinical observer that within the neurotic reaction patterns the two operate in a reciprocal relationship: the more fixed the defenses, the less the ebb and flow in the psychologic struggle, and vice versa. Given then (1) a test pattern in which the EA points to inner mobility, the outlook for change will (2) vary according to the test's indication of free anxiety and related active ego struggle, and also to (3), conversely, the state of the defensive structure, i.e., how free is the patient to permit the mobility which is his potentially as indicated in his EA? A detailed discussion of the psychological defenses as patterned out in the Rorschach test, with the attendant reasoning concerning treatment implications, is therefore in order now.

# CHAPTER 13

## The defenses and treatability. Constrictions

The exposition that follows is that of behaviors identified as defenses in the Rorschach test, together with my understanding of their roles in the total therapeutic experience. The behavior patterns were originally factored out in our researches in schizophrenia. Clinical psychiatrists and Rorschach test investigators independently described certain patients by the same list of behavior items. Among these items were some denoting the psychologic defenses as work of the ego, in accordance with the theories principally of Anna Freud[33] and of Fenichel.[32] Since these behaviors were formulated by psychiatrists, we have that warrant for their clinical validity. Since our method correlated the clinical judgments with those based on Rorschach test findings, we have this basis for inferring that these Rorschach test behaviors are, by the test's frame of reference, the ego's defenses. In later studies, Molish has, independent of myself, been testing out the defense findings first reported in the 1954 monograph[15] and later revised (see Molish and Beck[51, 52]).

One outcome of our method has been the regrouping of all the behavioral descriptions into clusters that contain specific manifestations of certain larger traits into which the whole personality of each patient was factored out.* For the defensive operations, the levels of manifestation as we identify them are: A: constrictive; B: pathogenic; C: adjustive. These we may look on as the ego's strategies in its defensive effort. The individual behavior items are the tactics. I cannot here enter into the dispute as to whether defenses are ever anything but pathogenic. My main interest here is to relate how these defensive activities in any clinical picture, and more concretely, in any individual patient, affect the outlook for treatment.

A. The constrictive defenses are identifiable, for one thing, by a rigid hold on reality. Productivity (R), i.e., liberated associational activity, is reduced. The question may be asked as to how the examiner knows whether the productivity (R) represents the patient's actual developmental ability or is a reduction from his potential. A judgment as to the probable intellectual functioning of the patient can usually be made from internal evidence in the test. When the test is not done blind the expected intellectual

---

* Five such major traits emerged. In addition to the (a) defense organization, they are (b) associational integration, (c) fantasy activity, (d) emotional state, and (e) social adaptation. I am limiting myself in this writing to the details concerning the defenses.

level can be known from extratest information about the patient's intellectual and social, as well as vocational, levels.

Other indications of constrictive defenses are:

The ability to synthesize percepts meaningfully, to grasp relations between data (Z) is hampered, or lost.

Thought content is narrowed or sterile (percentage of animal forms rises above expectancy).

Selective attention is channelized by the most obvious (Approach: D!).

Orderliness (Sequence) is excessively methodical to the point of being invariant (always W, D, in that order).*

Perceptual accuracy (F+ per cent) is very high. The patient is painfully certain of those realities which he does report.

All the foregoing traits make up a character armor. The patient encases himself in this psychologic wall and wards off any idea or impulse that might divert him from his accustomed ways. So, he is safe from the disasters with which his anxiety threatens him, although he is not by these tactics removed or secured from the anxiety itself. That persists and necessitates his maintaining his armor intact.

In so keeping up his guard, the patient shuts off any outflow of feelings to others (number of color-determined responses is small or totally lacking) and he permits himself few imaginative flights or none (M). Hence, another characteristic Rorschach test finding is excessive concentration on the external world (lambda index is high, beyond normal range) at the cost of inadequate response to the inner world (narrow EA). The limited free emotional experience that we find in some clinical pictures is actually the pathologic result of a pathogenic defense.

So closely held a defense would point to resistance to change, and therefore to a pattern not responding to treatment effort. This inference is supported by the clinical realities in the conditions in which psychotherapy has great difficulty in making a start. These conditions include deep depression and severe neurotic repression. And these are the patients, too, whose Rorschach test patterns are distinguished by the constrictive behaviors. A depressed individual's test is, we keep in mind, marked also by other indications. The defenses above described do not in themselves spell depression. Then, too, certain other features critically differentiate a depression from a neurosis with repression. Yet, given the Rorschach test indications for character armor defense, this defense is one of the clinical dynamics in the

---

* Strictly speaking, Sequence, or orderliness, can usually not be judged in these Rorschach test patterns for the simple reason that, when a patient attends only to D in all ten cards, there can be no Sequence, because he does not vary his approach. Such all-D approaches are by no means rare findings. But, more frequently, one or more W, the simple ones (those in Figs. I, V, IV, VI) are also used.

illness whatever the form of the illness. It can be added here that in one of the schizophrenias many elements of this pattern appear—many, but not all; distinguishing differences also appear. The logic of the resemblance is, however: is the schizophrenia itself, the entire illness itself, a defense? I shall return to the question of schizophrenia below.

With their character armor Rorschach test patterns, some patients also produce responses of a kind not typical of these defenses. These are the associations that are fantasy determined (M) or the product of lively affect (color-determined). A healthy recreational, or wish-fulfilling, theme may appear in the fantasy, and a cheerful, sprightly note in the associations of lively tone. Here is the test's evidence that more salutary trends can pierce the armor. The patient can relax from his stiff psychologic posture. To this extent he can change. The content theme may not even be one from which an adjustive social attitude is to be directly inferred, e.g., it may be an impulsive aggression idea or an immature heterosexual wish. The over-all indication is, nevertheless, that the depression is reactive or that the conflict is an outgoing one. The patient can change.

In some of these tightly held defense positions, a variation in the pattern is manifest in an excessive attention not to the most obvious (D!) but to the over-all stimulus without perceiving its significant elements (W!) or in too much absorption with the minute (Dd!). These findings characterize the more obsessively structured neurotics (cf. p. 208). This Rorschach test behavior still delineates a narrowing of the field of attention but patients so reacting are pinning their safety on either the generalized, abstract concept (W) or on an exhaustive regard for all possible elements (Dd). Clinging to these habits they are resistant to treatment. Again, however, their total emotional life may yield evidence of responsiveness, and so of changeability. As I show below, the quality of the color-determined and of the fantasy associations and the themes in them necessarily influence the judgment as to a person's inner responsivity. So do other test findings, those that bear on the health and developmental level of the ego. But assuming certain conditions are indicated in these other test spheres, then the rule holds: treatability can be appraised in the test by (a) the emotional structure (EA) and (b) the defense organization.

Among the test behaviors that uncover the crippling defense tactics, restriction of the field of interest may stand out prominently over the other constriction findings. The patient's thought content will be dominated by only the simplest everyday ideas. This is Rorschach's "stereotype," manifest in the test in a percentage, much above expectancy, of the most common, the easiest percepts—the animal forms. Or even if the percentage of animal forms is within the expected range, the interests may still be narrowly channelized by some particular topic. This may appear in the test as a perseverative idea (tree, stone, some particular bird or animal) which was seen in one of the earlier test cards, or it may be an expression of some symptomatic need (anatomy associations), or it may be vocationally determined. These latter are personalized stereotypes. All are used by the ego as a way of eschewing mental adventuring. This limited functioning becomes an intellectual habit, a mental process, and the only way that the person can carry on. Change is foreign to his ways.

Another area of mental activity which the constriction defense may attack is the thinking, usually apparent as interference with speech. The response total will, in these instances, be lower in the free association than the examiner has reason to expect. In the Inquiry, the patient may confirm the expectation by producing several new associations. The interference may make itself known in the time findings: very slow time per response, or time per first response. Clinical anxiety can readily be deduced from these test behaviors. Any special foci of the anxiety, as disclosed in the particular points at which these test behaviors are observed, offer differential information as to the reactivity of the patient. Should no such foci show up, it is likely that the clinical condition is generalized and more severe: a depression is most likely, or a well-established, persistent, chronic neurosis. The reactivity at whatever point is sign that the ego is sensitive enough to be mobile. Ingress via psychotherapy is possible.

The crippling of the thinking may be more severe, reflecting general damage to the personality psychologically. It betrays itself in the test behaviors by which the blocking is known, but with the difference, for one, that the failure centers around no specific personal dynamic. The inquiry does not elicit new associations. The constraint shows up also in the language forms, unspontaneous and sterile. These patients show "impotence of verbal expression, little elaboration of responses, and stereotyped phrases" (Molish[50]). Emotional life in these patients' Rorschach tests is severely inhibited, to the point of the invisible (EA at near zero). The outlook for a psychotherapy in which it is hoped that the patient can himself soon invest effort is not favorable.

Defense tactics of another order, but also having constrictive effect, are the denials. In themselves, these defenses do not necessarily impede treatment and, in fact, they may be evidence that the personality is in a mobile state, one favorable to treatment. In their simplest forms the defenses consist of (a) the rejecting of an association, sometimes in the free association, more frequently in the Inquiry; (b) forgetting a response in the Inquiry, or explicitly denying it; and (c) altering a phobic or a conflictual association, or one otherwise affect-laden to an innocuous one. These shifts have been observed both in the free association and in the Inquiry. Thus, a "tiger" or a "lion" will be made into "a cat;" "lightning" into a "jagged line;" "a snake" into "a worm." When these denials are found in neurotic reaction patterns, the ego's sensitivity and struggle over social values are to be inferred. Where there is ego as consciousness of values, the patient is unhappy over things in himself as they are, and he is willing to cooperate with the therapist in the therapeutic program.

A more formidable and arresting kind of denial consists of those which some patients achieve in reaction to anxiety shock, whether occurring to the black or the chromatic figures. The massive disturbance mobilizes equally massive counterdefensive strokes. The Rorschach test behaviors are: notably faster speed of the first response and marked increase in the total productivity. Molish reports the increased productivity (R) with increased attention to the minute (Dd) as especially elicited by the black test figures in obsessive compulsive patients. He astutely observes that this denial is "a reaction formation to the presence of a dangerous situation; a denial of painful experience." The patient condemns, as it were, the unpleasant fact to nonexistence. All denials are an expedient by the person's ego to neutralize the sense of threat which his own thoughts are stirring up within him. The increased absorption in the small point (Dd) of the obsessive patient is the exacerbation of a symptom under traumatic conditions. As the emotions press on the ego, a character weakness has freer reign. Similarly, some patients release fantasy (M) in strikingly greater amounts at anxiety shock points, or they may communicate such fantasy living for the first time. In them, the disturbance, by temporarily loosening the ego from its moorings, is permitting the use of an activity which these persons have hitherto been repressing. Whether this recourse to fantasy living when under anxiety shock is other than a simple escape into the autistic world may vary from patient to patient. Even as such escape, it is still defensive, removing as it does the thought out of conscious awareness and preventing any attrition incident to the related emotion. It is a true denial in some patients, since by translating it into the language of fantasy they are denying its existence in reality. To the criticism that this is avoidance rather than denial, I would attempt no rebuttal. The distinction between these two defense tactics, clinically, is frequently not one with a noticeable difference. This question arises also with reference to naming the colors or describing them in the chromatic cards and naming or describing the shadings in the black cards. In instances, these behaviors are denials, true efforts by the ego to talk its way around the fact of anxiety being stirred up. But see also above concerning these behaviors as affect avoidance (pp. 141, 148).

Molish also holds that shifts of mood within the strongly affective reactions, whether hypomanic or depressive, are denials. "The alternate cramping of affect (on shading) and expansion of affect (on color) ... is a denial of the contradictory affects, an attempt to attain serenity." While I have myself observed these shifts of moods in patients so affect-dominated, I have not been struck by these shifts as defensive. Rather, I have taken them to be a spontaneous manifestation of the two mood qualities within these cyclothymics, brief alternations into the affect contrary to that which is at the time dominant. Further observation of these patients and their variations with a view to clearing up the significance of the changes will be of importance from the viewpoint of diagnosis and hence treatability. If Molish's surmise is correct, a denial as evidence of the ego's sensitivity over a nondesirable mood state becomes a promising note to the therapist.

# CHAPTER 14

## Recourse to the pathogenic

The defensive method that is most refractory to change in an individual's percepts about himself is that strongly held behavior habit known as paranoid projection. Organized by a usually vigorous intellect, founded in premises which to the patient are unassailable, it rests on a logic equally unshakable. A stubborn determination is a major trait in these persons. This provides that fixed psychologic medium with which they stick to their convinced attitudes. The disastrous fallacy in their position is the falsity of their major premise. It is a distortion of reality. The distortion is psychodynamically induced; the patient must so believe in order to be at peace with himself. Such are the perverse contrivances which the human ego can construct by means of the rich cortical processes at its disposal. The contrivance serves the inescapable human need to be able to respect one's self. It removes thus that unbearable pain, the one that goes with losing value in one's own eyes. With so strong a dynamic in it, and rationalized by the logic that follows impeccably from the major premise, and firmly maintained by the stubbornness trait, it can be seen that these persons *will* not change. The paranoid, whether or not schizophrenic, is among the patients least amenable to treatment.

In the test, certain themes in the fantasy (M) associations will be a first lead to paranoid ideation. The principal themes are: hostility and activity of the eyes, especially if these recur; sometimes this thinking is screened by tangential topics (binoculars). The lead in these latter is to the paranoid's suspiciousness. Less frequent are "ear" associations. Currently I am following the hunch that these are specific for suspiciousness. Rather more frequent is the "nose." When this recurs, it is likely to be a displacing, but from what organ will vary with the patient. It may be a clue to paranoid thinking—the patient "smells" in the other the ego-alien trait in himself. This interpretation is also in the hunch stage. When any of these activities, scorable as fantasy (M in accordance with Rorschach's criteria), are perceived as being in animals, the paranoid thinking is being screened. The patient is repressing the meaning of his idea more deeply, defending against his unhealthy defense. Whether such repression is a relieving feature, a promising finding for treatability, depends again on the total mental health of the patient. In an integrated person, flexible in psychologic structure, it reflects ego stamina, that foremost ingredient in a treatable patient. When the test record liberates signs of deeper regressions

216

(M—, unique originals, personal themes) that are far from the known norm for the figure being attended to, the paranoid thought as structured in animal content is only more bad news. The usually more repressed ideas, those in the deepest unconscious, are being released. Unconscious and conscious are too nearly a single stream.

Among other paranoid themes are: the devil, religious ideas in which omnipotence is a motif, plotting, concealing, masks. While their probability of being of paranoid flavor is the stronger if produced as fantasy (M), any of these ideas may also emerge in nonfantasy determinants. More than one of these topics is likely to appear, and some will be of fantasy source. The very important, confirming finding in that of any paranoid patient must be sought in the structural processes.

These processes are manifest in the Rorschach test picture in the following triad: high Z score, unique F— responses, a high average to above average white space count. That is, the patient is perceiving relationships, he is twisting reality, and he stubbornly holds to his attitudes. When the individualized F— is in the same associations as in those in which he organizes relationships, the evidence is that much more certain: the patient is seeing relationships that are not there. Since a grasp of relationships depends on a high intelligence, it can be seen too why some of the patients with most elaborate paranoid ideas are also those with very high intellectual endowment, whether measured psychometrically or by their achieved social level. When with the above triad the test record includes much fantasying and especially fantasying in which the percept is inaccurate (M—) we may look for delusional trends. The patient is not only distorting reality but actually living the false idea, whether wish or fear, in the unconscious. When one theme persists in the fantasy and is found also in nonfantasy associations, the lead is to systematized delusions. For purposes of judging treatability, it is important to inspect the delusions within the framework of the patient's history. Does the content have any direct relation to his life situations? To the extent that it does, he has been using this maladjustive expedient in resolving some stresses. To this extent the treatment outlook can be more hopeful than when the delusion is on a topic remote from him. In some anatomy associations, Molish reports that bodily functions may be being "used as physical models for the projection." The content in these, he states, is "elaborated upon in an unique fashion, generally dealing with pathological digestive and sexual functions." In his chapter on schizophrenia, Fenichel (ref. 32, pp. 428–429) provides some clinical examples of this kind of projection. I have myself encountered a few such anatomy associations but without enough in the test record to support the reasoning that the response was a projection. All these responses have appeared in the test records of schizophrenics or of neurotics in severe disruption and permitting themselves deep regressions. From the, so far quite fragmentary, evidence for this kind of projection, the surmise is in order, however, that it stems from a paranoid habit of mind.

Paranoid ideas are, of course, found in many persons in whom no such malignant general process has developed. The ideas appear symptomatically not only in schizophrenics but also in neurotics and in persons in relatively healthy integration. They live without other evidence of a habitual misconstruction of their sense data, they do not blame others for their own unacceptable wishes, and they construct no delusions, systematized or otherwise. The associational themes of paranoid flavor are in themselves expression of only fleeting such thinking. In the amount of their occurrence in any one test record and the degree of the pathology in them, they will provide evidence of the potential for pernicious trend in the patient. In themselves they will, however, not be definitive indication against treatability. As always the conclusion on this point must be drawn from all the evidence, and it is the structure of the entire reaction pattern that yields the critical differentiation.

Defensive withdrawal into a fantasy world need not be paranoid in structure or theme to be quite pathogenic. A recourse to imaginative living as an autistic solution is a fairly common major defensive strategy. It permits some satisfaction of frustrated wishes, or it can be a theater for acting out resentments. Whether this activity is a pernicious defense or a healthy use of a talent depends on the extent to which it is characterized by certain pathologic features, either in structure, in theme, or in both. It may follow the path of structural regressions. These again are principally those fantasies in which the form is inaccurately perceived (M−), those seen in a part-human (M with Hd), also, but less frequently, such an association in a small detail (Dd with M). Regressions, both structural and in content, are those in which a true human activity is perceived as in an animal (M in A).

Among specific themes that may dominate the inner world into which the patient has withdrawn are the following:

*Primitive eroticism.* Crude genital, whether male or female, percepts; intercourse in which only the genital organs of the two sexes are seen, not the entire human forms; erotic activity or copulation between animals; anal themes, including defecation and urination. Some oral themes belong here (Molish): Fig. X, D 6: two kissing fish, small, guppies. Fig. VI, D 1: a pelvis, and, D 2, a penis (sure they are connected! I don't know how I pictured it. Realistic of a penis, pelvis is not too accurate.). Fig. X, D 5: a rabbit, and D 4: snakes, are caressing its cheeks (I don't think he knows it's happening, is not paying any attention to them). Fig. VII, D 6 and

D 10: a vagina ... and it should be on the other side ... just reversed (rump, too much skin, seated, round. I've never seen anyone sit that way).

*Oral reunion.* The mouth or lips as pleasure organs are accented in the fantasy activity, and specific "sucking" associations may appear. "Breasts" may recur in such records, whether or not of fantasy structure. Food topics, especially as sweets, drink, may also appear in nonfantasy responses, supporting the indication in the fantasy for the oral-reunion yearning. Molish observes that the fantasies identified as of this significance "must be strongly experienced, regressive and bizarre in nature, and generally are monotopical." In his interpretation these responses uncover the patient's effort at "the deepest oral reunion with the universe; a restitution experienced in the past, receptive manner."

*Rebirth.* As the term indicates, the fantasy centers around birth. These responses are likely to be extremely regressive, both in structure and in theme. The perceived birth is frequently that of an animal, especially a lower organism: a tadpole; a moth emerging from its crysalis. Occasionally it is a human birth or a woman about to deliver a baby; more frequently, a human embryo in utero. In these the line of distinction between "rebirth" and "oral" reunion can at times not be made. Example: Fig. X, Dd 25: might be a face ... a fetus ... something sucking or drinking ... (getting nourishment ... attached). Whether any of these fantasies have either of these meanings to the patient can usually not be established from the test alone. At the best it is a lead, to be confirmed in further therapeutic exploration. In the example, Fig. IX, D 4, "a little baby, putting a spoon in its mouth (a new-born baby, the skin is pink)," the seventeen-year old girl who so associated may be disclosing her normal biologic interest in child-bearing. But other evidence in the test—a poignant fantasy of being rejected by her mother, strongly felt security needs, and the structure of the pattern as a whole—open up the question of the more regressive rebirth longing. The girl was under threat of a schizophrenic breakdown.

*World destruction.* The grand and catastrophic performances of nature form the themes in these associations, whether in fantasy or in other emotion-determined responses. When a severely disorganized schizophrenic is the source of these, the lead to be explored is that he is identifying with these natural forces. This thought content is defensive activity which enables the patient to transfer to the external world the ideas about himself which are so distressing. By the transfer, it is the world at large and not he himself that is collapsing. The defensive preoccupations here achieve the psychologic economy of relieving the patient's suffering. Examples:

Fig. VII (D 11): Two people holding hands, but (D 6) there again the dark and light in the middle appears to be something falling down on them, lava from a volcano, or a mountain stream which comes down between them as though their feet are immobilized in the earth. (They are happy at the moment, but they know something is going to happen.)

Fig. VIII (W): A forest is on fire, and there is the top of a fir tree, and the fire is rising up to it and eating it away.

*Cosmic identification. World reconstruction.* Associations for either of these themes resemble one another and the line of distinction is a fine one. The ideas are of a kind connoting reconstruction of the world's moral tone. A religious motif is frequently central to the content, although it may again be nature in her grandeur. In the cosmic identification associations, the affective quality is usually pleasurable. It reflects the subject's elation or excitement as he identifies with the reconstruction forces, possibly sensing himself the agent for them. In reconstruction thinking the affect may be either pleasurable or painful. Examples:

Fig. VIII, inverted (D 2, then W, and finally Dd 29): A figure here almost facing the earth, on Judgment Day ... the earth ... the people on earth would be entering the kingdom of heaven, and are judged that day on their sins and virtues, a glorious conception ... Paris, the Eiffel Tower (because of the colors something unusual will happen, and I just thought of Paris because of my fondness for it).

Cosmic identification and possibly also world destruction are the possible meanings for which this association can be further explored.

Fig. VIII, inverted (the white spaces within D 3): Two martyrs tied against a stake, tied around with a rope. It looks like they are going through some form of torture, and these are the flames, the white flames, Christian martyrs who are dying ... like some in the Bible, who died for their Christianity.

*Body distortion. Depersonalization.* Deformations, disintegration, dismemberings, or decay of the body form are perceived. The basic content may be human or animal. When seen as "dead" the cause will be seen as one of violence, e.g., Fig. VI, W, as "a squashed insect," or "an animal run over and flattened out." These associations again are defensive and serve the patient's psychologic economy. They are his means for sloughing off his own unhappy mood and preoccupation with himself, transferring them to the image invoked by the test, whether human or animal. The affective quality in these associations is usually painful. Inasmuch as the patient is thus displacing the sense of his own deterioration, an affinity between this defense tactic and world destruction can be observed.

More frequent than in fantasy responses is another variety of depersonalization. It is manifest in anatomy themes of highly pathologic quality, much emphasized. The patient may do this either qualitatively, in lurid description of anatomic details, especially in their unpleasant or repulsive aspects. Or quantitatively his record will overaccent this topic. As a rule, both these characteristics are present in the test record. When both anatomy content and depersonalization fantasy themes are found in the same record, they confirm each other as defensive measures. In relation to treatability, the anatomy association is the more unfavorable finding. I have observed it in deteriorated schizophrenics, some patients with brain pathology, especially those in advanced stages, and the acutely depressed when approaching the psychotic level or already having reached it. The Experience Actual in these patients is scant to the zero point.

When anatomy is being accented and the indication of the record as a whole is severe psychopathology, a probable hypochondriasis is to be inferred, a difficult condition to treat. Molish reports depersonalizing fantasy as also occurring in anxiety hysterics. The psychologic structure in the latter is more integrated, the dynamics more amenable to therapeutic effort, and the total outlook for treatment therefore more favorable. Depersonalizing fantasy taken by itself is not necessarily a pernicious sign. It is suspect because it is most frequently found in patients in whom personality disintegration is far advanced, especially in schizophrenics. The Rorschach axiom that a symptom's meaning can only be known from the entire personality always holds. In fact, caution is most essential when a pathologic sign is found by itself in an otherwise less malignant total pattern. Samples of body distortion associations:

Fig. II (D 1 with Ds 5): The face of a cat, the eyes ... peculiar that there is a blank space where the brain ought to be. It would be frightening, it would produce a sense of fear. ... I just see the eyes staring (at me, in some ways it reminds me of my mother. I am afraid of her ... I just rather would not have anything to do with her).

Fig. I (W, with additional attention to D 3): It appears to be a cat's head with a portion of the head torn away ... in the mouth is the bottom of a woman's torso from the waist down (it is eating the woman; the rest of her is in the cat's mouth, half swallowed; it is not a tiger, but a garden variety).

For a sample of pathologic anatomy content:

Fig. IV (all the Dd): The mottling represents a sickness, cancer.

The treatability of patients withdrawing into any of the topics described in the preceding paragraphs is not to be judged from these themes alone. Pathogenic as they are they may still be reflecting the patient at a crisis and turning point. He may be engaging in a restitutive effort, regressive as it is. The patient is, in his psychosis, restating the dream the poet has formulated with reference to "this sorry scheme of things entire;" he would "shatter it to bits, and then remake it nearer to the heart's desire." That is, the patient is groping for resources whereby to attain some of the satisfactions which he has missed, to rebuild what circumstance has shattered, to start over. To the extent that this is so the therapist has the opportunity which he needs. This hope may, of course, prove to be not justified. The fantasies and the other pathologic thinking may be the symptoms of regressions into which the patient's mental life will recede ever further from the real world. Fantasy, as all thought content which is heavily emotion-saturated, is a two-edged tool. It may open up and irritate deeper wounds, or it may cut through the impeding defenses and open the way toward mental health.

*The obsessional behaviors.* These are symptomatic for another major group of defense patterns. Persons so organized differ from the paranoid individual in that they do not misconstrue reality. On the contrary, they overdo themselves in adhering to it. At the same time, it is due to this very characteristic that these defenses have a pathologic quality. They hem in and entangle the person's intellectual processes, rendering him ineffective, narrow and encased, adhering to rigid, immutable ways. The paranoid transforms the world into one conforming to his presuppositions. The obsessional shuts out the portions of it which do not fit into his well-ordered, and sometimes perfectionist, and highly systematized universe.

In the test the findings are: very high productivity with much attention to the minute, including the infinitesimally small, usually disregarded by the healthy. Some records consist of a very diarrhea of associations as the patient's attention is chained to every mote within his field of vision. In this exhaustive regard for everything, he assures himself against missing anything. He includes all but is blind to the interrelationships, the larger and deeper meanings of what he perceives. He sees everything and apprehends nothing. In his inordinately large productivity and overattention to the insignificant the patient is binding his anxiety. He is at the same time binding all his mental processes.

These records, productive as they are, are thus impoverished in terms of achievement: there are few if any of the difficult whole responses (instant or additive W); synthesizing ability (Z score) is well below what might be expected from so productive a protocol; interest breadth (range of content and its originality) is restricted. It is all quantity without quality. As he interminably holds on to and associates to the test card, unable to give it up, the patient betrays that compelling need which is epitomized by Fenichel[32] in the opening paragraph of his chapter on "Obsession and Compulsion:" the ego is so compelled "otherwise it feels menaced by terrible threats." The compulsion may show up in the Rorschach test in the associational content in a recurring theme, in an idea to which the patient must cling under pain of the dread unknown. The emotional value which this content carries is, in some persons, apparent in the test record itself and throws light on the personal need behind the compulsion. The affect in these emotions is, in the majority of cases, of painful quality. Phobic ideas (large-mouthed animals, ghosts, weird monsters) are frequent among these topics. So also are anatomic percepts. The subject will further betray his anxious state through excessive precision, whether in identifying the portion of the test figure to which he is reacting or in describing what he sees, and he will enumerate the details, e.g., the animal's nose, eyes, ears, hair, tail. Or he may excessively qualify his associations. All of these may serve as binding mechanisms for deeper, more debilitating anxiety and thus save the patient from panic.

Another set of behaviors in the Rorschach test consists of attention to the bilateral symmetry of the test figure. The subject having associated to one of the lateral details must associate to the symmetrically corresponding one with the same content. Sometimes the response under this ritual symmetry follows immediately. At times the patient produces it only after some intervening associations, giving the impression that he is being driven by something which has been fermenting in this interval. My theory is that the second response is an undoing of the anxiety generated by the first. For a rationale of this theorizing I fall back again on Fenichel: "Something positive is done which, actually or magically, is the opposite of something which, again actually or in imagination, was done before" (ref. 32, p. 153; and see also p. 292 and p. 294). Another behavior which has the earmarks of undoing consists of the subject's continuing to talk around his association excessively and beyond any requirement for clarifying what he saw. He gives the impression of fearing to let go of the thought and as if elaborating on it is relieving him of the apprehension which it has aroused.

Finally, and especially important from a viewpoint of structure in the test findings, these patients have an almost inescapable penchant for balancing inner living (M) evenly with externalized feelings (sum C). This even balance, Rorschach's ambitendency of the *Erlebnistypus*, is found in the obsessive compulsive neurotic whether the amount of either component, fantasy (M total) or the total for the color-determined associations (C sum) is high or low. Psychologically we speculate about emotional pulls inward and pressure outward balancing off and neutralizing the person: he can go in neither direction. Clinically, this is his paralyzing doubt. It is the complete defense against any dangerous action and succeeds at the same time in defending against all action and against all enjoyment of life's values. Some of these patients produce Rorschach test records with much fantasying (M) and many associations in which the feelings are reaching outward (C). Their potential for emotional experience (EA) is broad. But, as they are organized psychologically, this rich emotional vein is no asset.

It cannot be exploited in treatment. The obsessive whole psychologic structure of the person nullifies this wealth.

Persons set in obsessive compulsive defense patterns are in fact among the most difficult to treat. These patients pull all the stops in the tactics identified (p. 210f.) as constrictive defenses. But where in the constrictive defense state the patient avails himself of some of these tactics separately, the obsessive compulsive person organizes a number of them, if not all, into a tight psychologic structure. As the histories show in many of these persons, the neurosis goes far back into early childhood, i.e., the structure has deep and lasting foundations. The balancing of the emotional forces, the inner living (M) against outward reaching (C), provides an equilibrium of tensions that insures the permanent maintenance of the total psychologic condition attained. Hence, ideas from the outside, referring here to the therapist's effort to bring new insights, cannot shape the structure or disturb the psychologic balance. The patient courses serenely in his unvarying orbit. For purposes of treatment, such Rorschach test findings mean, therefore, that both patient and therapist must set themselves for a long schedule, with no prediction possible as to course or outcome.

*Flight from fantasy.* See also concerning blocking of the fantasy activity (p. 211). By "flight" we identify the following behaviors: the person first associates with fantasy (M) but changes the response in the Inquiry to one which is strictly form-determined (F). Or he rejects or forgets the fantasy determinant when he is being questioned later. Or he owns to the association but refuses to elaborate or explain, usually with affect and always with finality. In essence, these behaviors are denials of the inwardly lived experience. It is thus a defense against a defense which the fantasy process itself it. The patient fears to face the wish—it may be dangerous—or the fear may be too distressing. So he flees. The high energy (by the Levy movement scale) with which some of these associations are invested attests to the intensity of the emotion which is being eschewed. The painful affect in some is structurally indicated by the shading determinant blending with that of fantasy (M.Y). Or the theme may directly denote a painful state of mind: "ghosts pulling at a lady," in figure I. The body distortion fantasies (p. 220) and the depersonalizing to which they testify are feared by some patients, as they show in their flights from them.

Another structural finding consists of those fantasy-determined responses in which the stance is one of immobility. The action in the M, and the patient, remains fixed at dead center. The patient cannot commit his mind, cannot decide on any action implicit in the associations. Essentially he is neutralizing the fantasy of any meaningful trend in it; he reduces it to zero. The flight may be achieved to the point of full repression. It is seen in persons who do associate with some fantasy associations and freely

explain these. The content in these consists of antisocial or asocial ideas—
violence or unconventional sexuality. The rest of the record meanwhile
etches out anxiety in conflict over these very trends. Meanwhile, the patient produces other responses also having conflictual content and these
raise the question of being fantasy-determined. But technically they are
not quite scorable as such. Or the anxiety-carrying associations emerge in
true fantasy structure but only in the Inquiry. Thus, the patient's mind is
actually pregnant with more such imagination than he brings forth to the
light of day. The resemblances in this kind of repression and in flight from
fantasy to blocking of this activity (p. 211) are apparent only, since in
the blocking tactic the subject verbalizes very little or no fantasy.

Taken by itself the flight from fantasy can be a favorable indication of
treatability. The patient is fleeing from his sea of troubles; he is revealing
that he is in conflict. Values are in collision, and this attests to ego. But
it is an ego under hard stress. What must still be judged is how much of
stress is being exerted upon the ego relative to the reserves which it possesses. How tough, unyielding, are the defenses? And, therefore, how determined will the person be in resisting the fantasies which have been
pressing for liberation? That is, how resistive is he to facing those life issues whose import to him is measured by the very fact that he so deter-
minedly wants to keep them out of his awareness? And, again, how changeable, adaptive, is he at the conscious, intellectual level? How fluid
emotionally? These data are available in an adequate Rorschach test protocol, and it is within the personality framework which they shape out
that the flight from fantasy is to be judged for its light on the patient's
treatability.

*Verbalism.* A defensive maneuver which should, on the face of it, characterize persons not refractory to treatment consists of a variety of behaviors all of which can be subsumed under the term, verbalization. Among
the behaviors, clinical as well as those in the test, are pretentious language
out of context and usually recognizable as out of the patient's usual sphere
of understanding. A philosophical, sometimes abstrusely metaphysical
tinge accompanies these associations in some persons. The philosophizing
is recognizably facile. Or the patient perceives the test figures in terms of
abstract ideas, e.g., harmony or music for figure X; balance for figure VII;
springtime for figure VIII. It must be remembered, however, that in some
patients such responses do express some strongly felt symptomatic trend.
As such they are not facile; in fact, they are not defenses but expressions
of the person's current emotional urges. More readily recognizable as of
this order are the distress cries, "gloom" to figure IV, "dejection" to figure
V.

Among the superficial verbalist associations are some of the cosmic themes (above, p. 220), especially when they consist of trite moralistic formulas. Test structure for any of the verbalist associations is most frequently an excessive number of responses to the entire test figures (Ap, W!). The subject so responds without differentiating the relevant component details. It is a holistic intellectual procedure, one which misses the concrete essentials of the test and of life. Since the patient sees many whole responses he gives an impression of having high intelligence. But, as in its clinical counterpart, the inflated language, it is spurious, a shadow, signifying nothing.

Verbalism is a defense against the poignant sense of self-devaluing. The patient, unhappy at perceiving himself as nothing, tries in his deluded way to be something. This attests to ego, and as such would seem to promise ability to respond to the treatment effort. Without ego, no treatability. However, ego alone is not enough. The empiric facts are that these verbalist behaviors are found in patients who clinically are in disordered or regressed states. Their egos are the prisoners of their pathologic needs. The ego is being used, therefore, not to achieve critical understanding of values but to promote symptoms. It is a restitutional type of activity. In itself, a verbalism is thus not evidence of treatability and may in fact be the clue to a deep maladjustment, one too deep for the person to be able to learn to change. Yet, as a restitutional effort, it may also be a hopeful sign: the patient is striving to reestablish himself as a meaningful unit in his society. Obviously, other findings must, as always, be evaluated: the ego's reserve, the intellectual adaptivity, the fluidity of the emotional structure, the total reaction pattern.

*Overevaluation of the self.* A defensive self-extension is in some persons their most manifest character trait. These patients are only too obviously compensating for anxiety-toned feelings of inferiority. The need for the compensation is structured in the test in a more than normal quantity of the vista-determined responses, and the vista plays a larger role in some of these than does the form (VF), i.e., the inferiority is intensely felt and the ego is having difficulty in mastering it. In instances the feeling is entirely out of control (V, undiluted). When the shading (Y) determinant blends with the perspective percept the person is suffering that much more painful mood over his disadvantageous self-appraisal, and this renders the defensive measure the more urgent. Heavy qualifying and especially self-qualifying, overt self-devaluing, apologetics, and resignation attitudes will also be found in these protocols.

The defensive operations emerge in, again, an excess manipulating of the large idea (W) without appropriate discriminating attention toward elements (D, Dd). It is the drive for intellectual self-display. But the quality of the percepts is mediocre in content (the butterflies, the animal skins);

they are seen in those test figures easily grasped in totality (figures I, IV, V, VI, and even VII), and not infrequently they lack form accuracy (F−). They do not show the synthesizing ability commensurate with this display of large viewpoints (few Z responses aside from those scored for the W's). In brief, the flourish of superiority lacks supporting evidence. It is a reacting beyond capacity, an overweening ambition which overvaults itself.

In some subjects the overevaluation of the self is achieved by way of more subtle and extravagant behaviors: in fantasies of cosmic identification, religious preoccupations, realities construed in accordance with the patient's wishes. (See also above concerning withdrawal into fantasy). The subject experiences in these regressive daydreams the exhilaration of grandiose conceptions. Qualitatively observable behavior consists of a very emphatic manner of associating. The subject asserts with a finality not to be gainsaid. The extreme form of this is reached in patients in hypomanic conditions; their own egocentric self-reference is their *raison d'être* for much of what they see.

As to treatability in these affect-dominated persons, the self-assertion is a symptom of the excitement and upward mood swing. It contributes to a diagnostic picture which carries with it certain principles and known procedures favorable to treatment. The regressive daydream identifications tell of a more malignant total condition. Taken by themselves, they are, in fact, likely to be findings of a discouraging quality. What rays of hope may be gleaned from these has been noted above (p. 221f.). The potential in these patients for change will necessarily vary with the residuals of ego, information which is to be sifted out from the rest of the test record.

Those subjects who compensate by pushing into the world—the men with ideas too big for their intellectual breeches—are suffering neurotic anxiety over their roles in the social milieu. As neurotics, with egos in active conflict, they are realistic within normal range and emotionally in flux. In them, the facts as elicited by the psychologic test findings in addition to those in the Rorschach test and supported by the subject's history are that the inferiority feeling is no fiction. The subject has ambitions actually beyond any which he can accomplish with his endowment. The psychologic test findings are helpful in these individuals in designing a treatment goal, one realistic for the subject's abilities. Then there are those persons in whom the inferiority attitude is truly a fiction, in the Adlerian sense. It is a construct of the neurosis and rationalizes an inner impediment, a dead weight, on the person's ability to aspire, to carry on effort commensurate with his intelligence. Behind this rationalization is an anxiety of older formation. This defense pattern in the Rorschach test is thus the road sign at a major intersection. It points to a direction which the therapist and the patient will follow in the interest of the patient.

*Symptomatic aggressiveness.* The principle that a strong attack is the best defense has long been practiced as a psychologic mechanism. It is used by some patients described in the section immediately preceding, those who overvalue themselves. They are aggressive in life, in their vocational and social and personal transactions. A keen observer detects in their striving to show themselves as being more their suffering for being something less.

In the test, their white space count (s) is high; their externalized feelings clearly exceed in quantity those that they introvert (C sum > M); and the dominant feeling tone is one of irritability (CF), with a visible dosage of impulsivity (undiluted C). Strong feeling surges are mobilizing behind the opposition trait. Themes of violence and aggression appear in the associational content of some, but not all, of these protocols. When they do, the aggression trends are not far from the conscious thought processes, and in view of the irritability or impulsivity, near the point of breaking through the ego's controls. Their symptomatic character is the more definite when the percepts for these themes are inaccurate (personal F−).

*The aggression-passivity closed circuit.* In some patients who are symptomatically aggressive against their inferiority of character structure, the clinical observations disclose a passive anxious withdrawal trend. It is usually screened in the everyday life behavior. Clinically, it has been formulated as follows: the patient is conscious of inferiority feelings, reacts with narcissistic protest, which draws him into overcompensating behaviors, with the attendant overt self-extending effort. This takes the form of competitive aggression, which, in turn, stirs guilt anxiety, bringing in its train dependency needs. Accompanying these needs are inferiority feelings, and the patient has returned full circle, and repeats. I have been unable to trace down the source of this formulation, and probably it has simply grown, as concepts do in any science, and the original writer of it is unknown. In their Rorschach tests these persons are more than normally sensitive to the shading determinant (YF and even Y associations, in some patients exceeding the number of their FY). Their test pattern is defined by their inferiority feelings (V-determined responses), opposition needs (s), energized by exciting feelings (CF or C), with ego integrated within neurotic limits (F plus especially, but with other evidence of ego control) and their passivity (Y). The reasoning from these test data is: the person becomes aggressive (s high, with CF and C) and this urge stirs his anxiety, against which he defends by passivity (Y) withdrawal, which is, however, a devalued feeling (patient senses himself being not man but mouse) and awakens the associated inferiority feelings (V). Now the need for compensatory self-respect is again aroused (ego forces), once again releasing the emotion-driven opposition (s with CF and C) and the aggression trends. So the chain reaction returns to its starting point, stays within its

groove, and the process continues in this closed circuit. It is the endless
repetitive pattern of the neurotic in his insoluble conflict, much like that
of a squirrel on a revolving platform in a cage. The squirrel and the human
neurotic differ in an important respect: the animal's torture is imposed on
him from the outside; the neurotic's has its motive force within.

Can this circuit be opened up by therapy, the patient redirected? The
treatment problem in these persons is the general one of the treatability of
a neurotic suffering acutely from inferiority feelings (see the exposition on
this point, p. 226f.). The passivity trait may compound the therapeutic
difficulty. It depends on how extensively it permeates the patient, and how
deeply. If it involves him seriously enough, it affords another avenue for
pathologic escape: he always withdraws at junctures requiring initiative
and forceful action.

Taken by itself, this cluster of test behaviors is not necessarily either a
deficit or asset for treatment purposes. It can be one or the other, depending on the structure and depth of the neurosis as a whole. Again, we must
evaluate the findings for all of the personality components: the emotional
resources, inner flexibility, intelligence endowment and breadth, ego reserves, state of the ego's defenses, and the others.

*Religiosity.* This term is itself a definition. Some of the behaviors to
which it refers are items in the cosmic identification and in the world reconstruction defenses. More rarely, it will appear in a world destruction
association. "Devil" themes, when fantasy responses, require tracking down
for the religious connotation—His Satanic Majesty as arch-enemy to the
Deity (Milton's concept). Such "devil" responses are also paranoid, a
projection by the patient of his own unalterable hatred toward other men.
Most commonly, however, the religiosity associations uncover (a) the aid-
seeking, dependent needs, and (b) a leaning on religious institutions. Examples of such responses are: prayer, altar, crucifix, priests or other min-
isters, angels, God.

When emerging as cosmic identification, world reconstruction or world
destruction ideas, the religiosity defense is, for treatment purposes, of the
quality described (p. 219f.) for those expedients and it similarly influences
the outlook. The paranoid trends in the "devil" associations, like all such
trends, are pathologic. They introduce a hardship into the treatment, or
compound any that are already present.

Religiosity as stemming from an aid-seeking trait may also be an unfavorable finding insofar as it discloses a person seeking solution through
supernatural means. In invoking the deity, to what extent is he resigning
his own effort, failing to exercise his own powers? In Thomas Mann's *Joseph*, that self-confident hero, deeply imbued with the religious spirit he
had soaked up in the formative years of his life from his father, is ever

crediting his progress to his God. But he is also explicit in stating that he must work along with God, help the Almighty in carrying out His divine design for Joseph. Three days in the pit, sold into slavery by his turbulent brothers, transported to a land and to a people strange to his ways, Joseph is always supremely sure of himself. His trust in his God is simply his trust in himself. It is never an appeal for help.

A pure dependency solution may, then, be pathologic and have its source in a very weak personality. It may, on the other hand, be a legitimate cry for help. These are seen in patients going through a crisis: the menopausal years, a sensed decline in a man, a blow such as a sudden change of fortune can inflict on anyone. In their extreme forms these are the depressive reactions, and it is in these conditions that the dependency needs are especially articulate and the appeals for help most poignant. Jonah is a supreme example, both in communicating his depressed mood and in his looking to a greater power for his help. In the blackness of the whale's bowels, he laments,

> The waters compassed me about, even to the soul;
> The deep was round about me;
> The weeds were wrapped about my head.

> I went down to the bottoms of the mountains;
> The earth with its bars closed upon me forever:
> Yet hast thou brought up my life from the pit, O Jehovah my God.

The therapeutic question in these cases is whether to support the dependency need. The lunge into this condition can be reversed in some of these patients. The religiosity associations are a signal to the therapist to give this support temporarily, bring relief from the oppressive mood, help the individual mobilize his ego reserves, and start him again on a course toward independence. This kind of defense is, therefore, not so much an indication in itself of treatability as a lead to what is to be the goal of the treatment, assuming that the personality structure as a whole warrants the effort.

# CHAPTER 15

## Defenses more adjustive

The concept of the psychologic defenses is one of very recent origin. Whether it had been known as such prior to the advent of psychoanalysis, I do not know. It is associated in current writings almost exclusively with psychopathology. Its importance to normal life is ignored or receives notice only incidentally. Fenichel[32] distinguishes between "successful" and "unsuccessful" defenses and comments: "The successful defenses are of less importance in the psychology of the neuroses; they are actually less understood" (p. 141). Anna Freud[33] lists nine defense methods* described in the psychoanalytic literature prior to her writing, and she adds a tenth which, she states, pertains to *normal* (my italics) life rather than to neurosis. Her tenth one is: sublimation or displacement of instinctual aims. In designating this one kind of behavior as normal she and Fenichel are in agreement. He says, "The successful defenses may be placed under the heading of sublimation" (ibid).

There are, then, defenses which are normal. Like the brother who, in the parable of the prodigal son, stayed home and never regressed into delinquencies, they pass unnoticed. Actually the concept has a significance well beyond the field of psychopathology and is of universal scope. It embraces all the conventions that humans in any one society observe in their relations with one another, those courtesies and polish that are of the weave and texture of everyday life. For, defenses these are. Our psychologic defenses save us from ourselves. The amenities of our everyday lives also so serve us. They are behavior patterns, products of the ages, affording to each person the measure of his esteem from all the others. The price each pays is the restraint on his appetites. Were it not for these observances, we would be in our everyday interrelations what we are in our unconscious. And there, quoting Ernest Jones, we are "selfish, jealous, impulsive, aggressive, dirty, immodest, cruel, egocentric, conceited, inconsiderate" (ref. 40; pp. 120–128). In a word, not fit to live with. Our egos command us to dress up in behaviors dictated by a norm. This is the civilizing effect.

Defenses are normal behavior, therefore, with the accent on the syllable *norm*. They devolve into the pathologic in those human conditions that

---

* The nine are: regression, repression, reaction formation, isolation, undoing, projection, introjection, turning against the self, reversal.

are pathologic as wholes. In neurotics and psychotics they are exaggera-
tions, distortions of the normal defenses, or an inappropriate show of
them, usually both. They are caricatures, as is so much in the pathologic
states, of normal behavior.

The adjustive defense patterns are defined in their Rorschach test
correlates in the following behaviors.

*Creative autisms.* A first line of defense in many persons is that which
they set up in their fantasy world. Rorschach saw his *Bewegung* or move-
ment-determined response (M) as a stabilizer of the feelings. By retiring
inward with them we can have our wishes as though satisfied or we can
mull over our fears, while at the same time carrying on our daily work.
The judgment to be made for each individual is: do the autisms in his
movement associations disclose high concentration around some one topic,
or do they range over many interests? Absorption in some one special
interest, in instances monotopically, characterizes both neuroses and
psychoses, and the theme can usually be identified for the pathologic need
which it represents. If the range of themes is wide, then the fantasies—
autistic though the purpose which they presently serve—can be an
imagination which is also a broad vision and opens up a perspective beyond that of the subject's immediate needs. As always, the judgment will
vary with other findings in the record: the patient's respect for reality and
the inference as to whether he can use his fantasying as a medium in working through his life's reality problems (M total as compared principally
with F plus per cent, but also P, per cent animal content, and lambda).
These same Rorschach test findings will be a gauge to the subject's
ability to contain his daydreaming. Does he distinguish it from reality,
or does it run away with him? Is it an end in itself, his stopping point,
so far as effort is concerned? In the healthy, their inner living becomes a
point of departure for action in the external world, and they can transmute their daydreams into socially integrated and constructive accom-
plishments. The Rorschach test factors, in addition to the relation between
fantasy and reality grasp (M and F plus), that need to be judged in this
connection are: The amount of fantasying relative to the totally released
associational activity (M/R). Does the subject live too much in his
inner world? Does his use of fantasy amount to being no more than an
autistic withdrawal? How introversive is the subject as compared with
how extratensive he is (M/C, which is also the *Erlebnistypus*)? Can this
person express his feelings with anything like his readiness to introvert
them? The inability to do so is not necessarily maladjustive, but healthier
individuals do reach out with their feelings, whatever their introversive
habits. The amount of imaginative living is appraised relative to the
intellectual achievement potential (M/Z). Is his fantasying consistent

with his basic intellectual potential? Imaginative activity unless carried on within a framework of large understanding can become superficial fancies or vagaries at best; at worst, flights unanchored to any detectable social value.

A limiting value on the quantitative balances and their significance as adjustive defenses is set by the quality of the fantasy responses themselves. The requisites are: structure of the percept is sound (M plus) in all or nearly all of these responses; content in nearly all is the whole human form (H); in males, the direction of the activity (if this can be judged; it cannot always) is in the majority of instances extensor (the pull away from the center axis of the test figure) as in females it is flexor, turned toward this axis; energy investment (Levy scale) is in the majority of the fantasy associations at median or higher (4 or more); the content is not extravagantly bizarre, although it may be highly original to the point of being individualized.

Autistic living is a defense and serves as a psychologic economy need. It is a tranquilizer, probably the world's oldest. It permits the subject to relieve his tensions by experiencing his feelings even as he holds them in. In stabilizing the individual, it enables him to control himself. Getting along better with himself, he gets along better with the world. In relation to treatment prospects, it must be clear that the closer to optimum the above-noted balances (total of movement responses in proportion to: total productivity, the sum of the color-dictated associations, the hold on reality, and the higher intellectual achievement as seen in the synthesizing ability, i.e., in W and in Z), the more promising the outlook. Norms have been published for these variables.[4, 12, 45, 68]

For the movement association, idiosyncratic activity that it is, the optimal range is very wide. No fixed measures can be stated other than those for the known healthy ranges of some of these variables: the grip on reality as reflected in perceptual accuracy is to be above the critical minimum of neurosis (F plus per cent not below 65 to 60) and this behavior is to remain below the rigidity levels (i.e., F plus per cent not above 90 to 95). Total productivity will vary with the freedom of the intelligence, kind of neurosis, kind of psychotic involvement. A minimum of emotional liberation is essential (sum of color values), and there are of course limits to emotional release if one is to be termed healthy. Even when the total is within healthy limits, emotional stability varies also with the nuances of the feelings, and these range in the test from impulsivity (undiluted C) to lability (CF) to a mastery over the feelings (FC). As a general rule, the greater the imbalance, using optimum points as a standard of reference, the less favorable the treatment implications. In the inner living ratios, for example (EB), either extreme depicts a patient presenting difficulties.

When the total of color-determined associations is high while the fantasy responses are at the zero point or close to it, the patient is (a) not communicating his innermost needs, those that he has relegated to his unconscious and that are the roots of his neurotic symptoms. At the same time, he is (b) excessively reacting to the world emotionally, is too extravert. He is here, there, and everywhere, all at the same time but no place in particular. Should the record pattern out to be one with a notably high number of fantasy responses while color total is at or near the zero point, the outlook could be even worse: an inability to make emotional contact with others, an immersing of the self in the inner world, remaining incommunicado in it. Nor does it follow that an even balance of fantasy associations and total of color responses is optimal. The empiric facts are that this is the inner equilibrium of the obsessive compulsive, including those patients who are most obdurate to treatment support (see above, p. 223). The healthy distribute among those persons whose fantasying (M total) exceeds the outward expression of their feelings (C sum), and into those whose externalized feelings are greater than their fantasy total, as well as some in whom the totals in these two findings about equal each other. The persons who are most readily treatable may follow any pattern in respect to their emotional balances. Inner fluidity is the thing.

Finally, fantasy is a gift which, Janus-like, faces in two directions. It can be the medium whereby the subject regresses and remains deeply sunken in his private life, out of touch with the greater world beyond him. Or it can be the ore in his unconscious out of which the subject produces something new, of creative quality. Healthy or sick, it is the theatre for the play of his tensions. The freedom of fantasy is an open vent, relieving tensions. To many persons, this freedom is denied. In some, it may be sheer lack of the ability, although this is as yet a moot point. The nature of the imaginative process, as inherited ability, is still among the psychologic mysteries. In many, however, the cause is clearly psychologic inhibition. The patient is himself shutting off this freedom. He cannot indulge himself in this relief. And then again, freedom is not an unmixed blessing. The unbridled misconstructions of some schizophrenics are among these fruits. Once again, we must know the whole person.

*Adaptive aggressiveness.* Whether we call it initiative, enterprise, or aggressiveness, the trait is a necessary one for an individual if he is to survive in human affairs and if he is to reap some fruits from his abilities. The question always is, how much of this trait does the subject under observation use, and how appropriately? Is it a useful tool in his healthy adjustment to his world? Exceeding certain limits it becomes maladjustive and can bring down the wrath and reprisal of those about the individual.

The Rorschach experiment calls out a well-defined congeries of behaviors that identify the aggressive person. One consists of the out-reach-
ing feelings (the color-determined responses). Again to be noted are the
total quantity released (C sum) and this quantity relative to the amount
of introverted feelings (EB).

Second is the opposition trait, or, better still, self-assertion as shown in
associations to the white space details (s). Does the person use this trait
within the normal range?[11, 15] What in the content of his associations
provides leads to thoughts of aggression? The specific topics vary in theme
and may disclose dangerously assaultive urges: club, knife, axe, gun. Or
they may uncover the conversion or sublimation of these offensive urges
into vocational and creative achievements which the individual is as-
serting with self-confidence.

This latter is a sample, as I see it, of what Fenichel[32] calls a successful
defense (p. 141f). The assumption is, however, that the content is found
in a person possessing also the necessary psychologic structure: free
emotional energy, self-assertion, ability to externalize the feelings. Even
so, the significance of these feelings as evidence of an adjustive aggressiveness will vary with other findings. Suppose a person does show this
psychologic structure but also suffers from feelings of inferiority (the
vista-determined associations, the self-devaluing comments) and manifests shock reactions of a neurotic kind, plus the fact that his feelings are
predominantly those easily set off, only partly ego-restrained, and sometimes entirely uninhibited (the number of undiluted color associations and
color-form associations together is greater than the form-color associations), in such an instance we can predict aggressiveness for this patient,
and it will be symptomatic, maladaptive, dangerous. Or let it be a patient
with the ingredients of the aggressive structure who is passive, excessively
submissive (shading-determined responses, expressions of resignation, too
many P responses) and we can look for occasional outbursts that are over-
aggressive, maladaptive, possibly assaultive (see above, p. 228, concerning the passivity-resistance circle).

The questions which need to be answered—and the Rorschach test
elicits the necessary data in many* of the response patterns obtained by
it—are: Is the ego adequate to hold the aggressive urges under control,
to steer them into directions consistent with socially honored values? Can
the person restrain and delay the discharge of his drives?

As to the significance for treatability of an adjustive aggressiveness,
it is patent that a person who has made this trait his life pattern is not
likely to be a candidate for treatment. He will not need it. He has de-

---

* Not all. Nor can I hazard a guess as to the percentage in which it does or does
not.

veloped successful defenses, in Fenichel's sense. The descriptions above
serve, therefore, as points of reference for judging the amount and the
quality of aggressiveness in persons who do present themselves for psychologic treatment.

*Symbolism.* When is a symbol a symbol? A puzzle, this, which many a
Rorschach test protocol poses. The alternative question is: does the apparently symbolic language refer to what is for the patient the real
thing? For a clear-cut example in the literature, the apples were to
Sechehaye's Renee[63] "mamma's breasts." To that schizophrenic girl, the
apples were not a *symbol* of breasts but the real thing. This is no longer
a defense but concretistic thinking. Quoting Fenichel: "Schizophrenic
thinking is relatively more concrete and active than normal thinking,
not yet capable of realistic abstractions, less preparation for subsequent
action and more a symbolic equivalent of action. Its concrete character
is 'relative' only in so far as its concrete images do not correspond to
objective realities, but are formed or influenced by the wish-fulfilling
magical qualities of primitive thinking" (ref. 32, p. 422).

To illustrate by one of the most common of symbols, when a schizophrenic woman says she sees a snake while she means a penis, she is seeing
a penis with the affect that that organ arouses in her. In an example from
Bleuler, a woman hallucinated that her father abused her sexually, that
"he thrust a spear into her lower abdomen." Bleuler continues "that the
attack with the spear was a sexual one is proved by the completely erotic
expression of the patient as she related the hallucination which, in its
contents, gave no such direct evidence apart from the frequent occurrence
of such things in sexual context. While the patient related her tale, she
hid her face with a guilty embarrassed laugh" (ref. 19, p. 412). To this
psychotic woman, the spear was no symbol of the penis. It was the penis.

When phallic symbolism forms the thought content of a neurotic
woman, she does not know that the affect which she is experiencing is
that which, owing to her personal needs, she attaches to the male genital.
The idea of that organ is repressed, totally unconscious, and totally disguised in the symbol which provides the defense. As such, it insulates this
woman from conscious awareness of her ideas and of the related wishes
which are guilt-encumbered.

The problem of symbolism for the Rorschach test student who tries to
identify the defensive purpose in it and to establish what its function is
in contributing to treatability is: to what degree is the affect which is
being experienced by the patient known by him to refer to the object of
personal, dynamic meaning to him, something related to one of his life's
issues? To return to my opening question: when is a symbol not a symbol

but the real thing? Are the apples apples to the patient, or are they real breasts to her?

How is the Rorschach test investigator to know when the particular percept disguises the person's repressed wish and serves him as defense? The only practical rule is to fall back on the symbolic meanings which are generically assigned to certain associational topics. The psychoanalytic writers have made the principal modern contribution in this field, with the anthropologists not far behind. One need only refer to Freud's *Interpretation of Dreams* and to his *Psychopathology of Everyday Life*, as well as to a number of his shorter papers and to Jung's theory of universal significance derived from a primordial psychologic matrix. Bleuler[19] cites a great number of examples culled directly out of his wealth of clinical observations. The Bleuler samples at the same time breathe a sharp caution to the Rorschach test examiner. The samples are idiosyncratic. Each has its particular meaning to the individual patient, fashioned by the life experience of that person.

Can we assume a universal significance for any symbol? The sheer fact that cultures differ in their symbolisms for the same percepts—colors are an obvious example—must set up a further warning about the notion of universal meanings. Objects having important dynamic meanings in one culture adduce no such response in another. The underlying dynamism is just as powerful but the imagery varies. For example, Freud (ref. 34, p. 81) cited the German word "Frauenzimmer" as the equivalent of "zimmer" and he referred to the "symbolic meaning" which it possessed for the girl, Dora, obviously her vagina. In German, as the translator adds in a footnote, "Frauenzimmer" is a slightly derogatory term for woman. In the United States the term, translated as "woman's apartments" or "woman's room," would awaken no reaction. But our slang has its dynamic equivalent. It speaks of "her box." In another context (ref. 34, p. 166) Freud refers to the German expression "das Kleine" (the little one) for the penis. The American slang practices no such screened modesty. Probably our most common appellation is *the tool*. One cannot help speculating over a possible source of this identification in a society whose most endogenous philosophy is pragmatist. The American, certainly to the time of the closing of the frontier, survived and prospered in proportion to his facility in using his tools.

To have recourse to anthropology, Lowie (ref. 49, p. 286–287) reports "to the Crow the feather is the 'greatest thing in the world'." This writer also points out that when a Hidasta woman says that "Indian corn and the wild geese were one and the same thing" she was not being "prelogical," but that in the given context both topics were associated "in the same sacred complex and stood for that complex." The important words are, of course: *in the given context*. Lowie also here shows that the same color, *black*, can have the significance of sadness to a Menomini and of joy to a Crow. "We must be on our guard," he writes, "against assuming that even in the simplest cases the interpretation is fully determined."

This sentence could have been written about content in the Rorschach test. The content is always only a starting point, not an answer. To translate the associational themes in the test directly into symbolisms identified in psychoanalysis or in anthropology can be a source of serious error. The interpreter will wander far from the realities of the patient's life problems. This individual whose test findings he is presently evaluating may be the rare exception to the general rule. The question, it must be emphasized, is what does the association signify to *this* man or woman? The feather to the upper flares of figure VI or to the extension upward in figure VII is a commonplace and has a neutral affect to the usual subject. But to a Crow Indian? Only the subject can answer the question concerning the affective loading of any theme to him.

What the Rorschach test offers in this field is, therefore, points of departure for further exploration. Can the percept be established as symbolic? If so, it helps build up the picture of neurotic repression. It is the work of a person still in conflict, his ego still fighting, and to that extent he is neurotic, and to that extent more treatable. Or does it turn out to be concretistic? It may still be a lead to the focus of the schizophrenic's pain, his sensed deprivation, that which started him on his tortuous and maladaptive path. As such, it is a communication which helps the therapist in understanding his patient. And understanding is, of course, the *sine qua non* in the therapeutic effort.

*Recovery from anxiety impact.* A major test of any person's character stamina is his behavior under stress. How does he handle himself in an emotional crisis? How effectively does he rein in his feelings, establish his equanimity, and attend to the realities of the moment firmly?

The experience of taking the Rorschach test offers a number of such challenges. Most obvious are those identified as the color shock and the shading shock phenomena. What are the signs that the patient is regaining his self-control? The evidence is to be found, usually, in the test figure following the one that triggered the discharge. But at times, and more especially in the stronger personalities, the recovery sets in within the shock figure itself. Other exigencies within the test experience also put a person on his mettle. They include phobic ideas, especially those that are regressive fantasies (see p. 209). When these are of acutely painful affect, they spell out the potential for panic. The anxieties will be in response to impulsive or oversensitive emotional processes (see p. 214) and to inferiority feelings when these are sharply experienced (p. 226). The themes in these emotion-determined associations may provide leads as to the personal dynamic behind the anxiety process, although they do not necessarily do so. Some associations that excite the emotions appear to be of more conscious origin, or perhaps it is that the test does not penetrate to the emotional determinants (scoring is simply F, whether F+ or F−). The themes in these are always unique to the patient. The anxiety reaction is also in evidence in the intellectual disturbance. The ego falters.

The test behaviors that tell of recovery are principally: the critical perception (F+), conventionality of outlook (P), a loosening of the inhibitions (T/1R is speeded up, and the delays between responses are much shorter); it is also seen in liberated productivity (R). The recovery behaviors are then the opposites of those by which we identify color shock and shading shock, and they have been described by various writers.[2, 9, 11, 21, 48, 57]

The essential question is whether the ego is able to reorient the individual to the real world and direct him toward goals consistent with his abilities and mental welfare. But the examiner needs to be on the alert for overreactions. They are not recoveries. These are apparent in a constrained attention to the point of rigidity (Ap), a rigid orderliness to the point of inflexibility of pattern (Seq), a narrow adhesion to the most realistic in the perception (F+ at 100 per cent), constriction of the emotional expression (low C sum), suppression of the imagination (few M), impoverishment in the thought content (high animal form percentage or concentration in some other particularized interest). These behaviors do not make for adaptive contact with one's world. The ego is still under duress. The individual has not freed himself from anxiety's affliction. (See in this connection the description of the constrictive and pathologic defenses, p. 210f.) The question becomes thus: can the person when subjected to anxiety-provoking events steer an even course between (a) free anxiety, in which the patient is not governing himself at all and is entirely out of control and (b) that paralyzing dead calm in which he cannot move at all? It must be accented that a person reacting adaptively to events known to stir anxiety does not by that reaction show himself lacking in anxiety. He is able to hold to his course when experiencing this always discomposing emotion. These are the persons who can master themselves in a crisis. Theirs is the optimal defense.

It is scarcely necessary to add that a person manifesting this supple ego, with its reserve of strength, will be a good risk in a therapy effort.

*Sublimation.* Assuming a total response pattern that points to a healthy integration by the subject of his intellectual endowment and his emotions with healthy social goals, we must naturally be inquisitive as to how this individual is defending against his own unwanted aggressions, his undesirable sexual impulses, his symptomatic ego extension. The assumption is that all are liable to these trends. Among the behaviors in the Rorschach test by which they disclose themselves are the delays or the circumlocutions around associations in these interest spheres. The themes are within the categories of those reported in the psychologic literature as symbolic. Just as any neurotic does, the subject is defending against repressed needs by screening them in symbolism. But in repressing them he is not having recourse to the severely constrictive or pathologic defense patterns which involve or cripple the personality. A modicum of pathogenic defenses will appear, scattered symptoms. Enough sexual themes will appear to uncover an affect about the topic.* Aggression topics may, but do not necessarily, emerge as such. But if the aggressive structure is patterned out (p. 234) while the thinking centers around some special topic, the surmise is in order that the aggression is being displaced.

The question next is how constructive socially are these displaced interests? In other words, what are the subject's life goals? A lead toward the answer may be found in the fantasy responses (see in this connection pp. 232f.). Not only the quantity of fantasying but also its quality, the energy invested in it, the dominance of dependency poses or of the self-assertive ones, and the themes—all must be judged. The information we look for is, does the patient resolve his frustrations by fantasy living? Is this autistic? Or is it the point of departure for some effort at activity outside himself? Is he in his entire organization as a personality capable of transmuting this autistic inner living into something creative in the larger world? Does his imagination have the qualities of perspective and of vision?

This is sublimation. It is still defense, successful defense (Fenichel) against the ever conflictual, ever tragic, experience which is the human destiny. These are some of the personality components with which he rises to his sometime greatness, even as he is so often struggling against his smallness. The answer which we are seeking for any one individual when we study his Rorschach test protocol is: on which side is the balance? Camus, in one of the closing paragraphs of *The Plague*, notes: "What we learn in a time of pestilence (is) that there are more things to admire in men than to despise."

What Camus is saying from his existentialist point of view is that

---

* We do not here include those persons, usually of highest intelligence level, who overload the associations for each of the ten test figures with penises, vaginas, or other sex percepts. These individuals too are defending pathologically against their sexual anxieties by flaunting their freedom.

human experience is chronically a pestilence. It has been the merits of Rorschach's test that it focuses a glass not only on those elements which we despise in men but also on those which we admire. It need hardly be added that, given a Rorschach test record from which we can deduce the potential for sublimation, both in terms of the structural psychologic processes and of the personal goals which human-kind has always valued, the question of such a person's treatability would be quickly answered.

# CHAPTER 16

## About transference

As it is for so much of our psychology of the human personality today, the wellspring for the concept of transference is Freud. The transference relationship must evolve in the treatment of every neurotic. It is a condition *sine qua non* for the success of psychoanalytic treatment. This is the core of Freud's thinking on the subject. As with so many of Freud's concepts, many streams of thought have flowed from it. Some stay close to the main river bed. Others take a different direction. But as we read them what we find is that they differ in flavor but not in the essential concept. What is still being dealt with is the transference process.

In an illuminating article, Orr[55] surveys the vicissitudes of the transference concept starting with Freud's several statements. The more notable changes of direction away from Freud are those of Horney; Rioch representing the thought of the Sullivan group; and Silverberg. In one respect, Silverberg is the most radical. One of the two characteristics which, as he holds, always attaches to transference is that it is of painful affect. As will be seen in the citation below, it can according to Freud be either painful or pleasurable. If pleasurable feelings attend it, according to Silverberg, this is because they actually contain hostility. His second essential in the transference is that it is irrational. This is in accord with Freud's formulation. But Silverberg appears to depart from Freud in holding that transference is not limited to the therapeutic situation. It may enter into any interpersonal relationship. He would speak, therefore, not of *the* transference but *a* transference. This departure is not as great as it looks. In the Freud-oriented writers, as I read them, transference is seen as universal in human relations. They have narrowed down a sector of it in order to use it as a therapeutic technique.

Among the writers whom Orr surveys, a notable number take what is essentially Freud's position. Such differences as appear result from efforts to define and clarify and in the emphases placed on related psychoanalytic concepts. The names include those of Ferenczi writing jointly with Rank, Hendrick, Fenichel, French, and Nunberg. It is this, the "classical" concept, which I have been using in studying transference readiness in the Rorschach test behavior and language. For a sample, I restrict myself here to one quotation from Freud:

"If further proof were needed of the truth that the motive force behind the formation of neurotic symptoms are of a sexual nature, it would be found in the fact that in the course of analytic treatment a special emotional relation is regularly formed between the patient and the physician. This goes far beyond rational limits. It varies between the most affectionate devotion and the most obstinate enmity and derives all its characteristics from earlier emotional erotic attitudes of the patient's which have become unconscious. This *transference* alike in its positive and in its negative form is used as a weapon by the resistance; but in the hands of the physician it becomes the most powerful therapeutic instrument and it plays a part that can scarcely be overestimated in the dynamics of the process of cure" (ref. 34, p. 122).

This is the psychoanalytic concept of transference. The Rorschach test, conceived in the mind of a psychoanalyst and by him developed into its usable form, is structured on psychoanalytic principles.

For about eight years now I have been making observations of test data with a view to their indications for transference. The notes below report these observations and something of the rationale that backs them up. How pertinent this application of Rorschach test findings to the transference relationship is, I do not yet know. I have only recently ventured into this tough and complex terrain. The present observations are really *a priori* reasoning, having their orientation in (a) the thinking of clinical psychoanalysis, and (b) known Rorschach test principles. It is within these two conceptual frameworks that we (c) apply transference theory. The descriptions below of the relevant behaviors in the test are, therefore, essentially hypotheses for verification. I have now been using them a long enough time to feel warranted in publishing them for others to try out.

First, a definition of transference in my own language is necessary. In a transference the patient lives with relation to some individual as if that individual were one who had been of decisive life importance to him as an infant and young child. In the analytic situation this present-day individual is the therapist, and the person of importance in the patient's childhood was his father or mother, or someone who stood in such a parental role to the patient. The emotions which as a young child the patient experienced toward this parent he now experiences about the therapist. They can be pleasurable or painful emotions, accepting or rejecting, either or both in the same patient toward the same therapist. They are intensely felt, especially if painful. As the patient enters on the transference, his resistance to the therapeutic process noticeably mounts. He eschews insightful understanding. A most important condition is that the memory, or rather the imago, of the person critically important to the patient in infancy persists in his mind at the present time. Pleasurable affects which are being experienced in the transference turn out, as the therapy proceeds, to be erotic in flavor and they have their roots deep in the unconscious.

The Rorschach test behaviors are:

(1) The whole personality structure must be a neurotic reaction pattern.

This is a presupposition binding on all the observations that follow. Any of the behavior manifestations following may appear in the test protocol of a patient with one of the psychotic conditions but they cannot be indicative or predictive of a transference except in the neuroses.

(2) Anxiety shock. The reactions will appear at figure IV and figure VII, either or both. When the shock is pronounced at figure IV, the examiner should be alert for its possible appearance in figure VI, D 9, and also in figure IX, D 4. In addition, disturbance having its source in anxiety will be in evidence at associations involving a human form, especially when either the masculinity or femininity of the form is explicit, and more so if elaborated as part of a significant theme. The test in these instances is activating the critically significant imago, triggering the memory of that all-important person to the patient, whether father or mother, which persists from infancy and early childhood as the nucleus of the conflict and the neurosis.

(3) Energy in the fantasy-dictated associations (M) is high (Levy scale) as evidence of the very strong emotions being invested in this inner living. The content in these fantasies, too, will be recognized as bearing on personal issues that are severely exercising the patient. In the other emotion-determined responses there is a preponderance of those in which the emotional determinant is dominant over the form element, with instances in which the form element is lacking all together (Y, YF; V, VF; C, CF). In the color-determined responses (C, CF) the content may be either painful, of anxiety source (lightning, fire, explosions) or of pleasurable affect (any of the flowers, dance scenes). In the shading-determined associations (Y, YF; V, VF) the content has a painful connotation as a rule, or at best is neutral.

The strong influence of the affective variable in the determinant is the test's information that any transference experience which the patient is developing is being intensely lived. It is the more intense the more conflictual and unresolved the neurosis is. These are inferences which we draw in turn from the severity of the anxiety shock and the degree to which the anxiety thus activated is free.

(4) The defenses require close scrutiny. They will be in the main of a constrictive variety. How tight, armor-like? To what degree is the patient engaging in delaying, denying, insulating tactics? Can these defensive maneuvers be detected as provoked by conflict of personal, and probably conflictual, significance? If the patient has recourse to symbolisms, are these the kind that point to repressions? In the avoidances or flight from fantasy, what is the patient avoiding, fleeing? The lead in such flight may be either concerning attitudes around the imago or over some other remembered event now being unearthed out of the unconscious.

In all these tactics the patient is shutting himself off from communicating his disturbing ideas to the world, which always means the therapist also. He is resisting the therapy. He will not liberate what he has repressed because, by reason of his emotions, he cannot, not yet. The very fact that he has repressed it is, of course, index to the pain which the recall would inflict on him and the anxiety it would stir up.

(5) In some test protocols the delays, avoidances, denials can be identified as highly centered around some one topic. The lead is obtained from either structure or content, usually both. Thus, the disturbance in a woman may be at phallic imagery (figure VI), or in a man at female genital ideas (figure VII, D 6), or at a menstrual blood percept (figure II, D 3). The anxiety reactions at these points may be entirely structural, the usual shock phenomena. But elsewhere in the test the associational content too will betray the heterosexual conflict. When aggression is a factor, the themes usually disclose themselves directly. However, it is at times inferred from the structural reactions, i.e., overreactive defenses or trends to rigidity at figures known to elicit aggression ideas (figures IX, II, IV, III, VII, I, X, VI). In these reactions and themes the test is highlighting the foci of specific conflict to the patient. They are useful in alerting the therapist that trends are emerging which are a signal that the transference is impending.

Affective quality in the associational material released under these conditions needs to be observed. Are they topics carrying pleasurable and gratifying connotation? Or are they painful, anxiety-toned, conflictual? These observations may have a special significance if the affects, whatever the quality, relate to the person of dynamic significance in the patient's memory, the imago. In the anxiety-toned associations, the hostile and aggressive attitudes held toward the emotion-laden imago are being transferred to the therapist. In the pleasure-toned transferences, a discriminating judgment is necessary as to whether the topic is a socially healthy, constructive one. What is its ego value? The pleasure may attach to a regressive need.

(6) When the affect is pleasurable with relation to the important imago, the pleasure may derive from an erotic loading toward this person. This content may be at conscious level and directly recognizable for its symptomatic significance. It may be screened in symbolism or more deeply in individualized fantasy themes. Its essence, in any event, is that of a communication out of the unconscious. It is thus a means whereby to trace the affect to its root source, i.e., to an attachment formed in infancy centering around a critical person which is still persisting. As an erotic or more specifically sexual wish it is regressive. This is what, in the transference, is attaching to the therapist.

(7) The relation of ambivalence to transference is an important one, insofar as it uncovers an ability on the part of the patient to shift from a hostile, antagonistic attitude toward his therapist to one in which he seeks aid, comfort, and possibly affection. Freud emphasizes that this is a shift possible only to persons of neurotic structure (ref. 34; p. 321). Such a shift is contraindicated in paranoid conditions, since in them the patient preserves his antagonisms.

(8) The therapist, having induced the patient to engage himself in the transference relationship, has the task of disengaging him in the terminal phases of therapy. This phase is a temporary illness through which the patient is led on the way to health (Freud). The aim is to have the patient slough off the immature aggressiveness and primitive eroticisms and anchor himself in constructive ego values.

Here again it is the test's function to throw light on the patient's equipment in this sphere. What ego values does he hold? How tolerant of stress is the ego? The signs of these are to be sought in both content and process. In the content we look to the range of interests and to their social values. But content alone, all the breadth in the world, does not help a structurally inadequate ego, and evidence for ego stamina must be sought in psychologic process.

(9) A principal ingredient in the ego's strength is clear and accurate as well as logical thinking. In the Rorschach test language this is: (a) F+, or perceptual accuracy, an activity requiring concentration and discrimination, both of which are conditioned by higher cortical processes; (b) the ability to grasp relations between percepts and to see the meanings in relation to one another, as well as in relation to a larger situation in which they participate. This is the synthesizing ability. (c) A broad mental horizon, something which in turn testifies to a broad intellectual background and experience, is essential. It helps the individual in terms of vision and perspective such that the ego is in a position to judge relative values. Freud accents the importance of rational thinking (ref. 34; p. 322). A minimum of intellectual endowment is essential for the grasping of differential ideas evoked within the therapeutic experience.

(10) Finally, there is that most important of all ingredients in the transference potential: the ability to relate to another person with one's own emotions so as to understand the other person's feelings. Such an understanding implies more than simply knowing with the intellect. A high intelligence quotient is not enough. What is required is a feeling *with*, which amounts to putting one's self in the place of the other. It means experiencing his experiences, their affective quality whether pleasurable or painful, the intensity with which the other enjoys or suffers them.

And here we are back at the emotional resources of the individual, both his outward-reaching, his seeking contact with others, and his wish-fulfilling fantasies. It is the fusion of C and of M, the person's Experience Actual, EA. Both C and M communicate feeling tones derived from the id reservoir. M differs from C only in converting the ore which the feelings are into the gold that is creative imagination. These responses thus stem from the person's basic emotional essence. And while in this lies a great danger since they can be the expression of self-regarding gratification, of the pleasure principle or of primitive aggressiveness, they are also the intensity of the self-sacrificing adolescent, the idealist, and the artist, of all those who experience powerful visions of universal scope. In the test, then, the emotional range should be varied and minimal in its expression of unrestrained feeling or of autistic daydreaming. The associations should express regard for social forms and an imagination that carries social values. Content in these color- and fantasy-determined associations should also be such as connote healthy interests and, along with the other content, divulge a wish to be in rapport with the world at large. Human form responses (H) should be numerous and also of a wide range in theme, disclosing a capacity for a broad sympathy with others. Freud speaks of the capacity for love as an ingredient in the transference. Federn, developing his concept of ego boundary and extension of ego boundary, arrives at essentially the same conclusion: love is of the essence of the ego.

The transference can be a transition from illness to health by opening the patient's understanding to values beyond those which have been holding him in their viselike and self-defeating grip. It is the experience whereby the ego extends its boundary so as to include persons beyond the self and sees their welfare as his own. The problem of therapy, so seen, becomes in fact the task of extending the ego's boundary. And, as just noted, ego in this sense is knowing with the emotions. It is thus that I understand both Freud's and Federn's "love." When these thinkers so theorize, they are actually restating very ancient wisdom, for love is the oldest known among therapeutic agents.

# References

[1] ALLPORT, G. W.: Personality. New York, Holt, 1937.

[2] BARTLEY, S. H.: Personally determined character of visual response. Am. J. Orthopsychiat. *17:* 371–387, 1947.

[3] BASH, K. W.: Über die Bestimmung und statistische Verteilung der Introversion und Extratension im Rorschach-Versuch. Internat. Ztsch. f. Rorschachforschung. *1:* 333–343, 1953.

[4] BATES, L. B., MÉTRAUX, R. W., AND WALKER, R. N.: Adolescent Rorschach Responses. New York, Hoeber, 1959.

[5] BECK, S. J.: The Rorschach Test as Applied to a Feeble-Minded Group. Archives of Psychology. New York, Columbia University Press, 1932.

[6] ——: Configurational tendencies in Rorschach responses. Am. J. Psychol. *45:* 433–443, 1933.

[7] ——: Introduction to the Rorschach Method. Res. Monog. No. 1. Am. Orthopsychiatric Assn., 1938.

[8] ——: Thoughts on an impending anniversary. Am. J. Orthopsychiat. *9:* 806–807, 1939.

[9] ——: Rorschach's Test, Vol. II, A Variety of Personality Pictures. Grune & Stratton, 1945.

[10] ——: Emotional experiences as a necessary constituent in knowing. *In* Reymert, M.: Feelings and Emotions. New York, McGraw-Hill, 1950.

[11] ——: Rorschach's Test, Vol. III, Advances in Interpretation. New York, Grune & Stratton, 1952.

[12] ——, RABIN, A. I., THIESEN, W. G., MOLISH, H. B., AND THETFORD, W. N.: The normal personality as projected in the Rorschach test. J. Psychol. *30:* 241–298, 1950.

[13] ——: The science of personality: nomothetic or idiographic? Psychol. Rev. *60:* 353–359, 1953.

[14] ——: Personality research and theories of personality structure: some convergences. J. Proj. Techn. *19:* 361–371, 1955.

[15] ——: The Six Schizophrenias. Res. Monog. No. 6. Am. Orthopsychiatric Assn., 1954.

[16] BENEDEK, T.: Adaptation to reality in early infancy. Psychoanal. Quart. *7:* 200–215, 1938.

[17] BENJAMIN, J. D.: A method for distinguishing and evaluating formal thinking disorders in schizophrenia. *In* Kasanin, J.: Language and Thought in Schizophrenia. Berkeley and Los Angeles, University of California Press, 1944.

[18] BERNARD, C.: An introduction to the study of experimental medicine. New York, Dover, 1957.

[19] BLEULER, E.: Dementia Praecox. New York, International Universities Press, 1950.

[20] ——: Textbook of Psychiatry. New York, Dover, 1951.

[21] BOHM, E.: A Textbook in Rorschach Test Diagnosis. New York, Grune & Stratton, 1958.

[22] BRUNER, J. S.: Perceptual theory and the Rorschach test. Personality *17:* 157–168, 1948.

[23] BRUNSWIK, E.: Perception and the representative design of psychological experiments. Berkeley and Los Angeles, University of California Press, 1956.

[24] BRUSSEL, J. A., GRASSI, J. R., AND MELNIKER, A. A.: The Rorschach method and postconcussion syndrome. Psychiat. Quart. *16:* 707–743, 1942.

[25] BYCHOWSKI, G.: The problem of latent psychosis. J. Am. Psychoanalyt. A. *1:* 484–503, 1953.

[26] CAMERON, N.: Experimental analysis of schizophrenic thinking. *In* Kasanin, J.: Language and Thought in Schizophrenia. Berkeley and Los Angeles, University of California Press, 1944.

[27] CHAREN, S.: Pitfalls in interpretation of parental symbolism in Rorschach cards IV and VII. J. Consult. Psychol. *21:* 52–56, 1957.

[28] DARWIN, C.: The Expression of the Emotions in Man and Animals. Philosophical Library, 1955.

[29] ——: The Descent of Man. New York, Burt, 1874.

[30] FEDERN, P.: Ego Psychology and the Psychoses. New York, Basic Books, 1952.

[31] FEIGL, H.: Principles and problems of theory construction in psychology. *In:* Current Trends in Psychological Theory. Pittsburgh, University of Pittsburgh Press, 1951.

[32] FENICHEL, O.: The Psychoanalytic Theory of the Neuroses. New York, Norton, 1945.

[33] FREUD, A.: The Ego and the Mechanisms of Defense. New York, International Universities Press, 1946.

[34] FREUD, S.: Collected Papers. London, Hogarth, 1950.

[35] GRINKER, R. R.: On identification. Internat. J. Psycho-Analysis. *38:* 1–12, 1957.

[36] HALLOWELL, A. I.: In Klopfer, B.: Developments in the Rorschach Technique, Vol. II. Yonkers, World, 1954.

[37] HOCH, P. H., AND POLATIN, P.: Pseudoneurotic forms of schizophrenia. Psychiat. Quart. *23:* 248–276, 1949.

[38] HOLT, R. R.: Some statistical problems in clinical research. Educational and Psychological Measurement *10:* 609–627, 1950.

[39] JACKSON, J. H.: Selected Writings. London, Hodder & Stoughton, 1931, vols. I and II.

[40] JONES, E.: Papers on Psychoanalysis. New York, William Wood, 1938.

[41] KANNER, L.: Problems of nosology and psychodynamics of early autisms. Am. J. Orthopsychiat. *19:* 416–427, 1949.

[42] KLOPFER, B., AND KELLEY, D. McG.: The Rorschach Technique. Yonkers, World, 1942.

[43] KLOPFER, B.: Developments in the Rorschach Technique. Yonkers, World. 1954, 1956. vols. I and II.

[44] KLÜVER, H.: Contemporary German psychology. In Murphy, G.: An Historical Introduction to Modern Psychology. New York, Harcourt, Brace, 1930.

[45] LEDWITH, N. H.: Rorschach Responses of Elementary School Children. Pittsburgh, University of Pittsburgh Press, 1959.

[46] LEWIN, K.: Field Theory in Social Science. New York, Harper, 1951.

[47] LISS, E.: The genesis, evolution and dysfunction of learning and remedial measures. Am. J. Orthopsychiat. *24:* 767–771, 1954.

[48] LOOSLI-USTERI, M.: Le test de Rorschach appliqué à différentes groupes d'enfants de 10–13 ans. Arch. psychol. *22:* 51–106, 1929.

[49] LOWIE, R. H.: Primitive Religion. New York, Boni and Liveright, 1924.

[50] MOLISH, H. B.: Schizophrenic Reaction Types in a Naval Hospital Population. Bureau of Medicine and Surgery, Navy Department, 1956.

[51] ——, AND BECK, S. J.: Mechanisms of defense in schizophrenic reaction types as evaluated by the Rorschach test. Am. J. Orthopsychiat. *28:* 47–60, 1958.

[52] ——, AND ——: Further Explorations of the "Six Schizophrenias": S-3. Am. J. Orthopsychiat. *28:* 483–505; 809–827, 1958.

250 THE RORSCHACH EXPERIMENT

THE RORSCHACH EXPERIMENT

250 THE RORSCHACH EXPERIMENT

# Author Index

251

# Index to Notes

NOTE: The numbers in the *Index to Notes* refer to chapters and the notes for that chapter. The **boldface** number is that of the chapter. For example, **3** 9 refers to note 9 in chapter 3; **10** 21 refers to note 21 in chapter 10. Since each note refers to a statement in the *Interpretation*, a reading of the note itself will not be sufficient. In order to derive the information intended in a note, the reader will always need to refer back to the text statement which it annotates.

Affective ratio, **3** 9, 22; **4** 26; **6** 33; **8** 7; **9** 15

Aggression content, **10** 30, 53, 55

Ambivalence, **5** 32

Anatomy content, **4** 85; **8** 25

Animal per cent (A), **3** 51; **4** 41, 53, 72; **5** 44; **6** 55; **7** 1; **8** 32, 33, 42; **10** 14

Anxiety, **3** 32, 33, 48; **4** 82; **5** 28; **7** 28; **9** 19, 31, 32, 39; **10** 26, 54, 78. *See also* Neurotic shock; Shading shock.
  binding of, **4** 44, 62, 63; **5** 18; **9** 41
  free, **5** 27; **7** 29

Approach, **3** 49; **4** 58, 71, 73; **5** 27, 44; **6** 10, 43; **7** 3; **8** 38; **9** 50; **10** 3, 14, 58

Avoidance, **5** 33, 51; **10** 54

Behavior, nonscorable, *see* Motor symptoms.

Black, **9** 32

Brain pathology, **3** 4; **5** 42; **7** 39; **10** 2

C, CF, FC, **3** 10; **4** 20, 23, 24; **5** 24, 26, 29; **6** 30, 58; **9** 15, 24; **10** 16, 18, 19, 51

Changes in repeated tests, **10** 14, 22, 64, 68, 69, 77, 82, 83

Color
  blends (Y, V, T, M), **3** 16, 30, 36; **4** 4; **8** 9; **10** 36
  content in, **3** 15, 22; **5** 30, 31; **6** 34; **8** 45; **9** 20, 50; **10** 22
  defense against, **3** 44; **4** 65; **5** 25; **9** 19, 41
  naming, **7** 23; **9** 41
  reaction to, **3** 7, 8, 14, 22, 64; **4** 33; **5** 23, 28, 48, 66; **6** 21, 22, 25, 29, 32, 34, 57; **8** 5, 6; **9** 14, 16, 18, 20, 38, 50; **10** 17, 21, 53 *See* Figures VIII, IX, X; *also* FC.

shock, *see* Neurotic shock.

Constriction, **3** 6, 51; **5** 8, 44; **6** 10, 38, 55; **9** 2, 4, 50; **10** 54

Content, **3** 51, 52, 56; **4** 28, 81, 86; **5** 10, 11, 27, 38, 40, 44, 49f., 59; **6** 53; **7** 8; **8** 32, 45; **9** 3, 8, 50; **10** 61, 70, 71f., 75, 76, 82
  symbolism, **3** 62; **6** 40; **10** 56, 76

Dd and Dds, **4** 73; **10** 1, 3, 69

Defenses, **3** 42–50; **4** 82; **5** 7, 33, 35, 37, 44, 63; **9** 4, 7, 28, 41, 50
  constrictive, **6** 38, 55, 63
  phobic, as binding, **4** 44, 62, 63

Delusions, **9** 50

Denial, **3** 44; **4** 16, 59; **5** 7, 33; **6** 38; **9** 41; **10** 54

Diagnostic indication, **5** 19, 21, 22, 47, 58; **9** 48, 57, 58; **10** 13, 69, 73, 80, 84, 86

Displacing, **4** 61, 63; **6** 18

Do response (Rorschach's), *see* x.

DW, DsW, **4** 17; **6** 46; **7** 20; **10** 14

Ego, **5** 43, 60, 61, 63; **9** 9, 11, 32, 37, 41, 49, 50; **10** 13, 14, 15, 18, 38, 51, 57, 58

Emotions, **5** 24, 26, 64; **9** 14, 39, 50; **10** 20, 22, 23, 36

Experience Actual, **3** 64; **5** 64; **7** 38; **9** 54; **10** 86

Experience Balance (EB), **3** 56; **10** 23, 86

Eyes, **3** 45; **6** 17, 39; *also*, 216

F, as moderator of feelings, **3** 12, 22, 36; **4** 3; **5** 21; **6** 31; **7** 26; **9** 17; **10** 18, 36, 45

F+, as control, **3** 11; **4** 8, 13, 21, 25, 40, 45; **7** 24; **10** 1, 58

# General Index

See more especially the *Index to Notes* for the following topics: color, content, defenses, fantasy, neurotic shock, regression, shading, shading shock, space responses, texture, vista.

Aggressiveness, 121, 125, 160, 161, 228, 234f.
Ambitendency, 208, 223
Anxiety, 26, 29, 84, 86, 104, 106, 118, 166, 213, 238f., 244
  bound, 47, 208, 209, 222f.
  free, 42–43, 46, 85, 160, 166, 208
Approach, 202f.

Behavior, qualitative, 6
Blind diagnosis, 6f.
Brain pathology, 99, 100, 101, 102, 103, 106, 107, 205

C, 11f.
Changes in personality, 167, 172f.
  *See also* Treatment
Character neuroses, 206f.
Constriction, 84, 122, 210f., 213
Content
  healthy, 28, 32, 43, 49, 64, 86, 88, 107, 123, 126
  meaning to patient, 46
  personal, 13, 28, 31f., 45, 48, 108, 160, 174, 232
  regressive, 118, 161
  suicidal, 89
  symptomatic, 43, 49, 72, 104, 121, 125, 166, 218f.
  *See also* Sexuality; Stereotypy

Defenses, 29f., 46, 47f., 87, 104, 122, 160f., 210ff.
Dependency, 42, 119, 230
Depression, 84f., 86, 205

Ear, 126, 216
Ego, 4, 7, 31, 42, 64, 99, 102, 106, 108, 118, 122, 123, 124, 160, 161, 165, 200, 204, 246
  and defenses, 87, 214, 216, 225, 226, 227, 239

Emotional state, 30, 43, 45, 63, 86, 90, 103, 105, 107, 117f., 118, 124, 166, 173
  *See also* Color in *Index to Notes*
Erlebnistypus, *see* Experience Balance
Experience Actual, 16f., 18f., 21, 50, 127, 204f., 209, 211, 212, 213, 221, 223, 247
Experience Balance, 3, 8, 10, 11f., 14f., 16, 18, 106, 127, 232

Fantasy, 43–44, 85, 119, 234
  autistic, 120, 232f.
  as defense, 122
  inhibited, 28, 30, 44
  *See also* Fantasy and M in *Index to Notes*
"Father" imagery, 29, 89
Feeblemindedness, 21, 26, 103, 126, 205
Field theory, 3

Gestalt, 3, 4, 11
Guilt, 85, 89, 104

Hostility, *see* Aggressiveness
Hysteria, 206f.

Impulse neuroses, 206
Inferiority feelings, 29, 174, 226
Inquiry, 102, 213, 224f.
Intellectual integration, 32, 71, 99, 100, 101, 104f., 124, 160, 166
  decline, 105, 106
Intelligence, 20, 85, 90, 217, 246
Interests, *see* Content
Interpretation, structure of, 7

Language, *see* Speech patterns

M, 11f., 20f., 232f.
Manic depressive, 206, 227
Meaning, 10, 13, 21f.
Mood, 27, 45, 63, 84–85, 86, 87, 107, 160, 166